REFRAMING SCREEN PERFORMANCE

REFRAMING SCREEN PERFORMANCE

Cynthia Baron

AND

Sharon Marie Carnicke

THE UNIVERSITY OF MICHIGAN PRESS
Ann Arbor

TO OUR FAMILIES AND FRIENDS

Published in the United States of America by
The University of Michigan Press
Manufactured in the United States of America
⊗ Printed on acid-free paper

2011 2010 2009 2008 4 3 2 1

A CIP catalog record for this book is available from the British Library.

Library of Congress Cataloging-in-Publication Data

Baron, Cynthia.
Reframing screen performance / Cynthia Baron and Sharon Marie Carnicke.
p. cm.
Includes bibliographical references and index.
ISBN-13: 978-0-472-07025-1 (cloth : alk. paper)
ISBN-10: 0-472-07025-8 (cloth : alk. paper)
ISBN-13: 978-0-472-05025-3 (pbk. : alk. paper)
ISBN-10: 0-472-05025-7 (pbk. : alk. paper)
1. Motion picture acting. I. Carnicke, Marie, 1949– II. Title.

PN1995.9.A26B35 2008
791.4302'8—dc22 2007031014

ACKNOWLEDGMENTS

I want to thank Cindy Baron for walking into my office one day to ask how theatre studies could help clarify acting in the cinema; this conversation was the genesis of this truly collaborative book. Moreover, I have little doubt that without LeAnn Fields's generous enthusiasm and unflagging patience, this book might still remain in our desk drawers; our gratitude to her as our editor is deep.

The Society for Cinema and Media Studies afforded us many opportunities to test our ideas in panels, workshops, and informal conversations; this work formed the foundation upon which we built our first draft. Additionally, many colleagues supported our work on acting in the cinema by publishing our articles: Alan Lovell and Peter Krämer, Diane Carson and Frank P. Tomasulo, Martin Barker and Thomas Austin.

Finally, we acknowledge our universities for providing sabbatical leaves to begin and end this project.

—Sharon Marie Carnicke

While it perhaps goes without saying, we are indebted to the screen actors and filmmakers whose work we discuss, and to the scholars and practitioners cited throughout the book whose writings opened up new ways of thinking about cinema and about performance. Readers will find special thanks to various colleagues tucked in the endnotes, but there are many other people to thank, most especially, Sharon Carnicke for her friendship, expertise, and willingness to allow the project to evolve until it reached fruition.

I share Sharon's gratitude for the support we have received from generous colleagues and welcoming institutions. Along with those already listed, I would also like to thank the University Film and Video Association, and want to express my sincere appreciation to Paul McDonald, Tamar Jeffers McDonald, Jim and Libby Dachik, Sara and Jonathan Chambers, Ron Shields, Daniel Williams, and Emily Baron for their ongoing assistance.

Special thanks to LeAnn Fields for believing in the work, and to Marcia LaBrenz and the entire production team at the University of Michigan Press for making the book a reality.

—Cynthia Baron

Earlier versions of sections of this work were previously published: "Acting Choices/Filmic Choices: Rethinking Montage and Performance," *Journal of Film and Video* 59 no. 2 (2007) (reprinted by permission of *Journal of Film and Video*); "Capturing Natural Behavior on Film?" *Theatre Annual: A Journal of Performance Studies* 59 (2006) (reprinted by permission of *Theatre Annual*).

CONTENTS

INTRODUCTION

Walter Benjamin was right—with film, like sports, "everyone who witnesses its accomplishments is somewhat of an expert."[1] Hidden in safe anonymity, sports fans confidently analyze players' strengths and weaknesses, just as film audiences blithely rate actors' performances. For decades, film stars have been the object of both scorn and adoration. By now, there is far more information about screen actors' personal lives than about the way their performance choices affect our interpretations of films. While every day thousands of words and images join the swirl of attention focused on stars' very public private lives, this book goes in a different direction. It offers ways to discuss the remarkable details of the performances we all encounter in films.

Screen performances are an integral component of film, contributing to audiences' interpretations just as framing, editing, lighting, production, and sound design do. Many filmgoers will find that idea obvious and wonder why an entire book would be devoted to clarifying just how actors' performances shape our impressions. But a complete hearing is needed. Why? Because the simple, straightforward proposal that actors' gestures and expressions are on a par with other filmic elements challenges the influential view that screen performances are created in the editing room. To suggest that acting is a component of film goes against accepted ideas about the "nature" of film and the time-honored notion that live performance is the province of "true" acting.

What caused these established positions to be at odds with the commonsense view that acting matters in film? One factor is that scholars writing about cinema have often separated acting from all other aspects of film, treating the actor's work as resistant to descriptive analysis and lacking an objective, critical vocabulary.[2] While academics readily accept that crew members rely on craft knowledge, they have often overlooked ways that screen actors use their training and experience to create vivid gestures and expressions. Another factor is that uniquely "cinematic" strategies have been seen as the foundation of "film language." Scholars agree that framing choices convey impressions, as when low-angle shots make characters seem more imposing than shots that look down on the subject. However, books on film do not discuss the way actors' use of sharp, sudden, staccato bursts of words can often signal alarm, while smooth, sustained, legato vocal rhythms can convey moments of calm.[3]

Academic writing about stars and audiences has illuminated a great deal about films and the moviegoing experience. However, only by challenging traditional views of film and performance can one shed new light on acting in the cinema. By discussing films from different genres, periods, and national cinemas, this book looks closely at screen acting and shows how performance details interact with other filmic choices. It returns to insights on art and performance elegantly formulated by the Prague Linguistic Circle (1926–48) and draws on a circumspect selection of acting terms and concepts. With these foundations, the book gives filmgoers of all types accessible, comprehensive ways to analyze acting in the cinema.

Some might object that vocabulary developed in theater and performance studies cannot be used in film analysis because cinema and theater are entirely different art forms, cultural products, and economic industries with separate histories and audiences. They are not. Long before *Sunset Boulevard* (Billy Wilder, 1950) was transformed into a Broadway production in 1994, research on "film nomenclature, production practices, consumption, and formal and stylistic elements" had clearly demonstrated that cinema shares deep affinities with theater.[4] As singular films such as *Children of Paradise* (Marcel Carné, 1945) and *Topsy-Turvy* (Mike Leigh, 1999) lovingly reveal, cinephiles not only recognize but celebrate cinema's origins in boulevard theater and comic opera.

Practitioners' shared use of acting vocabulary also warrants crossing the divide between theater and film. However, as discussions in the book will show, drawing on craft vocabulary to describe acting in individual films need not involve any claim about the techniques the actors themselves might have used. Instead, examining performances in light of terms borrowed from script analysis, for example, helps a viewer identify and reflect on the myriad acting choices in completed scenes. Similarly, using the Prague school's incisive distinction between performer and performance element leads to systematic thinking about screen acting because it clarifies, once and for all, that evocative gestures and expressions are fully present in film. Identifying "true" acting with expressive performance details illuminates the common ground between stage and screen acting that far surpasses the much discussed but finally inconsequential contrast between performers' presence on stage and absence on screen.

Essentially all of the terminology used in this book has been available for at least fifty years. One might ask: if tools for analyzing film acting were at hand, why weren't they used? Terms and concepts that could have clarified acting's integral role were not brought into cinema studies because influential views on film and acting made it nearly impossible to take screen performance seriously. For example, in 1936 cultural theorist Walter Benjamin effectively discouraged future scholarship on screen acting when he confidently asserted that the film actor simply "represents himself to the public before the camera."[5] Describing with dismay the "mechanical contrivance" that separated actor and audience, Benjamin intoned, "Any thorough study proves there is indeed no greater contrast than that of the stage play to a work of art that is completely subject to or, like the film, founded in mechanical reproduction."[6]

Contemporary film reviews show that critics still find themselves on shaky ground when they discuss screen acting. In most cases, they give serious consideration to screen actors' work only when the films themselves have sufficient cultural cachet. For example, performances by Kate Winslet and Leonardo DiCaprio in the special-effects blockbuster *Titanic* (James Cameron, 1997) were not widely discussed. Even though Winslet received an Oscar nomination, critics' observations about the actors' contributions were often squeezed in as an afterthought to commentary on other aspects of the film.[7] By comparison, critics generally paid close attention to Winslet's performance in *Iris* (Richard Eyre, 2001), a literate British drama with "quality" acting guaranteed by the casting of Jim Broadbent and Dame Judi Dench.[8] Similarly, DiCaprio's film performances became a viable subject for critics after he became associated with auteur director Martin Scorsese through leading roles in *Gangs of New York* (2002), *The Aviator* (2004), and *The Departed* (2006).[9]

Today's critics concentrate on performances legitimized by external validation because authorities of the past so completely discredited screen acting. In the early years of cinema, film director Vsevelod Pudovkin, playwright Luigi Pirandello, and cultural theorist Rudolf Arnheim all argued that film actors should be seen as stage props and film performances as constructed by others.[10] Echoing their positions, Walter Benjamin shared his alarm that a filmic reaction of being "startled by a knock at the door" could be created by a director firing a shot behind an actor without warning; responding to that possibility, Benjamin lamented, "Nothing more strikingly shows that art has left the realm of the 'beautiful semblance.'"[11]

With film performance anathema to several prominent figures who witnessed the rise of motion pictures, it is not surprising that anxiety about the illegitimacy of screen acting filters into even the most laudatory contemporary assessments. For example, reviews of Nicole Kidman's Oscar-winning performance in *The Hours* (Stephen Daldry, 2002) praised the nuanced expressivity of her eyes, face, voice, and body but also consistently remarked on her false nose, almost as if it created Kidman's performance; as critic David Edelstein smugly observed at the time; "If she wins the Oscar, it will be by a nose."[12] Charlize Theron's Oscar-winning performance in *Monster* (Patty Jenkins, 2003) generated the same anxiety and controversy, with much attention given to the effects created by makeup artist Toni G and Theron's weight gain. Interestingly, reviewers' doubts that Theron's portrayal could be considered acting actually prompted Roger Ebert to condemn fellow critics for suggesting that because one could identify the techniques that physically transformed Theron for the role, the actress herself had not created the performance.[13] Ebert's objection to questions about Theron's acting highlights the still uncertain status of screen performances. Are they instances of authentic acting? Or are they the result of filmmakers' sleight of hand?

Critics' lingering concerns about the legitimacy of screen acting begin to suggest the even more deeply rooted skepticism scholars have expressed about screen acting. For example, writings by film theorist Christian Metz amplified Benjamin's observation that the "audience's identification with the actor is really an identification with the camera."[14] Still influential today, Metz formalized the position that meaning in the cinema arises primarily from shot selection and shot-to-shot relations.[15] However, his view that cinema directs spectators' interpretations by means of frame selections and editing combinations made it difficult to explain variations in viewers' responses. Efforts to explain those variations include scholarship grounded in psychoanalysis, phenomenology, feminist theory, and various forms of reception studies.

This book reckons with performance to explain variations in audience response, recognizing that interpretations of filmic gestures are influenced by viewers' personal associations with comparable social gestures and their acquaintance with the gestural conventions of pertinent aesthetic traditions. While Metz emphasized framing, editing, and the organization of looks (camera, actor/character, spectator), this book examines the specific qualities in actors' gestures and expressions that convey characters' thoughts, moods, and temperaments. Because Metz ignored performance in his focus on narrative and "cinematic" strategies, this book explores interrelations between shot selections and gesture choices, miking decisions and vocal inflections, editing patterns and differing uses of facial expression, gesture, and movement.

A full accounting of audience responses and film acting involves a thorough look at the dynamic, mutual interactions among the many elements within shots, scenes, and films. While framing and editing are not the basis of "film language," neither is performance. Rather, interactions among countless textual and extratextual factors shape audience interpretations. Composite arts such as theater and film consistently have "various systems of signs in simultaneous play," and thus require the kind of functional analysis exemplified by Prague school structuralism.[16] Prague semiotics is particularly suited to discussions of screen performance because Jan Mukařovský's 1931 essay on Chaplin's performance in *City Lights* represents "the first attempt" to apply the concept of performance element "in a concrete analysis."[17] Guided by the lucid formulations of Prague theorists, one can see how performance details extend, support, and counterbalance impressions, meaning, and significance created by other filmic choices.

Part 1 of the book examines perspectives on film and acting that have precluded effective analysis of screen performance. Examples from a range of films help to show that performances are composed of observable physical and vocal gestures that warrant analysis. Part 2 highlights acting in films from different time periods and aesthetic traditions as it outlines the way Prague theories illuminate interactions between acting and other filmic choices. Part 3 examines several contemporary films to illustrate how taxonomies developed by Delsarte, Laban, and Stanislavsky allow one to effectively describe the acting choices that convey characters' thoughts and feelings.

Together, the discussions show that rich vocabulary for analyzing film acting already exists. Practitioners, scholars, and filmgoers should find the application of Prague concepts and acting/directing terms valuable. Readers should also encounter a new vision of cinema, one that recognizes the mutual interdependence of all filmic elements. Just as editing choices are best understood when cinema is seen as a composite form that features simultaneity, redundancy, and contrast, acting choices are illuminated when they are recognized as filmic choices, connected to other screen details through changing, mutually interactive relationships of subordination, equilibrium, and parallelism.

The book aims to *reframe* screen performance by replacing, for a moment, the familiar focus on stardom with concentration on actors' observable performance choices. Through this alternative frame, the light but sustained quality of an elderly woman's frail, clasping and unclasping hands becomes a filmic element on a par with the tight framing of the long take that draws attention to her hands. Focusing on acting rather than stars, the glazed expression in the eyes of a young man portraying a character out of his depth becomes a cinematic detail of equal importance to the camera movement that pans slowly past him. Attending to acting choices as filmic choices, one sees that the sudden rising inflection in a youngster's voice works in tandem with the cut to a close-up of the child's wide-eyed expression.

By reframing *screen* performance, the book also seeks to dispel assumptions about media specificity, modern perception, and the divide between stage and screen. While aesthetic traditions in film, television, and mediated performance art differ, all of these forms use gestures and expressions to shape audience impressions. They all combine performance details with framing, editing, and sound design choices that often enhance opportunities to search performers' gestures and expressions for emotional resonance.[18] While discussions throughout the book focus on feature films, that choice is not meant to diminish the importance of performances in other media forms. Documentaries, reality TV, televised sports, animated films, and avant-garde videos also generate a heightened interest in the minute details of gestures and expressions.

In theater and film, combinations of performance and nonperformance elements operate together to clarify and amplify the connotations already embedded in the individual components of the production. Discussions throughout the book emphasize the interlocking coordination between the various aspects of cinema because people have tended to think that films, like other aspects of modern life, simply fragment experience. While framing and editing choices can disperse attention, they also have a dialogic or reciprocal effect: the same processes that isolate sounds and images actually focus audience attention on the minute details presented moment to moment. Audiences know that emotional significance and narrative information will be doled out in bits and pieces. As a consequence, viewers notice the slightest shifts in performers' facial expressions, the smallest changes in their vocal intonations. They make meaning out of the selection and combination of all filmic details, sifting through slight changes of framing as well as changes in actors' energy.

The book also seeks to reframe screen *performance* in ways that acknowledge its multiple meanings.[19] For example, screen performances are like musical or theatrical ones in that they represent the material embodiment of scores or scripts that serve as exact blueprints or open points of reference. Moreover, because most films belong to narrative traditions, screen performances generally involve character portrayal in some way. Also, owing perhaps to cinema's origins in the spectacular pictorial traditions of boulevard theater and comic opera, film performances have often featured displays of exceptional skill, grace, and physical beauty. Additionally, because films frequently rely on recognizable gestures and expressions, audiences often access and interpret screen performance in light of social norms and familiar human behavior. At the same time, screen performances reflect surrounding aesthetic traditions and conventions of individual cinematic genres; as a consequence, audiences who care about film and the performing arts most deeply enjoy the craft in screen performances. This book endeavors to extend that appreciation of acting in the cinema by illustrating ways to analyze and discuss screen performances with other actors, directors, scholars, and filmgoers.[20]

PART ONE

CINEMA'S VARIED USE OF GESTURES AND EXPRESSIONS

CHAPTER ONE

CRAFTING, NOT CAPTURING "NATURAL" BEHAVIOR ON FILM

In the 1970s, poststructural film theory debunked the notion that film practice necessarily involves a process of recording reality. Yet this now-established view has not resulted in a widespread "concomitant re-examination" of assumptions about acting in film.[1] While a growing body of scholarship recognizes the craft involved in screen performance, the contrary belief that cameras and microphones merely capture natural behavior continues to dominate writing about cinema. This chapter provides an overview of the central biases that condition predominant views about acting in film and a brief survey of how those views have been circulated in the popular press. Thus, we lay a foundation for repositioning actors' work as part of the complex interactions between performance and nonperformance cinematic elements.

IF IT IS NOT LIVE PERFORMANCE IT IS . . .

Differences between stage and screen acting have often been framed by the normative institution, theater, which has laid claim to the positive attributes.[2] Live stage performance has been associated with legitimacy, complexity, and authenticity, while screen performance has often been viewed as something other than true acting. For example, Bert O. States compares a film actor to an "aerialist who works with a net."[3] Believing that actors are protected by the net of cinema technology, he argues that film audiences are also protected from the "toil and fabrication" that goes into performances; according to States, film "leaves us with the record of an actuality into which we can safely sink."[4] Summing up beliefs about the unique and intrinsic worth of stage acting, States proposes that audiences of live performances are "privileged" to have experiences not available to cinema audiences.[5]

Writing about film acting in an essay first published in 1936, Walter Benjamin articulated his era's dominant view by identifying mechanical reproduction as the central component of acting in film. Summarizing the ideas of contemporaries Rudolf Arnheim and Luigi Pirandello, Benjamin argued that "the camera introduces us to unconscious optics as does psychoanalysis to unconscious impulses."[6] Drawing on their observations, Benjamin proposed that the screen actor should be considered an inanimate stage prop, chosen for its characteristics and inserted in the proper place. Arguing that actors in film were as passive and insentient as the tables and chairs in a scene, Benjamin lamented that in contrast to actors in legitimate theater, the film performer does not portray "himself [as] the character of his role" but instead "represents himself to the public before the camera" in a way that allows natural behavior to be captured, reproduced, and exhibited.[7]

Today, screen performance is sometimes thought to reveal physical grace, but not true acting skill. For example, States argues that film performance "is no less a thing of beauty than that of the stage actor," but that acting in film can never achieve the sublime beauty created by actors who face the "danger" of live performance.[8] For States, screen performance will never be authentic acting because it does not require actors to endure the ultimate test of live performance. Instead, at its best, acting in film features the skillful virtuosity of "autonomous performance" (moments that emphasize spectacle, action, or display more than character and narrative) exemplified by Astaire-Rogers dance numbers or scenes with an Armani-suited Chow Yun-Fat gunning down waves of faceless opponents.[9] But as the case studies in James Naremore's landmark *Acting in the Cinema* (1988) demonstrate, even Hollywood studio films contain evidence that counters the equation between screen acting and display of physical grace. Analyzing performances by a collection of actors—Marlene Dietrich in *Morocco* (1930), James Cagney in *Angels With Dirty Faces* (1938), Katharine Hepburn in *Holiday* (1938), Marlon Brando in *On the Waterfront* (1954), and others—Naremore deftly illuminates a remarkable range of expressive techniques and effectively makes the case that film acting can be far more complex than simple performing.

Some observers who acknowledge this complexity still categorize screen performance as "received acting," that is, as performance in which the representation of characters does not arise from the agency, talent, or labor of actors, but instead through the costuming, makeup, lighting, framing, editing, and sound design choices made by other members of the production team.[10] As Michael Kirby points out, from the 1960s forward, performance art has highlighted instances when people are prompted to say that someone is acting "even though he is *doing* nothing that we could define as acting," and that there are occasions when the matrices of costume, set, and action are "strong, persistent and reinforce each other [so that] we see an actor, no matter how ordinary the behavior."[11]

Looking at screen performance from this perspective, some have found that while film actors seem to be acting, they are actually just people in costume on film sets. However, Naremore has clearly shown that acting in film tends to feature "a degree of ostensiveness that marks it off from quotidian behavior" and that different levels of ostensiveness indicate distinctions between extras, supporting players, and leads.[12] His detailed analysis of *Kid's Auto Race* (1914), for example, offers a lucid illustration of the various degrees or levels of performative display created by the soapbox derby audience and participants, the fictional director of the newsreel that is supposedly being filmed, and what was Charlie Chaplin's first filmic portrayal of the Tramp.[13] Naremore's studies of the ensemble performances in *Rear Window* (1954) and *The King of Comedy* (1983) show how the specific rhetorical strategies used by the actors are keyed to narrative demands, larger stylistic choices, and established associations with the actors who were cast.

In brief, screen acting is not simply "received acting," even when films use individuals in ways akin to photographic models. Take, for example, the films of the modernist director Robert Bresson, who introduces the "use of 'models': non-professional actors trained in neutral line readings, automatic gestures, and emotional inexpressiveness."[14] T. Jefferson Kline observes that "the model was to become a kind of blank that, like the other images in Bresson's creation, would draw its meaning from juxtaposition . . . with other images."[15] The casting of nonprofessional actors was also designed to maintain the integrity of the interaction between cinematic elements and insulate audience interpretations from the persona established by a professional actor's appearance in a series of roles.[16] These types of films do not feature scores of moments when actors project their characters' subjective experiences. Instead, they minimize actors' presentation of character. Physical and vocal expressivity is noticeably delimited by framing, editing, and sound design used to convey and comment on the characters' inner experiences. As Doug Tomlinson explains, while "in traditional cinema, most editing structures serve and privilege the communication of character through performance, in Bresson's cinema, the converse is true: editing serves to de-emphasize both the importance and function of performance."[17]

Even so, the minimal physical gestures performed by Bresson's "models" can register as expressive acting work. James Quandt describes Bresson's films as "a cinema of paradox, in which the denial of emotion creates emotionally overwhelming works, minimalism becomes plentitude, [and] the withholding of information makes for narrative density."[18] Consider the way performances are presented in *Pickpocket* (1959), for example. Early in the film, Michael (Martin Lassalle) is shown lifting some cash from a woman's purse. Lassalle has been expressionless up to that point and, as Kline notes, "the click of the clasp [on the woman's alligator purse] is immediately followed by the only facial expression Lassalle is to provide in the entire film: a wincing of his eyes, which has an almost orgiastic effect in the bleak facial desert of his expression."[19] In the minimalist aesthetic, such a small performative gesture resonates largely.

By comparison, films by the poetic realist Jean Renoir are filled with moments when the actors' bodies and voices convey their characters' subjective experiences. Here, lighting, framing, editing, and sound elements are organized to enhance access to the details of the actors' gestures, expressions, intonations, and inflections.[20] Tomlinson proposes that "Renoir's interest in the art of performance—that desire to observe performers and their characters in space" was actually the foundation for "the director's extraordinary visual style—notably his use of mobile camera strategies and deep-focus photography."[21] Describing the humanistic and democratic perspective that infuses Renoir's films, Tomlinson notes that "Renoir's preference was not for the spectator to form an easy bond of identification with any one individual, but to *recognize*—through numerous characters—aspects of themselves and their society."[22] *The Rules of the Game* (1939) exemplifies that approach, for audiences are consistently given the "opportunity to choose their visual focus from among a multiplicity of simultaneous actions."[23]

For example, when the guests first arrive at La Colinière, the country estate of Marquis Robert de la Chesnaye (Marcel Dalio) and his wife Christine (Nora Gregor), we explore the contrasting and quickly shifting subjective experiences conveyed by the details of several actors' performances in the scene. One frame composition features Nora Gregor in a medium long shot (head to knees) with Roland Toutain, as the young pilot. Days earlier he had publicly intimated that his record-setting flight had been inspired by Christine. As Gregor begins to address the guests gathering in the foyer of

Bresson's *Pickpocket:* a moment of expressivity in a minimalist performance

Renoir's *The Rules of the Game:* opportunities to explore actors' performances

the mansion, Marcel Dalio and Jean Renoir (who plays the couple's amusing but penniless friend) casually move into the frame behind Gregor and Toutain. The blocking and frame composition allow us to study the postures and facial expressions of all four actors as Christine acknowledges her relationship with the young pilot and announces that it was friendship, not love, that inspired his heroic flight. Frozen in his spot, Toutain takes on a more dour expression as the speech progresses, while Dalio's nervous twitches dissolve into a calm and assured smile. Quietly attentive in the background, Renoir offers a counterpoint to Gregor, whose tense voice and small, jerking gestures convey Christine's anxious confusion as she is surrounded by her husband, potential lover, and newly arrived guests.

Despite the subtlety of acting in films by directors such as Renoir, all screen performance is still sometimes seen as "simple acting," which Kirby describes as instances when individuals do something for the sake of an audience but without complexity.[24] He contrasts "simple acting" with complex or true acting that requires actors to perform an activity, such as putting on a jacket, in a way that conveys the character's emotional and physical feelings at the moment.[25] Obscuring the varied ways actors contribute to film, Kirby proposes that screen performances often "ask very little of the actor" in terms of creative expressivity because characters' inner experiences are conveyed by "the camera and the physical/informational context" rather than the actor.[26]

However, comparative studies, such as Paul McDonald's analysis of the very different meanings created by similar moments in Janet Leigh's performance in *Psycho* (1960) and Anne Heche's performance in the 1998 remake, demonstrate that the key details of film performances can carry dense and significant meaning. Analyzing the scene when Marion unpacks her bags after checking in at the Bates Motel, McDonald notes that when Janet Leigh takes the envelope of money from the bag, she holds it in her left hand, "while her right appears to hover away from the money."[27] By comparison, once Anne Heche has the envelope in her hand, "she opens out her arms, swinging from side to side to look around for a place to stash the money."[28] McDonald persuasively argues that Leigh's "gestures suggest a moral struggle" while Heche's "loose swinging body indicates a sense of liberty."[29] In short, the different ways they handle the envelope express the character's feeling at the moment; these are not instances of "simple acting" because the characters' inner experiences are not communicated by the framing, lighting, editing, or set design, but instead by the specific observable details of performance.

Similarly, our comparative studies of films from different time periods, national cinemas, and production regimes in later chapters illuminate actors' contributions to films by demonstrating that framing, editing, and production design do not *do all the acting* in screen performance. Of course, film actors contribute to a complex, composite medium. Hence, impressions about characters' feelings and their environments are also influenced by nonperformance elements. Film audiences do encounter performances that have been mediated and modified by the work of directors, cinematographers, editors, and others. What has been obscured by traditional views about the stage-screen opposition, however, is how film mediates and modifies *some thing*, namely, discernible performance details with specific qualitative features that carry a delimited range of meanings and connotations. Films create meaning not by the combination of inert physical and vocal elements but instead through the selection and combination of recognizable human gestures and expressions that carry dense and often highly charged connotations that can be variously interpreted.

MANUFACTURING STARLETS AND LEARNING TRICKS OF THE TRADE

The mediated status of performance elements has led observers to elide the training, experience, and creativity that actors bring to filmmaking. Often overlooked is the bank of knowledge and experience that actors draw on to produce the gestures, expressions, and intonations that collaborate and combine with other cinematic elements to create meaning in film. The entrenched equation between authentic acting and live performance has caused both academics and journalists to identify film performance with almost anything other than actors' labor and agency. Focusing on the Hollywood entertainment industry, writing about screen performance often considers things more accessible than acting technique and more in tune with leisure interests, with the popular press consistently emphasizing film actors' beautiful bodies and winning personalities.

As early as 1910 "picture personalities" had started to coalesce around certain individuals and by 1914 the star had emerged, whose "existence outside his or her work became the focus of discourse."[30] From the 1920s forward, Hollywood studios directed audience attention to actors' picture personalities and private lives. Following the transition to sound in the late 1920s, alleged inside reports showed film actresses passively acceding to Hollywood's star factory and film actors drawing on their pluck and determination to get ahead. In the studio era, from roughly 1930 to 1950, articles in the popular press reflected and reified the established view that film performance consists primarily of instinctive behavior captured and projected on screen.

Two main rhetorical strategies can be detected in mainstream writings about film performance. As the following pages will show, in the 1930s and 1940s, inside reports about Hollywood highlighted how performers enhance their beauty and develop their bodies. In the 1950s, stories about Method acting emphasized a slightly different angle, the cultivation of players' instincts for expressive, natural behavior. These two rhetorical strategies are linked by a common view that gestures and expressions on screen arise naturally from the performers; neither fully exposes the artistic and technical training that was widely available to film actors during these decades.

Indeed, publicity surrounding screen actors has often actively suppressed information about training, preferring instead the myth of the born performer whose natural talents and genuine feelings are first captured by the camera and then presented on screen. Traditional ways of thinking about film and about acting have caused screen performances to be valued insofar as they appear truthful, sincere, and authentic. Performances by Hollywood stars in particular are prized not for their craftsmanship but as glimpses of idealized people. Film stars function as social hieroglyphs, objects of desire, and sites of identity construction. Screen narratives activate complex subjective processes insofar as they effectively circulate a culture's understanding of the human figure, countenance, and psyche.

An influential view of acting in the studio era can be found in mainstream magazines such as *Colliers, Life, Ladies Home Journal,* and *Saturday Evening Post.* In the late 1930s, articles purporting to demystify acting in the cinema began to appear. These behind-the-scenes reports spread the sanctioned view that film performance was mechanically reproduced instinctive behavior. The inside scoops confirmed beliefs that performers were not really acting and that the true labor, training, and creativity was expended by other people. Circulating the studio era's prevailing views of gender as well, publicity informed readers that actresses were produced by Hollywood's expert makeup and publicity men, while actors trusted their instincts and used a few tricks of the trade that they had learned along the way.

There were, however, other, hidden stories to be told about acting in Hollywood at that time. One of these chronicles the Hollywood studios' hiring of women with extensive stage experience to train young film actors and to work with established stars. In 1933, Paramount hired Phyllis Loughton

(Seaton) and Lillian Albertson as dialogue directors to assist actors in analyzing scripts for both the meaning and dramatic structure in advance of shooting. Loughton was also head of Paramount's talent department and later worked at MGM. Albertson went on to work at RKO. After working in Hollywood for more than a decade, she summarized the techniques and exercises she had taught actors to use in *Motion Picture Acting* (1947).

In 1935, Universal hired Florence Enright to design and oversee their actor-training program; that same year, Republic hired Lillian Burns (Sidney) as their drama coach. In 1936, Enright became head of the drama department at Twentieth Century Fox and Burns went to MGM as head of their drama department. These positions required Enright and Burns to serve not only as acting teachers, but also as private coaches for established stars. In 1937, Lela Rogers became head of the drama department at RKO. In 1938, Warner Bros. hired Sophie Rosenstein, coauthor of *Modern Acting: A Manual* (1936), to shape their actor-training program. In 1940, Columbia put Josephine Hutchinson in charge of actor training at that studio. In 1949 Rosenstein was named head of talent development at Universal; when she passed away in 1952 Estelle Harmon took over Universal's actor-training program. Josephine Dillon (Gable), author of *Modern Acting: A Guide for Stage, Screen, and Radio* (1940), worked as an independent drama coach throughout the studio era.

Another story concerns the many film actors who developed their craft at educational institutions outside the studio system. They studied at the American Academy of Dramatic Art in New York and the Pasadena Playhouse's School of Theatre established in 1928 by Gilmor Brown. They took courses with Maria Ouspenskaya, formerly a member of Stanislavsky's Moscow Art Theatre company, at her School of Dramatic Art, established in New York in 1929 and in Hollywood in 1940. They studied at the Actors Laboratory in Hollywood, led by former Group Theatre members Roman Bohnen, Morris Carnovsky, and Phoebe Brand, who had themselves studied the American Method in its earliest incarnation. With Mary Tarcai as head, the Actors Laboratory offered classes between 1941 and 1949. Other actors trained in programs at Yale University, the University of Washington, the Goodman Theatre School of Drama, the El Capitan College of Theatre, and the Marta Oatman and Max Rheinhardt Schools of Theatre. Actors also gained experience working at theaters such as the Provincetown Playhouse and the Dallas Community Theatre.[31]

Yet inside journalistic reports on film actors in the 1930s and 1940s provided little if any information on these two hidden stories. For example, a

1937 article in the *Ladies Home Journal* entitled "Star Factory" does not tell readers about the drama schools established throughout Hollywood after the transition to sound. Instead it explains that sound cinema required talent departments to start manufacturing actresses from girls-next-door who had "personality" and were young, attractive, and just intelligent enough to make "passable" actresses.[32] The piece assumes that film actresses lack intellectual curiosity, explaining that the RKO contract players read passages aloud from Shakespeare, Ruskin, and the Bible "without interest" but happily cooperate with the makeup and publicity men who set out to work miracles on them.[33]

Moreover, the report presents only men as agents of change, ignoring the many women who dominated actor training at the time: Lela Rogers (Ginger Rogers's mother), Lillian Albertson, Lillian Burns (Sidney), Josephine Dillon, Florence Enright, Estelle Harmon, Josephine Hutchinson, Phyllis Loughton (Seaton), Sophie Rosenstein, and the Russian expatriate Maria Ouspenskaya. In short, "Star Factory" conveys the idea that screen acting has little to do with training, skill, intelligence, or experience, while it hammers home the point that actresses are best thought of as inert clay to be sculpted. The article explains that a film actress is a "finished product, a masterpiece created and sold by Hollywood's master craftsmen . . . a hapless butterfly . . . a newly found missing link" whose screen test is studied by men who can be compared to entomologists or "a bevy of anthropologists."[34]

Nor does the article mention that script analysis was central to actor training at both the studios' drama schools and the feeder institutions such as Pasadena Playhouse and the American Academy of Dramatic Art. Instead, "Star Factory" compares a film actress to "a multi-gaited saddle horse being shown at an auction."[35] An actress who balances objects precariously on her head learns "the graceful, gliding walk that native women in the Indies have gained from the same exercise."[36] Ironically tucked in only as an afterthought to the extensive coverage of the "studio beauty brigade," the article notes that actresses in the drama school at RKO work with theater's "greatest teachers."[37]

The article's extensive pictorial spread makes that brief note entirely insignificant. Focusing on the process of manufacturing physically perfect models to be photographed, "Star Factory" features before-and-after pictures of Myrna Loy, Norma Shearer, and Greta Garbo along with a progression of photographs that take readers through the "manufacturing" process required to produce Joan Fontaine. Photos of experts working on her

Joan Fontaine in *Suspicion:* her powerless character echoing her studio-made image

makeup, hair, and wardrobe are followed by images of Fontaine walking with a book on her head, jogging with a coach, having her body positioned by a dance instructor, practicing the piano, being directed in a rehearsal scene, and, finally, posing for a publicity photo, an event that seems as if it were the ultimate moment in an actress's career. Fontaine's role as the passive vestibule of labor expended by RKO's talent department is, not surprisingly, entirely consistent with the picture personality that would emerge from the characters Fontaine portrayed in films such as *Rebecca* (1940), *Suspicion* (1941), and *Jane Eyre* (1943).

A 1937 *Life* magazine article begins by noting that "hundreds of girls and boys who get into the movies each year" need training.[38] Despite this introductory nod to craft, "Young Starlets Learn to Act at Fox Drama School" features just two paragraphs of text alongside three pages of photographs that show young women exercising (legs in the air, bottoms to the camera) and being taught how to stop frowning, blinking, popping their eyes, and letting their double chins sag. Captions under frame enlargements from a screen test analyze the mistakes made by a novice actress playing opposite an experienced actor. Two photographs show young men learning tricks of the trade: one contract player learns the secrets to on-screen kissing, another how to walk down stairs with eyes gazing upward.

While this article also includes a photo of drama coach Florence Enright, who started as a founding member of the Washington Square Players (a prestigious theatrical group that evolved into the innovative Theatre Guild on Broadway), it ignores her depth of experience and the significant fact that in her job as drama coach she helped film actors develop characterizations through careful script analysis. Nor does it mention the acting principles that guided the work of studio-era drama coaches as articulated in manuals by Rosenstein, Dillon, and Albertson.[39]

In a 1940 *Life* magazine article entitled "Terry Hunt's Job Is to Keep Movie Stars Lean and Healthy," film performers are again presented as if they are inert matter, bodies without minds. Studio-era notions of gender difference are succinctly communicated by the disparity between text and image. The copy describes how actors come to Terry to toughen up for roles as prizefighters and so on, while the pictorial coverage features a sheet-swathed showgirl in a steam room, a freelance starlet arching her back in a handstand, a third aspiring actress having her thigh measured, and a fourth doing a stretching exercise with Mr. Hunt neatly positioning her leg in an arabesque.[40]

Film actresses' complete lack of agency is the theme of another *Life* magazine article from 1948. In it, studio-era readers meet Colleen Townsend, who is "charming, intelligent and knows a little about acting."[41] The real focus of the story, however, concerns the publicity men at Twentieth Century–Fox who shape Colleen's career, leaving nothing to chance. Their publicity campaign ensures a happy ending: copy explains that "the long labor of the flacks begins to pay off" when Colleen gets a featured role. The photograph shows her in a petticoat being given "an approving look" by Fox's head of ladies wardrobe.[42]

Press coverage that equated Hollywood actresses with models continued into the early 1950s. A *Life* magazine article on "Apprentice Goddesses" opens with the line, "Like a sculptor in a polytheistic tribe, Hollywood can never afford to leave off making goddesses."[43] Vignettes about twelve actresses, including Debbie Reynolds, Eleanor Parker, and Marilyn Monroe, feature titillating photographs alongside text that carries the semblance of candid reportage. Whether the aspiring actresses will "click and soar into the big time or sink away to a limbo of domesticity" is determined by the men who create them.[44] The article explains that "even if they are not raving beauties, the starlets still have a chance because the studios have dress designers, dentists, hairdressers, posture instructors, [and] charm coaches who can mold the most unlikely material into the requisite form [of] divine."[45]

The article closes with another analogy that reiterates the mythic assumption that actresses are processed goods: "like a frantic oil prospector always drilling new wells, Hollywood goes on digging for the girls."[46]

In publicity about actors in the studio era, a man's performance is equated with natural behavior captured by technology, and the coverage highlights the development of his athletic skills. A Universal promotional brochure entitled "Hollywood Talent School" shows actors boxing and fencing while actresses look on approvingly.[47] Aspiring actors are presented as men born with charismatic personalities and the instinct to play themselves. Articles in the popular press about a matinee idol such as Dana Andrews are emblematic of this type of studio publicity. While the coverage touches on Andrews's training at the Pasadena Playhouse, it focuses on his persistence and determination by repeating an anecdote about a deal he made as a young man with his employer who paid for his training in exchange for a percentage of his earnings as a star.[48]

A 1948 *Saturday Evening Post* article entitled "Knockouts to Order" describes film actors' work with Mushy Callahan, Warner Bros.'s "impresario of boxing, brawls and general disturbances."[49] In contrast to the elaborate pictorial displays of actresses, the *Post* article includes only one photograph, a picture of Callahan boxing with Jack Carson. The many accompanying paragraphs characterize the actors who work with Callahan as "Hollywood tough guys" who learn "gimmicks" like snapping the head back as they are hit.[50] The article assures readers that the actors' performances arise from the men's own personalities. To explain how actors learn to create convincing fight scenes, "Knockouts to Order" offers tales of film actors' natural, manly behavior. Readers learn about the time Wayne Morris got carried away during a staged fight and injured another actor; they find out that a former prizefighter once hit Errol Flynn so hard the fighter broke his hand, while Flynn came through without a scratch.[51]

In this collection of behind-the-scenes articles, the binary oppositions of muscular men versus butterfly women and authentic stage performance versus manufactured film performance serve to support one another. Today, the overt gender bias in the studio-era articles comes across as dated. Yet the articles' implicit claim that screen performance is best understood as "simple acting," "received acting," or the display of physical grace might still convince some readers. The connection between Hollywood film acting and Strasberg's vision of Method acting, which emerged in the mid-1950s and has since become deeply entrenched, might be one reason that is the case.

STRASBERG'S METHOD: RADICAL DEPARTURE OR MORE OF THE SAME?

During the studio era, the American press rarely if ever published stories at odds with the studios' public position that acting in film is a natural, effortless experience for stars and starlets whose charm and physical beauty make them uniquely suited to the fantasies Hollywood provides for its customers. In the poststudio era, however, the press began to circulate stories that did not focus on the physical process of manufacturing stars but instead seemed to offer glimpses into the methods actors use to develop characterizations. By the mid-1950s, rather than presenting actresses as hapless butterflies or multigaited horses, journalists had discovered they could sell behind-the-scenes articles about screen stars learning to produce natural performances.

Indicative of such coverage is a 1957 *Life* magazine article about Natalie Wood entitled "The Strange Doings of Actress at Practice," which features a series of allegedly candid photos of her, Nick Adams, and Dennis Hopper. The images show the actors, who are all younger than twenty-four, rehearsing scenes, staging impromptu performances, and studying experienced actors in a film projected for them at a Warner Bros. screening room. The article explains that while the actors might seem to be at play, they are preparing to perform by studying ordinary people and making "speeches to street loungers to see how well they can handle audiences."[52] Readers learn that the young actors "prowl skid row seeking characters to re-create" and even "act brief and startling scenes" for people in elevators.[53] "Strange Doings" explains that in addition to observing people and practicing public performance, in the "evenings the trio meets in each other's homes and reads from the classics."[54]

Articles that refer to actor training like "Strange Doings" rarely appeared in the studio era. At that time, as acting coach Lillian Burns (Sidney) explains, "possibly only the executives at MGM . . . and the producers and directors" knew about the kind of work she did; and until the 1970s Burns herself "had chosen to remain silent about what really went on beyond the closed doors at Metro Goldwyn Mayer at its zenith."[55] Maria Ouspenskaya was one of the few acting teachers who had received attention in the popular press. She was mentioned, for example, in a 1935 article about actor Franchot Tone in reference to what the reporter refers to as "the Stanislawsky [*sic*] system."[56] A 1940 *Modern Screen* article describes Ouspenskaya's film appearances and mentions John Garfield, Eddie Albert, and Anne Baxter as her students.[57]

"Strange Doings" suggests that after twenty years of studio-supported training programs, certain aspects of actor preparation had become commonplace enough that they could circulate in the press without disturbing the studios' equation between films and pleasurable entertainment. The article also reveals the press's response to the public's sudden interest in acting, especially stories connected to the Actors Studio in New York.

Tidbits of news about the Actors Studio was doled out in celebrity pieces such as the 1957 article in the *Saturday Evening Post* entitled "The Stars Rise Here," which describes Marilyn Monroe's decision to take a break from working in Hollywood so that she could study with Lee Strasberg at the Actors Studio in New York. Underscoring the fact that one of the country's most visible celebrities had made a very public decision to spend time in acting classes, journalist Maurice Zolotow tells readers that Monroe "threw Hollywood into a frenzy of excitement [by walking] out on a studio contract that was paying her $100,000 a picture."[58] Articles about Monroe's time at the Actors Studio piqued public interest in what happened behind the Studio's closed doors, even as they ignored the fact that Monroe went to the Actors Studio in New York because the Actors Laboratory in Hollywood, where she had already taken classes, had been closed as a consequence of cold-war politics.[59]

Similarly, acclaim for Marlon Brando's performances in *Streetcar Named Desire* (1950), *Viva Zapata* (1952), *The Wild One* (1953), *On the Waterfront* (1954), and *Sayonara* (1957) made him a celebrity and confirmed his abilities as an actor. In the 1950s, the Actors Studio laid claim to Brando as one of their own because he had attended a few classes taught by director Elia Kazan. In the same way that stories about Monroe served to enhance the Studio's visibility, Brando's association with it facilitated its fund-raising and publicity campaigns. Such press also increased the stature of Lee Strasberg, the Studio's artistic director from 1951, even as it tacitly diminished the significance of other actor-teachers, in particular Stella Adler, who had been Brando's principal mentor since 1942.

There are, of course, many actors, directors, and acting teachers who can be linked in some way to Method acting in America.[60] Moreover, the Method developed by Strasberg is quite different from that formulated by Stella Adler or envisioned by Sanford Meisner.[61] Practitioners, for example, recognize that these three leading proponents of Method acting focused on different techniques for preparation, character development, and performance.

Describing their distinct approaches in the simplest terms, one might say that Strasberg popularized the use of affective memory and the substitution of actors' personal experience for characters' circumstances and objectives; Adler emphasized creative use of imagination, careful study of the fictional world disclosed by the script, and research into the historical circumstances referenced by the script; Meisner shared Alder's opposition to Strasberg's emphasis on the actor's personal emotion and developed his own unique exercises to help actors establish and maintain deep connections with each other during performance.

As do all these variations on the Method, Strasberg's approach differs from the System that Stanislavsky had developed in Russia over the course of his life. In brief, Stanislavsky viewed the actor as an artist with agency and his System as a multivalent guide to acting that avoids dogma and embraces many different techniques and styles of dramatic art, realism being only one. Strasberg's more rigid Method and his insistence on emotional truth represents a tiny fraction of Stanislavsky's multidimensional System.[62] Indeed, Strasberg's emphasis on losing oneself in the part and on affective memory is distinctly at odds with Stanislavsky's focus on the actor's duality of consciousness and on playable actions. What Strasberg viewed as primary, Stanislavsky had discarded after earlier experimentation; the Russian master saw that affective memory had made his actors nervous in ways that did not advance their artistic work.[63]

Despite Strasberg's respect for acting, he actually moved key elements of Stanislavsky's System from the actor's to the director's control, thus shifting artistic responsibility for performance. He did this in two basic ways. First, he asked actors to modify Stanislavsky's question, "What would I do if I were in the character's circumstances?" to a less analytical and more personal question, "What in my own life would make me behave as the character?" Strasberg's restated question generates a "personal substitution" from the actor's life, rather than the imaginative flight into the character's world that Stanislavsky's question encourages. Thus, a Method actor can substitute personal feeling and emotions for that of the character. Second, once a personal substitution has been identified, all the actor need do is relive that remembered emotional life, the affective memory, in front of the camera. The actor's remembered emotion then becomes material for the camera, the director, and the editor.[64] An actor need not think or feel like his or her character as long as the content of the actor's thought leads to the performance that the director desires. For example, Strasberg argues that the "proper execution" of the scene in *Romeo and Juliet* when Juliet takes the potion "demands the use of emotional memory," and he proposes that the actress "investigate the normal behavior of a girl going to bed and saying her prayers."[65] For Strasberg, unlike for Stanislavsky, the cast need not necessarily share a common understanding of the film's characters and story, since each actor can draw on different personal substitutions to generate the performance required. In this way, the close textual analysis taught by Stanislavsky and the studio-era teachers is diminished in favor of easily accessed emotion. Indeed, many Method actors find that intellect can spoil their motional instincts. In contrast, Stanislavsky believed that great acting drew upon mind, body, and spirit equally.

Studio-era acting teachers had actually taught techniques that were more compatible with the central principles of Stanislavsky's System. For example, they argued for the value of training the body and the voice because they saw actors' minds and bodies as unified, organic wholes. They believed that the script provided the blueprint for building characters and that preparation made it possible to integrate directorial suggestions and interact effectively with other actors. Studio-era practitioners also emphasized the dispassionate execution of performance that was facilitated by concentration on the character's circumstances, goals, and actions. All these ideas underlie Stanislavsky's teaching as well, giving actual agency to the actor as a creator of performance.

However, with press coverage obscuring the agency of film actors, the integral role of drama coaches, and distinctions between the positions of different Method acting teachers, Strasberg's formulation of the Method came to be seen as the first systematic approach to film acting. Subsequently, screen performances have often been categorized by the type of actor (more and less versatile stars, method actors, character actors, and nonprofessional actors), with variants of Method acting lumped together.[66] For example, outlining the Method for film students, William H. Phillips combines Alder's emphasis with Strasberg's in saying that "the Method actors tries to figure out the character's biography and psychology and immerses herself or himself in the role (for example, by not sleeping enough if the actor needs to create an exhausted or distraught character)."[67] Mixing Alder's and Strasberg's positions once again, Phillips explains that "Method actors try to become the character and feel and act as the character would, in part by using people they know as models and by remembering situations from their own lives that evoke the same emotion."[68]

A number of film and theater scholars have recognized that Method acting as envisioned by Strasberg not only conforms to Benjamin's vision of film acting, but is also "strongly associated with certain modes of film stardom."[69]

For instance, Christine Geraghty notes that the Method's "emphasis on [actors'] emotion expressed through gesture and sound (rather than words)" seems to suit assumptions about cinema and its "visual possibilities."[70] She also points to the fact that Strasberg's emphasis on actors' personal feelings and emotions has been a topic of interest to academics because it is "consonant with [commercial] cinema's promotion of stars as unique and authentic individuals."[71] In other words, even the performances of serious method actors come to be seen as instances in which technology records and produces "natural" behavior.

In the 1950s the American public's interest in the Actors Studio was a response to publicity that the Method represented a radical departure from the slapdash methods and inauthentic approach used by older generations of actors. Film actors appeared to emerge as agents of their performances insofar as they drew on their personal experiences to create natural behavior and emotion that could be selected by directors and recorded by cameras and microphones. Ironically, however, Strasberg's approach at base confirmed the picture of screen performance that studio-era publicity had established. Thus, the transition from that to articles about the Actors Studio was seamless. In both journalistic eras, film actors supposedly played themselves. The public visibility of Strasberg's Method amplified the idea that film acting arises from natural behavior captured on screen. Throughout, the press did not challenge the basic tenets of the stage-screen opposition, seeing film actors as models or personalities to be photographed. Yet the narrative might have been different if the aesthetic influences on early film acting had been more clearly understood.

CRAFTING "NATURAL" BEHAVIOR IN SCREEN PERFORMANCES IN THE LATE 1800S

In Europe and the United States, the first film screenings took place in 1895, during a period shaped by the arrival of the telegraph, telephone, phonograph, and peepshow kinetoscope, all devices that manipulated physical presence. Following the introduction of the telegraph in the 1840s, encountering other people in urban societies no longer required them to occupy the same space. Beginning in the 1870s, the telephone made disembodied verbal encounters even more immediate and lifelike. With the arrival of the phonograph, mediated audio performance became more varied and entertaining. By 1879, Eadweard Muybridge was able to project images based on glass-plate series photography, and in 1882 Etienne-Jules

Marey's chronophotographic gun was the first single camera to produce series photographs. Magic lantern productions—slide shows often accompanied by off-screen narrators—were popular throughout the fin de siècle period. Kinetoscopes were invented in 1891, and the first Kinetoscope parlors opened in 1894. Thus, by the end of the nineteenth century, various devices featured mediated appearances and encounters.

Initially, when individuals appeared in films their performance status went undefined. People shown in films were often directed to perform their actions in certain ways, yet institutional conventions that would have prompted viewers to see them as acting or portraying fictional characters were not in place. Richard de Cordova points out that "'individuals' appeared in films for over ten years before the notion that they were actors began to be put forward."[72] Looking at the situation in terms of audience, Miriam Hansen explains that "the film spectator, as distinct from a member of an empirically variable audience, did not come into existence until more than a decade" after the first projection of films before a paying public in 1895.[73] This development explains, at least in part, the later twentieth-century view that screen performance is not necessarily crafted.

It also suggests how human bodies in film came to be seen as somehow comparable to inert matter. Early cinema was one of many visual novelties of the period. Audiences in Europe and America encountered films alongside wax museum displays, department store windows, and even the presentation of dead bodies in venues such as the Paris morgue.[74] The idea that performance on screen was "acting" emerged only after filmmakers, not exhibitors, determined the sequence in which scenes would be shown, after fiction film became the standard form of cinematic entertainment, after films of longer length allowed for the development of characters' psychological traits, and after theater stars such as Sarah Bernhardt began appearing regularly on screen.[75]

In France, the end of theatrical censorship in 1906 prompted the film industry to enhance cinema's status by aligning it with theatrical practice; "the theater analogy, at the level of both commercial and critical discourse, became more deeply ingrained in France than anywhere else."[76] French film's association with theater led to Films D'Art productions distributed by Pathé beginning in 1908. These were the first films "offered by reviewers as proof that the art of acting could be translated to the screen."[77]

Prior to her landmark performance in *The Loves of Queen Elizabeth* (1912), Bernhardt had not been pleased by the "translation" of her performance in *Hamlet's Duel* (1900) or *Tosca* (1908; never released). But, with the acclaimed Film D'Art production of *La Dame aux Camélias* (1911), she changed her mind. Her critical and commercial success with Film D'Art became the logical extension of her theatrical career as a star at the Odéon, the Comédie Française, and in international tours. The star dimension of Bernhardt's theatrical performances anticipated and perhaps influenced the central place that personality would have in film acting.[78] As if prefiguring studio-era publicity and Strasberg's Method, Bernhardt's contemporary George Bernard Shaw observed that the actress does "not enter into the leading character, but substitutes herself for it."[79] Shaw explained that Bernhardt's stage performances did not direct audience attention to characters she portrayed but instead involved "the art of making you admire her."[80]

It is significant that film appearances by stars such as Bernhardt, whose theatrical performances were prized for the degree to which they displayed the star's personality, coincided with the perception that acting could be found in film. The connection laid the foundation for the expectation to see stars, not actors, in films. In the earliest years of Western cinema, audiences tended to assume that film captured and then reproduced the natural behavior of ordinary people. By the teens, screen appearances by theatrical stars modified that view to include the notion that film also recorded stars' personalities.

However, the exclusive focus on screen performance as something produced not by craft but by the mechanical reproduction of personality and natural behavior warrants further scrutiny, because acting in Western cinema also coincided with the development of theatrical naturalism on the stages of France. Many scholar-practitioners are familiar with the fact that director André Antoine was instrumental in creating naturalist staging practices in the late nineteenth century. In productions mounted between 1877 and 1894 at the Théâtre Libre, Antoine worked out naturalism's key conventions in landmarks productions of Strindberg's *Miss Julie,* Hauptmann's *The Weavers,* Tolstoy's *Power of Darkness,* and Ibsen's *Ghosts* and *The Wild Duck.* Antoine's productions featured city streets and domestic spaces. He designed rooms environmentally, doing away with painted backdrops and often setting furniture along the curtain line. His productions featured complete rooms with the fourth wall removed in a way that gave rise to the convention of the invisible fourth wall. He brought real objects onto the stage and gave his actors authentic properties: for *Jacques D'Amour,* he borrowed his mother's kitchen table; in *The Butchers,* he hung real carcasses of beef on stage.

To heighten the illusion that audiences were observing life itself, Antoine worked with actors so that their performances broke away from the declamatory tradition that had included direct audience address and ostentatious gestures. His performers spoke to each other using low voices and colloquial tones. Crafting performances in this new way, Antoine's actors moved as if the room's fourth wall masked the eavesdropping audience on the other side; they often turned their backs to the audience. Training, experience, and creativity were integral to these performances that came to exemplify theatrical naturalism, for Antoine proposed that seemingly non-crafted performances required close observation of nature.[81] Antoine argued that stage sets had to be "brought back to the actual dimensions of scenes of contemporary life" so that actors could "play in true-to-life settings, without the constant need to *strike poses* in the customary sense of the word."[82]

Under the codes of theatrical naturalism, actors' labor and agency contributed to the aesthetic revolution that made incidental activity (precisely the sort often found in film acting) vitally important. Ironically, this shift depended upon actors hiding their virtuosity from the audience in order to make it appear that realistic characters lived on stage. Craft remained, but great actors made it invisible. When this aesthetic was used in cinema, the undefined status of film acting and the subsequent institutionalization of stars as anchors for screen performance allowed the labor and agency of people appearing in films to go unnoticed. Craftsmanship based on the naturalist aesthetic made it possible for theater *and* film practitioners to abandon emphatic, expressive gesture and the former convention of striking attitudes to sum up "an emotion or narrative idea for the audience."[83] However, given the reception context, early on film actors often succeeded all too well in making their craft invisible.

CONCLUSIONS

When screen performances that suggest the informality of quotidian behavior are seen as belonging to an aesthetic tradition, one can recognize that they are not simply instances of natural behavior captured by recording equipment. When film performances are seen as the result of acting/directing choices that are informed by aesthetic tradition, one can also recognize that they are comparable to a film's editing and lighting designs, framing patterns, or musical score. Like these, performances too result from ideologically informed but conscious decisions made by individuals. As long as live performance alone is identified with training, experience, and craft, the work of film actors will continue to be discounted. If the hierarchical opposition between stage and screen persists, critics will likely always focus on the genius of directors, and journalists will valorize screen actors for their bodies, personal emotions, and personalities.

It may be that "the impenetrable barrier of the screen favors representational playing styles."[84] That should, however, not obscure the fact that "an invisible 'fourth wall' had descended between the drama and the auditorium" prior to performers' first appearances in film.[85] Moreover, filmmakers' reliance on acting styles that draw on fin de siècle stage naturalism should not be taken as proof that acting in the cinema is captured natural behavior; it should be seen as evidence that screen performances are often crafted to produce what appears as "natural" behavior.

CHAPTER TWO

GIVING PERFORMANCE ELEMENTS THEIR DUE

The examples cited so far from *Pickpocket, The Rules of the Game,* and *Psycho* together with the observations about stage naturalism's influence on screen acting begin to dislodge the presumed opposition between the simple, natural behaviors captured by film cameras and the complex, intentional performances crafted by stage actors. This chapter takes our argument one step farther. We recognize that the narrative meaning of filmic gestures and expressions can be clarified by surrounding framing, editing, lighting, costuming, and sound design elements, but challenge the idea that framing and shot combinations create acting in the cinema. We propose that performance elements acquire dramatic significance in films the same way they do on stage: through their relationship to the other formal elements in the production. To make the case that screen performance does not differ as substantially as it might seem from performance on stage, we start by dismantling the familiar notion that "the camera and physical/informational context do the 'acting' for" screen performers.[1]

One of the most deep-seated reasons for thinking that cameras and informational contexts trump the film actors' craft stems from anecdotes about the editing experiments of Soviet filmmaker Lev Kuleshov in the early twentieth century. These have been "cited so frequently [they have] attained mythic status."[2] Kuleshov's editing exercises are generally thought to have shown that the work of film actors is "practically superfluous."[3] Yet, this story is far more complicated. Kuleshov's own interpretations of his work have been obscured by inconsistencies in his writings, prevailing ideas about cinema's unique properties, the doctrinaire views of his primary translator, and the fact that he formulated his nonmaterialist ideas in ways that would circumvent Soviet censors.[4] Despite the fact that Kuleshov explained it was "incorrect" to read his experiments as proof "that the work of the actor is absolutely irrelevant," the simplistic interpretation prevails.[5]

Three types of experiments are discussed by film scholars. The first involves Kuleshov's use of "creative geography" or the "juxtaposition of separate shots taken at separate places and times" to generate impressions of unified spaces or causal relationships.[6] In one of these studies, Kuleshov "synthesized the body of a woman [from images] of several separate women."[7] He created the depiction of a woman "sitting before her mirror, making up her eyes and eye-lashes, rouging her lips, [and] lacing up her shoes" by combining images that showed "the lips of one woman, the legs of another, the back of a third, and the eyes of a fourth."[8] Film scholars tend to view this work as primary evidence that the montage, not the actor, performs. Kuleshov, however, did not see these experiments as suggesting anything about film acting. His primary interest was to show that "artificial landscapes" could be created through the combination of selected images.[9]

The second type of experiment was a form of commutation test: Kuleshov prepared pairs of images, keeping one image in each pair constant, while changing the other. The most famous series involves using "the completely expressionless face . . . of pre-Revolutionary matinee idol Ivan Mozhukhin" as the stable image.[10] Kuleshov found "a long take in close-up of Mozhukhin's expressionlessly neutral face" and decided to "intercut it with various shots," which, according to Soviet director Vsevolod Pudovkin, featured "a bowl of steaming soup, a woman in a coffin, and a child playing with a toy bear."[11] The experiment demonstrated to Kuleshov that connotations conveyed by images used in films were not entirely fixed. He found that when an image is seen in isolation, there are connotations "it possesses in itself as a photographic image of reality."[12] However, when the image is presented in combination with another, it can acquire "a different [narrative or dramatic] meaning."[13] In other words, just as interpretations of gestures and expressions in live performances are influenced by a production's numerous material details (costume, lighting, set, etc.), so too do interpretations of photographed gestures and expressions reflect the film's combination of production details.

While Kuleshov saw the commutation test as providing information about how connotations that arise from isolated photographic images can differ from those suggested by images in a narrative-based sequence, his colleague Pudovkin took the test as evidence that acting in film is distinct from stage acting. For Pudovkin, the varying audience responses to

Mozhukhin's expressionless face demonstrated that editing had created the performance. Since audiences saw "hunger, compassion, and sorrow . . . in the actor's impassive countenance," Pudovkin credited Kuleshov's editing for each effect.[14] The experiment became known for demonstrating "the Kuleshov effect," the idea that significance arises from combinations of images that have no intrinsic meaning.

While this commutation experiment perhaps foreshadows the use of actors in films such as *L'Avventura* (1959) by Italian modernist Michelangelo Antonioni, *Last Year at Marienbad* (1961) by French modernist Alain Resnais, and the body of work by Robert Bresson, which includes *Pickpocket* and *Lancelot of the Lake* (1974), it does not represent the way all films work. Rather, when modernist filmmakers choose to create meaning by combining actors' blank expressions with other images, they consciously, deliberately, and radically break from mainstream film practice.

Moreover, the Mozhukin experiment does not show that film actors' gestures and expressions are insignificant. Kuleshov's observations about a third type of experiment best expose this misunderstanding of his work by confirming the importance of actors' contributions to films. This investigation took place in 1916 or 1917 and originated from Kuleshov's debate with "the then famous matinee idol, Vitold Polonsky, [who] asserted that there would be an enormous difference between an actor's face when portraying a man sitting in jail longing for freedom and seeing an open cell door, and the expression of a person sitting in different circumstances—say, the protagonist was starving and he was shown a bowl of soup."[15] Kuleshov shot both two scenes with Polonsky and "exchanged the close-ups [of the actor's face] from one scene to the other."[16]

While the filmmaker noticed that Polonsky's "reaction of joy at the soup and joy at freedom (the open cell door) were rendered completely unnoticeable by the montage," Kuleshov's further conclusions about the significance of this experiment are especially important.[17] First, he recognized that Polonsky's face actually carried different expressions in the two scenes, despite the fact that these differences went unnoticed when placed within the sequences. Second, Kuleshov attributed the interchangeability of the two close-ups not to editing but to Polonsky's skill as an actor. Polonsky had crafted expressions that were apt for both scenes. Kuleshov explained that in another instance he was unable to interchange the two reactions of an actor because they were performed by a less experienced actor. In that case, Kuleshov determined that each reaction registered as "completely different" because of the "poor work of an actor."[18] For Kuleshov, the lesser actor's work proved it was "not always possible to alter the semantic work of an actor."[19] He thus acknowledged that meaning in the cinema does not depend exclusively on editing choices, but also on connotations in "the segments themselves [and] in the very action that is being photographed."[20] In other words, Kuleshov found that meaning does indeed reside "in the actor's performance."[21]

Writing about the implications of the Polonsky experiment, Kuleshov comments that "when the director does not know his work with actors well enough, when he does not have sufficient command of the technique of this work, he tries to rectify all his errors and tries to compensate for the inadequacies of his acting with montage."[22] Kuleshov observes that one of Soviet cinema's "distinguished directors—the director Pudovkin, working in his films principally on montage construction—[was losing] his previous ability to work with actors more and more with each new film."[23] Kuleshov notes that, when directors are doing "films with large formats" and "many performing personnel," the cast will likely include "people who are unqualified as actors."[24] He explains that in these situations, "the role of montage, correcting and adjusting the actor's job, is highly significant."[25]

Kuleshov contrasts situations in which editing predominates with instances "when an idea must be expressed through the actor's work above all."[26] His detailed commentary on "the training of the actor" illustrates his respect for the craft of film acting, which requires "the most exact calculation and regard of the entire action."[27] He argues that screen performance requires "precision" and "the necessary conviction of the actor's work."[28] He demonstrates his familiarity with acting traditions when he suggests that "for the work of the face and all the parts of a human being, the system of Delsarte is very useful, but only as an inventory of the possible changes in the human mechanism, and not as a method of acting" (see chapter 7).[29] Kuleshov proposes that "the most important aspect of the training of the technique of the actor" involves "work along the fundamental axes of all the parts of the human organism."[30]

Kuleshov also outlines training principles that suggest points of contact with the work of Rudolf Laban (see chapter 8). He encourages exercises in which actors "shift from high-energy movements to slack and weak movements"; actors, he writes, must be able to create with "reality and simplicity" a full range of gestures that "can be energetic, strong, light, and weak."[31] Noting that "the better an actor works, the more complete his technique, the more intricately he can construct his movements," Kuleshov cautions against "having inexperienced people perform complex roles."[32] He proposes that after adequate training, "disorganized, muddled, confused work will be done away with, replaced by expressive clarity, assuredness."[33] Closing his remarks in a way that might surprise some readers, Kuleshov finds the expressive clarity he seeks "demonstrated to the entire world by Chaplin, Lon Chaney, Adolphe Menjou, Mary Pickford, and other first-rate actors."[34] These observations on acting reveal that "Kuleshov was intensely concerned with the training of players" and that he held an entirely different view of actors' work in the cinema than that suggested by Pudovkin's interpretation of the Mozhukhin experiment.[35]

Yet, Pudovkin's one-sided interpretation has remained central to academic notions about film performance. Jeremy Butler suggests that this bias is due to the early-twentieth-century Soviet "eager[ness] to distinguish the cinema from the other arts" and a feeling that cinema "had to be justified as more than a mechanical reproduction of a stage performance."[36] The desire to position cinema as a unique art led Kuleshov and his contemporaries to discuss all aspects of cinema under the rubric of "montage," which they did not always identify with editing. For example, Kuleshov writes about the "montage" or "internal rhythm" of an actor's performance.[37] This internal rhythm must by conveyed through clear performance choices. Formulating a position that would become key to Bresson's careful work with actors, Kuleshov argued that "pretending [and] playing are unprofitable, since this comes out very poorly on the screen."[38] In his view, cinema could not accommodate "a pretense of reality"; seeing "theatrical performance, actorship, [as] poor material for celluloid," Kuleshov argued for "organized movement" to convey ideas and express characters' thoughts and feelings.[39]

A WIDE SPECTRUM OF SCREEN PERFORMANCE

Kuleshov's writings not only suggest new ways to think about the infamous "Kuleshov effect," but also offer guidelines for mapping out the various ways that gestures and expressions are integrated into cinema. While in some films, the "vivid expression of an idea [is] achieved through montage above all," in others "an idea [is] expressed through the actor's work above all."[40] The examples from *Pickpocket* and *The Rules of the Game* (see chapter 1) suggest how directors can make different use of actors' expressivity (the degree to which actors do or do not project characters' subjective experiences). These films also disclose how directors can make equally different use of cinematic expressivity (the degree to which other cinematic elements enhance, truncate, or somehow mediate and modify access to actors' performances).

Directorial visions display a range of strategies for integrating performance and other cinematic elements. At one end of the spectrum, where framing and editing predominate, directors use performance elements as fragments in the film's audiovisual design. The work of experimental filmmakers such as Maya Deren and Stan Brakhage represent a radical version of this aesthetic; some of their films depict human movement as nothing more than pieces in a collage that re-creates the "act of seeing" or suggests "impossible" time-space combinations.[41] Luis Buñuel's surrealist classic *Un Chien Andalou* (1928) represents a step closer to the center, for the players' trancelike gestures and blank, inexpressive eyes contribute to the weird impression created by the piece as a whole. Punctuated by leers and wide-eyed expressions of surprise, the performances fit into bizarre sequences created by jump cuts and illogical "creative geography," with the ephemeral moments of expressivity always fading back into the actors' deadpan faces.

Narrative feature films by modernist directors occupy another step closer to the center of the spectrum, for while they explore the expressive connotations conveyed by acting choices, they do contain moments when "the film actor may do very little."[42] As Doug Tomlinson points out, Robert Bresson's films are marked by "the flattening of both external elements of performance: the physical and the vocal."[43] Bresson "systematically downplays the importance of the human figure, generally rendering it the equal importance of the environment."[44] His editing choices minimize "the onscreen representation of cathartic or paroxysmal acts."[45] Bresson often denies viewers access to players' emotion-filled facial and vocal expressions; however, "the camera and the physical/informational context" do not create performances in Bresson's films; instead acting choices are carefully designed to coordinate with framing and editing choices.[46] Tomlinson calls this approach an "aesthetic of denial."[47] In modernist films marked by such an "aesthetic of denial," actors are required to suppress the expression of emotion, while framing, editing, and other nonperformance elements become especially important.

This aesthetic represents a specific approach to *presenting* performances, one consciously designed to obstruct conventional identification with characters. Films by modernist Michelangelo Antonioni also exemplify this approach to the presentation of performance. He severely delimits actors' evocative gestures and expressions in order to use them as graphic elements. He thus consistently denies easy or conventional access to characters' inner experiences. Frank P. Tomasulo explains: "Certainly, *all* film directors shape the performances of their actors by utilizing wardrobe, hairstyle, and props. What sets Antonioni apart is that he relies [on] découpage, camera angles, color, lighting, set design, sound track articulations, music, *and* pared-down performances to construct . . . characterization."[48]

Illustrating the key role played by staging and design elements in Antonioni's *Blow-Up* (1967), Tomasulo notes that in the aftermath of the erotic photo shoot with model Veruschka von Lehndorff (playing herself) and David Hemmings as Thomas the photographer, the film cuts "to a view of Veruschka sprawled out on the floor as the photographer lies collapsed on the sofa in the background. A phallic wooden beam appears to emerge from the woman's crotch, suggesting the impersonal, 'wooden,' and unconsummated nature of their make-believe 'intercourse.'"[49] Discussing Hemmings's expressionless face and voice throughout the film, Tomasulo observes that even in the rare expressive moment when Hemmings's knitted brow suggests curiosity, "the shot composition communicates the character's situation more directly [for] Thomas's face is trapped between two of the blow-ups, which impinge on his 'personal space' and occupy most of the frame."[50] Tomasulo notes that in *Blow-Up,* there are times when "props actually *take the place of* performance and communicate directly with the spectator."[51] For example, at the end of the film, Antonioni "eschews the use of dialogue" and relies instead on "elements of the mise-en-scène: in this case, a chimerical 'prop'—an invisible ball—is used to convey character and meaning."[52]

At the other end of the spectrum where actors' work is treated as a primary cinematic element, human movements and interactions often provide the basis for a film's visual and aural design. Here, nonperformance elements are orchestrated to amplify the thoughts and emotions that actors convey. Such films use lighting, setting, costuming, camera movement, framing, editing, music, and sound to give audiences privileged views of the characters' inner experiences. This approach to the presentation of performance focuses attention on the connotative qualities of actors' work, and thus in these films, actors do a great deal. Chaplin's performance in *City Lights* (1931) reveals the way that film comedies often subordinate not only plot to actors' performances, but also shot selection, lighting design, and editing choices (see chapter 4).

Actors' gestures and expressions often provide an organizing principle in films by American independent directors working in a "neonaturalistic" tradition. Analyzing an opening scene of John Sayles's *Matewan* (1987), Diane Carson shows how Chris Cooper conveys the "curiosity mixed with apprehension" that his character, Joe Kenehan, experiences when he first encounters labor strife in the town he has come to unionize.[53] In a wide shot that features Cooper leaning out from between two railroad cars, he moves "unhurriedly but promptly" to secure a clear view of a skirmish between local miners and laborers who have just left the train.[54] Highlighting Cooper's motionless figure throughout the scene, Carson points out that Cooper communicates Kenehan's "unease and tension [simply] through pinched lips and shifts of his eyes."[55] Organizing nonperformance elements to allow these facial gestures to register, Sayles provides enough space in the frame around Cooper for audiences to perceive the physical and emotional restraint in his passive but attentive posture; Sayles's editing too gives audiences sufficient time to explore the actor's concerned, then pondering, expressions.

Films by John Cassavetes similarly focus on the work of actors, in part because his framing and editing choices are so often keyed to actors' movements and dramatic interactions. Even thematically, as Jonathan Rosenbaum notes, Cassavetes's "cinema is centered almost exclusively on actors and scenes."[56] Locating a point of contact between Cassavetes and Orson Welles, Rosenbaum explains "that 'acting' was the subject of all their films—not merely because of their passionate interest in actors, but also because their view of human nature and behavior had a lot to do with performance and the notion that everyone is an actor."[57] Discussing *A Woman Under the Influence* (1974), Ivone Margulies proposes that Mabel Longhetti, played by Gena Rowlands, "is the ultimate example of [Cassavetes's] stance. She acts oddly, she has tics, she desperately tries to please, she becomes selfless, and then, in turn, her self escapes her, becoming too visible, too theatrical."[58] The film's framing and editing strategies allow Rowlands's nuanced performance to convey "the precarious line between a medical and a social condition" for women living under the influence of tyrannical but loving husbands, clueless but concerned families, and skewed social norms that make it possible for a desperate one-night stand to be used as evidence of a nervous breakdown.[59]

Consider, for example, a scene early in the film when Mabel shares a spaghetti breakfast with her husband, Nick (Peter Falk), and his work buddies. This scene illustrates the way that Cassavetes organizes his film around actors' performances. Rowlands is placed at the far end of the table, opposite and distant from Falk, framed on both sides by burly men in heavy work clothes. Her gestures and expressions reveal how hard Mabel is trying to fit into the reality of the moment, even though she still reels from her experience the night before. Having planned a special date with her husband, she

Gena Rowlands in *A Woman Under the Influence:* Mabel in a moment of reflection

Rowlands reveals Mabel's effort to put on a public face and fulfill her role as hostess

A second later, Rowlands shows us that, for a moment, Mabel has composed herself

had sent their children to stay overnight at her mother's, but she drank too much while waiting for Nick to come home, and then, empty and disappointed after he finally called to say he was working late, made her way to a local bar. There she met a lonely, divorced man, whom she allowed to come home with her. When she wakes to find this strange man but not her husband and children, Mabel slips into a state of confusion. Hung over and still disoriented when Nick arrives home later that morning, not to make amends but with his entire work crew, Mabel is forced to grapple with another challenge, playing hostess. Pulling herself together, Mabel throws herself into preparing the spaghetti breakfast. When they sit finally down at the table, the momentary calm sets her adrift again. In the space of three seconds, the expressions that pass across Rowlands's face and through her eyes convey Mabel's flutter of varied emotions. With her eyes lowered, a pensive expression suggests that Mabel is trying to sort out what happened the night before. A second later, Rowlands looks up and slightly toward screen left. The strain in her face and neck together with a grimace that might pass for a smile conveys Mabel's struggle to fulfill the role of gracious hostess. A second later, Rowlands's expression suggests a moment of fleeting composure as she smiles and looks up, as if to Nick at the other end of the table. Framed to allow audiences to explore Rowlands's subtle and swiftly changing expressions, the film makes it possible to see that performing a wifely role can be tough.

AESTHETIC INFLUENCE, GENRE, AND ERA

The contrast between modernists like Bresson and Antonioni and neonaturalists like Sayles and Cassavetes reveals the spectrum of strategies for presenting performance on screen. At the same time, similarities within the two aesthetic approaches points to the fact that films from the same production tradition, regime, or period often share comparable approaches to the integration of performance and nonperformance elements. For example, *The Letter* (William Wyler, 1940), exemplifies the style of performance presentation in classical Hollywood films that feature the deep-focus cinematography made famous in Orson Welles's *Citizen Kane* (1941). In this aesthetic style, camera movements, frame compositions, sound design, and often long-take editing patterns are organized around the actors' performances. Part way through *The Letter*, Leslie (Bette Davis) is confronted by Howard (James Stephenson), her lawyer and her husband's friend, with news that there is evidence of her romantic involvement with the man she had supposedly killed in self-defense. The film presents this dramatic encounter in one nearly continuous take. Unobtrusive camera movement, keyed to their movements around the jail's visiting room, is broken only by two brief insert shots. One shows Howard/Stephenson pause to shift tactics in his line of questioning; the other reveals Leslie/Davis grasping that her husband and many others will learn about her sordid affair.

The aesthetic conventions illuminated by *The Letter* are thrown into sharp relief by the few films that prove the rule through exception. For example, *You and Me* (Fritz Lang, 1938), starring George Raft and Sylvia Sidney, uses nonnarrative and nonnaturalistic sequences to offer social commentary. Inspired by Kurt Weill, Bertolt Brecht's collaborator and the composer of the film's musical score, *You and Me* represents one of the instances in which a studio-era film features scenes marked by a Brechtian aesthetic (see chapter 6). For example, it opens with an extended visual and aural montage that enumerates the evils of capitalist consumer society. Later, its "stick with the mob" musical number with George Raft and the gang of petty crooks combines expressionistic images of the men in prison, straight-on shots of individual actors chanting their lines, and the men singing as if members of a call-and-repeat chorus. Near the conclusion, Sylvia Sidney gives a didactic lecture on the reasons "crime doesn't pay," using a blackboard to show the crooks how their $30,000 robbery would net each man only $113.33. The combination of Sidney's businesslike manner and Lang's frontal framing makes her lecture approximate direct address to the viewer and allows her conclusion, that politicians are the "big shots" in crime, to become an observation about the fictional world and the society inhabited by the film's audience.

Studio-era conventions for presenting performances can also be brought to light by contrasting them with strategies used in more recent films. For instance, Michael Almereyda's 2000 adaptation of *Hamlet* starring Ethan Hawke exemplifies the contemporary "televisual" aesthetic. Like a number of films designed for consumption in today's media marketplace, *Hamlet* models itself on viewing experiences in our media-saturated environment. Almereyda's title character carries a video camera to record his experiences, thus creating moments when the same gesture or expression is shown in multiple frames within the scene. While some viewers might find the multiple images confusing, for others they amplify the emotional impact of the expressive gestures that are framed in different ways. Just as Hamlet pores over the almost ephemeral gestures and expressions featured in his tapes, audiences too explore the actors' fleeting physical signs of emotion that are pieces of a larger collage cluttered with frenetic camera movements and dizzying editing patterns. In his 1996 "televisual" adaptation of *Romeo and Juliet,* Baz Luhrmann also draws attention to his mediatized frame of reference when he opens with a sequence that presents the Montague-Capulet feud as material suited for television news. Further, as our extended study demonstrates (see chapter 5), Luhrmann employs a similar approach to performance presentation when he emulates televisual experience by shifting rapidly from one character's story to another. In his film, framing, editing, and sound design sometimes obstruct access to characters' experiences, while at other times these elements enhance the perceived intensity of their subjective experiences.

Contrasts in strategies for presenting performance also emerge in comparisons between genres. There are discernable differences, for example, in the energy emerging from the performances in 1930s screwball comedies and those in recent action adventure films. The antics of the eccentric characters in *My Man Godfrey* (Gregory La Cava, 1936), for instance, are presented via performances infused with buoyant, bubbly, and flexible energy. William Powell's relaxed but self-possessed portrayal of Godfrey, the butler, provides just the flimsiest tether for the loopy energy in the performances by Carole Lombard, Alice Brady, Eugene Palette, and Gail Patrick, who portray the unconventional Bullock family. Often the only person not moving, gesturing, or talking in a scene, Powell grounds Lombard and the ensemble with more measured, economic movements. Similarly, when compared to a film like *Aliens* (James Cameron, 1986), the airy, flexible quality in Lombard's portrayal of dilettante Irene Bullock becomes entirely distinct from the strong, direct quality of Sigourney Weaver's performance as crew member Ellen Ripley. Portraying Ripley throughout the *Alien* series (including the 1979 Ridley Scott film, the 1992 David Fincher film, and the 1997 Jean-Pierre Jeunet film), Weaver uses tightly bound gestures and expressions, thus establishing a physical vocabulary for her character. She often presses her lips together, thrusts an arm out to deflect an attack, or slashes through the appendages of the Alien in its many incarnations. Reflecting conventions of the action adventure genre, Weaver's performance choices have little in common with the light, dabbing inflections in Lombard's voice when Irene seeks Godfrey's attention.

While Hollywood films from different genres and eras present performances in diverse ways, there is one constant: actors adjust the quality and energy of their gestures, voices, and actions to fit their characters' shifting desires and interactions with others. At any moment of a film narrative, actors' work contributes to the trajectory of the dramatic action. It also reflects characters' narrative function, with secondary and background characters sometimes portrayed with less expressivity than central characters. By seeing acting choices as designed to suit narrative demands and aesthetic traditions, it becomes possible to appreciate the complex and varied relationships among facial expressions, shot selections, characterizations, and more (see parts 2 and 3).

This type of aesthetic analysis differs from studies of the way directors work with actors. Anecdotal accounts about directorial styles not only occlude performance elements' place in film representation; they can also be misleading. For example, the endless circulation of Alfred Hitchcock's infamous remark that actors should be treated like cattle merely reinforces entrenched assumptions about film acting (see chapter 1); it says little about his actual work with actors and fails to increase insight into ways that acting choices affect audience interpretations of his films. Doug Tomlinson notes that Hitchcock never confirmed or denied the remark but instead "played to it, delighting in the confrontations it provoked with critics as well as the attention it ultimately brought his name."[60]

Working relationships between directors and actors vary. Jean Renoir explains that some directors think first of framing and shot selection, while others "start with the actors."[61] Antonioni, who considers actors as "an element of the image—and not always the most important element," begins with framing and shot selection; directors like Renoir, who began their careers as actors, base shot selections on blocking developed in collaboration with the actors.[62] Some directors who emphasize audiovisual design place a high priority on actors' contributions, while some directors who attend to actors' vocal and physical choices do not welcome collaboration.

Directors who start with the camera but leave actors alone to do their creative work often see film actors as experts who bring specialized knowledge and talents to the enterprise. Henry Fonda explains that "they hire the best actors they can find and expect a performance from them."[63] For example, Robert Altman sees screen performances as work that emerges from "the combination of what I have in mind, with who the actor is and then how he adjusts to the character, along with how I adjust."[64] Directors who start with shot selection sometimes become master puppeteers who treat actors as objects for the lens. Describing his experience with director Fritz Lang, Fonda explains that Lang "would actually manipulate you with his hands" to achieve the image that he desired.[65] Stanley Kubrick, who saw "himself as a director who focuses intensely on acting," did not collaborate with actors.[66]

Ultimately, the status of performance elements is best clarified by analysis of the aesthetic choices actually seen on screen. From the standpoint of reception, what the actor does within the frame with body and voice, rhythm and movement, matters more than the presumed creative process. Moreover, as the varied examples from *Blow-Up, Matewan, A Woman Under the Influence, My Man Godfrey,* and *Aliens* suggest, treating film acting as a single class of performance that provides "a good example of nonmatrixed representation" and actors' performances as simple behaviors performed without reference to the "matrices of pretended or represented character, situation, place and time," disregards how seldom such situations occur in fiction films.[67] Instead, actual examples suggest the variety of ways that films use actors' gestures, expressions, intonations, and inflections, and consequently demonstrate that film acting does not have a single distinguishing trait. Most importantly, specific examples illuminate how performance functions as one aspect of a film's formal design. In sum, examining films from different production contexts illustrates that sometimes film actors do very little, while at other times meaning is conveyed, as Kuleshov wrote, "through the actor's work above all."[68]

VARIED RELATIONSHIPS BETWEEN PERFORMANCE AND NONPERFORMANCE ELEMENTS

To pursue the idea that acting is an aesthetic and meaningful component of film, consider how performance elements enter into audiovisual design. As films produced in varying styles, genres, and periods suggest, performance details do not have fixed relationships with other cinematic details or techniques, even within an individual film. In some scenes, especially in those where singing, dancing, or dynamic interactions occur, performance details might outweigh the impact of editing and framing.

An example of performance directing audience attention can be found when Donald O'Connor performs "Make 'Em Laugh" in *Singin' in the Rain* (Gene Kelly and Stanley Donen, 1952), using movements that become "increasingly assertive and energetic" as the dance develops.[69] As Richard Maltby observes, "Camera movement and editing are kept to a minimum: both simply recompose space to support O'Connor's performance."[70] Maltby notes that "minimal cutting" is a salient aspect of the scene: "a single long take covers most of the routine, with panning movements reframing space to cover O'Connor's actions."[71] Moreover, this scene is not an aberration because musical "sequences and comedy routines are often constructed like this, with the duration of the shots emphasizing the complexities of a sustained performance."[72]

At other times, when actors' performances do not overshadow choices about other aspects of a scene, a nonperformance element such as camera movement can become the dominant component. Jean-Luc Godard's *Weekend* (1967) features a scene in the French countryside; a moving camera tracks along a stretch of road that is filled with dozens of cars and trucks, some horse carts, a Shell oil tanker, vehicles towing sailboats and exotic animals in cages, and, finally, a few overturned cars next to bodies covered in obviously fake blood. The scene's bravura camera movement is ostensibly keyed to the progress of the sports car carrying the film's thoroughly rotten haute bourgeois protagonists, Corinne (Mireille Darc) and Roland (Jean Yanne). While their animated, angry gestures enhance the unpleasantness of the sequence, the scene functions largely as a Brechtian commentary on "the weekend" and capitalism's management of human labor. By highlighting the "cinematic" technique of camera movement, Godard also pays ambivalent homage to *Promenade of Ostriches, Paris Botanical Gardens* (1895), the Lumière actuality that documents a parade of local citizens and exotic animals. An irreverent young man closes this thirty-second actuality by tipping his hat to the cinematographer as he "accidentally" interrupts the filming of the parade.

While the scenes in *Singin' in the Rain* and *Weekend* represent extreme examples, cinema most often presents audiences with films in which performance operates in more equal concert with other cinematic elements. In *Philadelphia* (Jonathan Demme, 1993), Andrew Beckett (Tom Hanks) makes his lawyer, Joe Miller (Denzel Washington), confront his own homophobia. The scene takes place in Beckett's apartment with a recording of Maria Callas singing Maddalena's aria "La mama morta," from *Andrea Chénier* playing in the background. As Ronald E. Shields explains in his analysis, "the contrast between Joe's slow progress toward empathy and Andrew's emotional confession during the [Callas] aria scene can be traced in the careful use of lighting, blocking, and camera angle."[73] Shields observes that the scene ends with Andrew/Hanks "standing alone in the center of the room, leaning heavily on the [medical-drip] stand for support—a diva spent, standing alone onstage."[74] He notes that the beginning and the end of the scene are "established through a high-angle shot circling above the wooden floor of the apartment," and that at key moments Andrew/Hanks "pushes his medical-drip into and out of the frame—a lonely solo dance."[75] Describing the balance and connection between performance and nonperformance elements, Shields explains that "the use of a moving camera, the pulsating red light alternating with darkness on Andrew's face, and the layered line readings by Tom Hanks, all work together to bring the audience directly into Andrew Beckett's world, his hope, and his hell."[76] As this example suggests, it is sometimes difficult to determine which, if any, filmic element has priority.

At such moments, performance elements are integrally connected not only to framing and editing choices, but also to set design. For example, a complex interaction between performance choices and scenic color can occur, sometimes in concert and sometimes in counterpoint. In the scene from *Orlando* (Sally Potter, 1992) when the lithe young title character (played by Tilda Swinton) relaxes in a steam bath and recalls his drinking adventures with a Middle Eastern nomadic prince, Swinton's calm, yielding posture converges with soft, white towels and the beige tones of the steam bath that provides a sanctuary for the sensitive young man. Changing any one of these elements would alter the sense of the scene, as later scenes reveal.

Soon after the steam bath scene, Orlando has a brush with death; he regains consciousness only to discover that he has become a woman. He/she returns to England and the film's next segment features scenes in which Swinton's tense, agitated gestures are set against a calm monochromatic palette and soft light. The character's deep discomfort now registers against an ostensibly peaceful environment. With movement made almost impossible by her newly required corset and layered petticoats, Orlando finds that she is blocked in by the furniture in her mansion, and later deterred by the estate's manicured hedges as she attempts to escape her new and limited status as a woman in eighteenth-century England. As these contrasting examples indicate, an actor's gestures and expressions can be used differently within a film's formal design in order to contribute to the meaning of individual scenes. In short, the connotatively rich quality of actors' movements combines with other aspects of film to create meaning and dramatic significance.

FRAMING AND EDITING AS CHOICES ABOUT PERFORMANCE

Because performance details carry significance, film acting is something more than what is created by shot selections and shot-to-shot relations. Joining together a close-up on a young woman's startled expression with a sharp rise in the musical score reflects a directorial choice about more than frame composition and sound design; it is as much a choice about performance.

The image of an elderly man glaring, wide-eyed, his face half in light, half in shadow, similarly reveals decisions about lighting design and performance.

Aesthetic choices described in terms of framing or editing are often in fact decisions about the presentation of actors' performances. To understand framing and editing choices, it is useful to recognize when they are designed to feature performance. As Kuleshov might note, there are indeed times when framing, editing, lighting, costume, and sound design are keyed to the actors' contributions, for sometimes in the cinema "an idea must be expressed through the actor's work above all."[77]

Yet, instances when performance predominates are often overlooked. Noting that the first cine-semioticians were "blind to performance," Jeremy Butler observes that Christian Metz was "remarkably mute about the position of actors' performances . . . in his two groundbreaking books, *Film Language* and *Language and the Cinema*."[78] In fact, performance elements have no place in Metz's system. Placing emphasis on framing and editing as key to film, he believed that spectators' primary identification was "with the act of looking itself" and that identification with the story's dramatic characters was, at best, of secondary or tertiary importance.[79]

Building upon Metz, scholars focused on the idea that shot/reverse shot sequences (pairs of over-the-shoulder shots often used in dialogue scenes between two characters) position spectators to assume the (literal and figurative) point-of-view of the respective characters.[80] Metz's view that spectators identify with the look of the camera and/or the look of the characters became linked to the psychoanalytic concept of suture, the process whereby a thinking and speaking subject "is 'stitched' into the chain of discourse."[81] In the late 1960s, the concept of suture was applied to "the films of Robert Bresson as a way of designating a particular type of relation between the look of the spectator-subject and the chain of filmic discourse."[82] Robert Stam, Robert Burgoyne, and Sandy Flitterman-Lewis point out that applying the concept of suture to "films other than Bresson's has been problematic."[83] William Rothman has also raised "a general uncertainty as to the actual role of the 'system of suture' in classical film."[84] Indeed, if one sets aside the notion that audiences identify with the camera first and the characters second, one can see that shot/reverse shot sequences often represent instances when framing and editing are organized around actors' performances, when nonperformance elements are secondary to actors' gestures and expressions, and when "an idea must be expressed through the actor's work above all."[85]

Consider, for example, how *Far From Heaven* (Todd Haynes, 2002), an homage to Douglas Sirk's *All That Heaven Allows* (1955), features shot/reverse shots that give audiences time to examine the actors' facial expressions for cues that illuminate meaning and dramatic significance. By focusing on the social stigma of a love affair between a wealthy widow (Jane Wyman) and a young, bohemian gardener (Rock Hudson), Sirk gave dramatic form to the consequences of American patriarchy and economic class. Continuing that analysis in *Far From Heaven,* Haynes also critiques race relations and homophobic social and legal strictures. In his film, Cathy (Julianne Moore), a model housewife in Hartford, Connecticut, seeks solace from her gardener, Raymond Deagan (Dennis Haysbert), while she and her husband, Frank (Dennis Quaid) struggle with his long-repressed but newly rediscovered homosexual desire.

One shot/reverse shot sequence that features performance occurs outside the medical building where Frank has sought a "cure." While Cathy waits outside, Frank tells the doctor, "I'm going to beat this thing. I'm going to break it, so help me God." But afterward, as Frank/Quaid and Cathy/Moore leave the building, she is taken off guard when he abruptly stops on the front steps, refusing to see other doctors and shouting at her that he wants to get "the whole fucking thing over with." From earlier scenes, the audience understands that this is an unusual moment; Frank has rarely raised his voice with Cathy and very likely has never used curse words around her before. A three-second shot over Quaid's shoulder allows us to study Moore's face as her character registers the significance of this painful moment with her husband. As the shot begins, we see Moore's eyes open wide. Her head is drawn back and her neck is stiff. Cathy is stunned, perhaps even shocked. She has never seen this side of her husband. She had expected the doctor to bring back normalcy; she had expected her efforts to support and understand her husband to pay off. After a moment, Moore slowly dissolves the look of shock. Her next expression suggests her new realization that finding her husband in the arms of a man had set into motion a chain of events that will change her life. As the shot continues, a softening in Moore's expression conveys Cathy's growing awareness of her changed circumstances and her mounting sense of loss. Moore's eyes fill with tears; her mouth closes in a wistful smile. In the space of three seconds, Moore's evolving facial expressions make concrete her emotional journey as she comes to understand that she has already lost her husband.

Far From Heaven also contains scenes in which performances by actors in supporting roles carry equal if not greater weight than the framing and editing choices that surround them. Throughout the film, Viola Davis as

Julianne Moore in *Far From Heaven:* Cathy is stunned, shocked, out of her depth

A moment later, Moore suggests the emotional distance Cathy has quickly traveled

Sybil, the Whitaker's maid, often embodies the salient emotional tone of dramatic moments. For example, midway through the film, Sybil/Davis looks out a front window of the Whitaker house to see Cathy and Raymond happily setting off together on a beautiful fall afternoon. Framing Davis in a neutral, conventional medium shot, Haynes allows audiences first to see and then contemplate the slight frown on Davis's face. Her expression might suggest concern about Cathy's and Raymond's welfare, unease with Raymond's boldness, alarm about Cathy's inappropriate behavior, or even disapproval of their blithe ignorance of the repercussions that would arise from their afternoon together. Here, Davis's expression succinctly reflects a spectator's possible reactions to the central characters' ill-fated relationship.

Davis also functions as a mirror for the audience in a moment near the end of the film, after Sybil tells Cathy that the "colored" girl injured weeks before by local schoolboys is Raymond's daughter. While the audience has known about the attack and understood that it was a consequence of Cathy's indiscreet affair, only now does Cathy discover that white residents of Hartford showed their displeasure about her behavior by hurting Raymond's child. While Moore reveals Cathy's shock and frantic concern, in the final images of the scene the details of Davis's performance give physical expression not only to Sybil's sorrow, but also to what the audience might feel about the film's dramatization of the emotional pain caused by racism in America.

Echoing the neutral framing in the scene when Davis had conveyed concern about Cathy and Raymond's friendship, Davis is again framed in a medium shot that allows audiences to study her face and the qualitative features of her pose. Watching Cathy/Moore leave toward the lower-right corner of the frame, Davis stands in the front doorway of the Whitaker house and slowly closes her eyes, remaining almost completely still. Here again, the long take allows us to examine this simple, restrained facial gesture. With her head bowed slightly, her lips gently closed, her left hand on the half-open door, and her right hand at her side, she lowers and closes her eyes to create an impression of sadness. Her closed eyes also suggest that Sybil takes a moment to ponder the injury to Raymond's daughter, the futility of Cathy going to Raymond, and the injustice that Sybil herself experiences daily. As the shot holds on Davis, the details of her performance continue to provide cues to the scene's dramatic significance. After opening her eyes, Davis keeps her shoulders square, and leans forward slightly. Her change of posture suggests that Sybil is not overcome by her sorrow, or even by the social forces that cause it. By leaning, as if toward Moore in the near distance, Davis allows us to understand that Sybil does not disapprove of Cathy, but rather cares about her well-being. Davis's restrained, composed stance in the doorway conveys the sense that Sybil is a compassionate, clear-headed witness to the events surrounding her.

Design and framing elements extend Davis's work in this scene, but they do not do the acting for her. Costume supports the connotations carried by the details of Davis's performance. Her uniform's midnight-blue color and white, crisply starched cuffs and collar suggest restraint and inner strength,

Viola Davis in *Far From Heaven:* a slight shift in posture conveys her compassion

as do her facial expression and postures. Similarly, sadness is amplified by the image of Davis alone in the doorway, an image that remains on screen for a long time, dissolving very slowly into the next scene. Certainly, the dramatic significance of Davis's gestures and expressions are clarified by shots surrounding them, but her performance is active, not inert clay. It would be untenable to suggest that Davis does very little. In the brief seconds of a single shot, Davis conveys Sybil's sorrow and resolve, her private experience of grief, and her compassion for those around her.

Framing and editing can be choices about performance even in films known for spectacular displays of cinematic technique. Take, for example, the scene from *Moulin Rouge!* (Baz Luhrmann, 2001), in which Jacek Koman, as the Narcoleptic Argentinean, performs the Roxanne Tango. This scene gives physical expression to the emotional turmoil experienced by the leading characters, the courtesan Satine (Nicole Kidman) and her lover, the youthful writer Christian (Ewan McGregor). Convinced that her sacrifice will keep Christian from harm, Satine has agreed to spend the evening with the Duke (Richard Roxburgh) to secure his continuing support for their upcoming production of "Spectacular, Spectacular," which ends with a courtesan, played by Satine, falling in love with a penniless sitar player. Earlier scenes make clear that the Duke and the entire company all recognize that the sitar player is Christian's fictional double. Previous scenes also establish that the Narcoleptic Argentinean portrays the sitar player; thus it is fitting for the Argentinean to perform the writer's powerful and conflicting feelings in this time of emotional crisis.

In the opening moments of the scene, Koman focuses his full attention on Christian/McGregor as he tells him that a man "should never fall in love with a woman who sells herself." The clear, even, direct quality of his vocal delivery gives the sprawling, multifaceted scene a lucid, succinct, emotionally charged grounding. As an act of compassion and camaraderie, Koman performs the intense feelings he knows that Christian is experiencing. With strong, direct movements, Koman strides to the center of the huge, darkened dance hall, commanding the attention of the entire company of dancers who have been lounging at the sidelines. His dance enacts a story that parallels the writer's, that of a man in Buenos Aires who once fell in love with a prostitute. Early in the tango, grace and elegance express the man's ignited passion. As the tango progresses, however, tension in Koman's hands and arms suggest the beginnings of the man's jealousy. Christian and the mesmerized dancers watch, listen, and begin to join into the tango. Further on, images of Koman's anguished face now convey the lover's pain. As the tango moves into its final stage, the tight, twisted posture of Koman's body makes visible the despair of a man who falls in love "with a woman who sells herself." As it concludes, Koman's voice still fills the vast expanse of the dance hall; it seems to carry beyond, out to the tower where Satine meets the Duke, its rough, powerful, and rasping quality cutting through space as if representing the lovers' stifled cries.

In Jacek Koman's mournful rendition of "Roxanne," the harsh, gravely quality of his voice carries such strong connotations of pain that the film's audience might be led to experience empathetic feelings of pain or grief. The film amplifies the feelings prompted by the qualities of Koman's voice through its dizzying fragmentation of the visual aspect of the scene; as one of the few points of continuity, Koman's voice has a greater impact than it might in a scene with conventional editing. The film's aggressive editing also causes Koman's body to be one of the few points of continuity. The consequence is that fleeting images of Koman's expressive movements, gestures, and facial expressions take on a great deal of import, with framing and editing choices functioning as choices about the presentation of performance.

Jacek Koman in *Moulin Rouge!:* taking command of the scene and the situation

Koman enacting the passion the young writer feels for the beautiful courtesan

The tension in Koman's gesture communicates the writer's anger and suspicion

Calling out to “Roxanne”: Koman’s grimace conveys the pain of the jealous lover

Koman’s sidelong glance and constricted posture embodies the lovers’ despair

Jacek Koman, his voice traveling through space, anchoring the “Roxanne Tango”

FOCUSING ATTENTION ON GESTURES AND EXPRESSIONS

The way Koman's vocal and physical expression contributes to the Roxanne Tango sequence illustrates the principle that framing and editing often serve to focus attention on the images featured in filmic combinations. That principle is the subject of Sergei Eisenstein's 1929 essay "The Cinematographic Principle and the Ideogram." Here, Eisenstein contrasts the West's established method of fine art composition with the modern "cinematic" approach that he likens to a process in Japanese landscape painting. He contends that Western visual artists "take any piece of white paper with four corners on it [and then] cram onto it, usually without even using the edges . . . some bored caryatid, some conceited Corinthian capital, or a plaster Dante."[86] Eisenstein maintains that conventional films employ "this expiring method of artificial spatial organization of an event in front of the lens."[87] In contrast, like Japanese landscape painters, filmmakers sensitive to cinema's potential approach composition "from a quite different direction."[88] The Japanese process requires artists to select a "branch of a cherry tree," and then locate "compositional units" that illuminate the unique details of the branch (the gentle curve of its base, the twist of an attached twig, the bend of another twig with two leaves, and so on).[89] Eisenstein compares that process to cinematic framing, and he reasons that the "cinematographic principle" involves "picking out" significant details with "the camera [and hewing] out a piece of actuality with the ax of the lens."[90] In Eisenstein's view, framing does not fragment visual experience but instead illuminates the evocative qualities of actuality by focusing viewers' attention on its salient features.

Jonathan Crary comes to the same conclusion about modern film and media. His study presents an alternative to "the widespread assumption that, from the mid-1800s on, perception is fundamentally characterized by experiences of fragmentation, shock, and dispersal."[91] Analyzing patterns in modern Western culture, he determines that reception is not distinguished by "a state of distraction."[92] He responds to the one-sided emphasis on modern experiences of shock and dispersal by asserting that cultural-technological developments that fragment attention actually have a "reciprocal relation to the rise of attentive norms and practices."[93] In Crary's view, people living in media-saturated environments are not confused by or inattentive to the barrage of sounds and images that surround them because they have also grown up within "the disciplinary organization of labor, education, and mass consumption."[94] The naturalized presence of "attentive norms and practices" becomes visible when one reflects on "activities like driving a car or watching television" that require us to "cancel out or exclude from consciousness much of our immediate environment."[95] "Attentive norms and practices" enhance one's ability to set aside extraneous input and thus focus more effectively on the dense, constantly changing bits of information pertinent to the matter at hand, be it traffic conditions or narrative enigmas.

By recognizing the role of "attentive norms and practices," Crary is able to address "ways in which film and modernist art occupy a common historical ground."[96] Essentially following Eisenstein's line of argument, Crary proposes that modern film and painting require and reward the type of "concentrated attentiveness" central to industrial Western societies since the late nineteenth century.[97] Both feature fragments of telling details that must be made sense of; both involve attention that "is much more than a question of the gaze, of looking, of the subject only as a spectator."[98] In contrast to traditional compositions that use the borders of the canvas/frame to organize an event for the viewer, modern painting and films designed according to the "cinematographic principle" communicate with audiences by "picking out" significant details, by "hewing out" pieces of actuality, such as Koman's expressive vocal and physical choices in the tango sequence. In modern art and cinema, these details are themselves charged with expressivity that can be detected by attentive audiences. Single details need not carry full-blown narrative meaning to resonate with significance; as Crary notes, "by the 1880s, perception, for many was synonymous with 'those sensations to which attention has been turned.'"[99]

Crary's insight that "attentive norms and practices" focus audience attention on fleeting details (whether one is driving, watching television, exploring modern painting, or viewing film) has important implications for conceptualizing the role of framing, editing, lighting, sound, and acting in the scene from *Moulin Rouge!* and in cinematic scenes generally. The importance Crary places on "attentive norms and practices" supports our view that framing and editing choices can serve to "cancel out or exclude" sounds and images that would detract from the evocative qualities of performance details. With modern "attentive norms and practices" shaping reception, framing and editing choices in the cinema do not mute the expressive power of performance but instead concentrate attention on the connotatively rich features of actors' performances.

Eisenstein's observations about the cinematographic principle of composition and Crary's research on modern attention clarify the fact that cultural and aesthetic conventions facilitate concentrated attention on the gestures and expressions that become highlighted through framing and editing selections. While some scholars might draw on Christian Metz and thus imagine that cinema "can be characterized above all in terms of the *fractional* and *fusional* aspects of its cutting structure," Eisenstein's essay, Crary's research, and the case studies throughout this book provide a reasoned correction to the notion that editing is the most salient component of film.[100] Editing is one of many filmic elements. As noted earlier, Eisenstein identifies *the* cinematographic principle as framing that serves to highlight expressive details. Thus, even the simplest view of cinema needs to account for the effect of editing and framing choices, and those that color the evocative, connotative details of the "actuality" pictured.

The thrust of Eisenstein's argument and Crary's findings on attention has been confirmed and amplified by new research in neuroscience, which shows that perception of human movement, when encountered in the immediate environment or seen on screen, induces "the ability of humans to empathize with others, detect their mental states, infer their intentions, and predict their actions."[101] Eisenstein's position is that even when actors suppress emotion, and when ideas are conveyed largely through framing and editing choices, filmmakers still select and then feature *lucid human expression* to reveal character and communicate ideas. In Crary's view, modern attentive norms and practices enhance one's ability to explore fleeting but expressive human gestures so that one has the information needed to function effectively and perhaps even meaningfully in a media-saturated environment.

When viewers strain their bodies as they watch track runners race to the finish line or feel aroused when they watch performers lock together in passionate embrace, the hard-wired connection between performing actions and watching actions in person or on screen comes clearly into view. The findings on mirror neurons are extremely important to cinema studies because they support the view that audiences respond to human movements, gestures, and expressions shown in films. The research is also significant because it puts to rest the entrenched notion that film acting cannot have the same impact as live performance. The studies of mirror neurons not only debunk the notion that film acting lacks efficacy, they even show that performing actions, being present to watch actions, and observing actions on screen all trigger the same responses.[102]

The research in mirror neurons suggests that audiences do not respond directly to framing and editing choices but instead to gestures and expressions that serve as the locus of meaning. For example, in the shot/reverse shot sequence in *Far From Heaven,* interpretations and emotional responses are more directly linked to Julianne Moore's changing facial expressions than to the conventional shot selection and editing pattern. Far from being inert matter, the minute qualities of actors' gestures and expressions carry connotations that audiences analyze in relation to nonperformance elements and in light of narrative context. An important implication of the research into reception, perception, and cognition is that cinema facilitates the close examination of expressions, gestures, intonations, and inflections so that audiences can ascertain what goal-directed action they are watching and determine what emotional content is conveyed by the qualitative dimension of the performance details on screen.

CONCLUSIONS

The examples throughout this chapter reveal that films allow audiences to pay close attention to the gestures and expressions presented in films. The series of telling details within single shots in *A Woman Under the Influence* and *Far From Heaven* also indicate that screen performances can be quite complex, often creating the impression "of many things taking place simultaneously in the work of a single actor."[103] Yet in spite of this evidence, some might still hold to the stage-screen opposition, seeing film actors as essentially stage props whose gestures and expressions "acquire representational and characterological significance only in the editing room."[104]

Regarding the example from *A Woman Under the Influence,* it is true that watching the scenes that show what has happened to Mabel before the spaghetti breakfast provide a context for understanding and interpreting Rowlands's facial expressions at the table. But the previous scenes do not create her expressions, nor do they change the impressions audiences might get from those expressions. Without seeing the scene in context, audiences might not know why Mabel is so unsettled, but Rowlands's expressions would still convey the idea that a woman struggles to find balance and connection at this moment. Similarly, in *Far From Heaven,* contextual information prior to Frank's shouting at Cathy makes it possible for Moore's changing facial expression to have "characterological significance." But even if taken out of context, the qualitative details in Moore's face would remain the same. While it might not be possible to determine what had caused her feelings, it would still be clear that a stunned and unhappy woman is first shocked and then saddened by the man's shouts. While the film provides information that allows audiences to grasp the full significance of Viola Davis's changing expression and posture as she stands in the doorway, even if this shot were seen out of context, it would still be clear that a woman shifts from a private moment of reflection to an expression of outward care and concern.

The evocative gestures and expressions in the frame captures from *Far From Heaven* and *Moulin Rouge!* serve as a reminder that film technology does not transform inert material into screen performances. Rather, combining qualitatively distinct gestures and expressions with other formal elements in a film clarifies narrative meaning and dramatic significance. Performance elements take on representational significance when combined with other elements, much as do other cinematic choices in lighting, set, or sound design. However, acting choices carry certain connotations in and of themselves. For example, in the tango sequence, Mandy Patinkin's soaring tenor voice would convey rather different impressions from Jacek Koman's use of rough, gravely vocal expression. Consistently dense with connotation, performances, like other aspects of a film, are "evolving structures" that are best understood by examining "relations between components" (see chapter 4).[105]

The extended case studies in the later chapters of the book should clarify the fact that screen performance does not have a single, defining attribute, for they challenge the idea that "the camera and the physical/informational context do the 'acting' for the film actor."[106] They demonstrate that complex acting does occur in the cinema and that it deserves careful analysis. For instance, examining the given circumstances, objectives, actions, and units of action in film performances, such as those in *The Grifters* (Stephen Frears, 1990), reveals that film acting can display specificity, modulation, and frequent change (see chapter 9).[107]

Shot selections, camera movements, lens selections, and so on will amplify, sustain, or truncate the connotations carried by actors' gestures and expressions. Impressions created by set design elements will confirm or counterpoint those created by performance elements. Information established over the course of the narrative will support or contradict impressions conveyed by the gestures and expressions we see and hear at any given moment in a film. Yet that does not mean that framing, editing, and other filmic strategies do the acting. Rather, performance elements should be given their due as integral components of a film, with concrete details of voices, gestures, postures, and actions examined as aspects of narrative and audiovisual design.

CHAPTER THREE

THINKING SYSTEMATICALLY ABOUT ACTING

The perceptible details of screen performance come into view more readily when they are differentiated from fictional characters, actors, and stars. Distinctions between some of these categories are more obvious than others. For example, fictional characters are immaterial, intratextual aspects of a narrative, while actors occupy the material, extratextual world of everyday life. In addition, actors who pay bills, have parents, and get stuck in traffic are distinct from their larger-than-life star images, which belong to yet another immaterial realm, that of extratextual, cultural discourse. Characters, actors, and star images do share something, however: none of them are part of filmic discourse or representation per se. Only gestures and expressions, which are executed by actors and become associated with characters and stars, are part and parcel of films. To see how those performance elements contribute to audience impressions, one needs to think systematically about acting.

The dense array of connotatively rich gestures, postures, intonations, and inflections seen and heard in film are the material, intratextual elements that belong to filmic representation in the same way that lighting design and editing patterns do. Importantly, performance details contribute to the flow of narrative information; interpretations about characters' desires, their confrontations, and their choices depend in part on the sense that audience members make of actors' gestures and expressions. The selection and integration of performance elements in a film provide some of the most crucial information about what is happening, why, and what is at stake.

Interest in performance elements as indices of narrative information has been a circumscribed part of film scholarship for decades. As Jeremy Butler notes, writings by Béla Balázs in the 1940s anticipate contemporary approaches to performance as a text "composed of signifiers, such as bodily gestures and facial expressions—the raw material of acting—that are patterned into structures that have meaning for the spectator . . . when placed in the larger context of the sign system of an entire movie or television program."[1] Yet a collection of factors have hindered widespread analysis of observable performance elements; these include the misleading equation between film acting and captured natural behavior (see chapter 1) and the notion that gestures and expressions are inert matter that acquires meaning only as a consequence of shot combinations (see chapter 2). This chapter addresses two other impeding factors: first, the conflation of performance elements and characters, actors, and star images that seems tied to the use of linguistic-based models, and second, the notion that screen performance is, by virtue of the absent actor, "not-acting."

Conceptual models used in analyses of literature have contributed a great deal to film studies. But as Butler points out, the semiotic and structuralist approaches that "were imported from literary criticism" in the 1960s and 1970s were unequipped to address "the performative aspect" of cinema.[2] While these critical models did not by themselves delay work on screen acting, they contributed to performance being "neglected in favor of film technique and narrative structure" by sustaining the view that filmic discourse consists of *(a)* uniquely "cinematic" techniques and *(b)* narrative devices.[3] Of the "stylistic features unique to the medium . . . relationships between shots" remained especially important.[4] At the same time, the "artistic organization . . . of the causal-chronological order of events" was given priority.[5] According to the linguistic-based approaches developed to study literature, performance details simply did not exist. As a consequence, they did not generate terminology for analyzing gestures and expressions nor taxonomies that could illuminate the way performance details differ from characters, actors, and star images.[6] While distinctions among these categories are likely familiar to scholars, practitioners, and interested observers, a short review of differences that concern acting in narrative films will clarify the place of gestures and expressions in cinematic discourse.

Fictional characters and material performance elements occupy entirely separate realms of a narrative film. While characters exist in the immaterial narrative, observable performance elements occupy the same register or category as other perceptible filmic elements (lighting design, shot selection, and so on). Characters in narrative films are defined by their given circumstances. They have short- and long-range goals, tacit and explicit desires, stated and unstated objectives. They use tactics or strategies to achieve their objectives. They change tactics when they encounter obstacles to achieving their goals. Like characters encountered in a novel, characters in a fiction film exist within the world of the story. However, audiences learn about fictional characters from details in the representation. They make inferences about characters based on performance details working in concert with other cinematic elements.

Certainly, characters do not cause the gestures and expressions seen and heard in film. People do. The labor expended by extratextual, material actors, voice talents, and others create the performance elements from which audiences piece together information and impressions about characters. Despite Hollywood publicity, actors are not the characters they play but instead exist in everyday life. While an actor might be hired to portray a character determined to get rid of his roommate, on the day of shooting, the character's and actor's objectives are likely to be entirely different, with the actor aiming to do a good job at work and then be on time to collect his kids at daycare.

This same distinction between character and performer pertains to films in which a nonprofessional is cast because his or her physical appearance closely corresponds with ideas about how a type of character should look. In the mid–twentieth century, Italian neorealist filmmakers like Roberto Rossellini and Vittorio de Sica sometimes employed a form of type casting. For example, in *Bicycle Thieves/The Bicycle Thief* (Vittorio de Sica, 1948) factory worker Lamberto Maggiorani portrays the central character, Antonio Ricci, who tries in vain to get back the bicycle that had allowed him to be employed for one brief morning before it was stolen. Earlier, in the silent era, Soviet filmmakers such as Sergei Eisenstein and Vsevelod Pudovkin often relied on what they termed *typage* casting. As Kuleshov noticed, in contrast to experienced actors who brought "expressive clarity" to their work, when performers were cast simply because they physically fit their role, filmmakers were often required to use framing and editing to correct and adjust "the actor's job" (see chapter 2).[7] Yet even in these cases, when editing "corrects" the performer's work, the specific qualities of the nonprofessional's gestures and expressions affect audience impressions about the character. Moreover, however close the match, the person is not the character but instead a member of the production team.

While biographies, interviews, and behind-the-scenes reports offer interesting information about actual members of a film's cast and crew, they do not, of course, provide evidence about the fictional characters in the story. Instead, insights into characters emerge from watching films. A character might want to punch his boss, but audiences only know this because they see an actor's eyes glance to the side, hear him release his breath, and see him clench his fist. Audiences make inferences about what characters want or do not want based on the specific gestures and expressions in film; they make inferences about characters' temperaments and emotional states by observing the quality of the physical and vocal expressions crafted into filmic representations.

When these distinctions are reviewed, they seem quite obvious. Yet the absence in film studies of established and widely used terms to differentiate between characters, actors, and manifest performance elements has led to both rhetorical and conceptual confusion. It has also postponed sustained inquiry into screen performance. As noted earlier, beginning in the 1960s, scholars considered how framing and editing choices affect audience understanding of character and narrative point of view but left the role and status of performance elements largely unexplored (see chapter 2).

Initially, physical and vocal gestures were also overlooked in critical and theoretic writing when star studies became an active area of film scholarship in the late 1970s. Early cultural studies in cinema ostensibly differed from analyses that focused on spectators' purported primary identification with the camera and secondary identification with characters. However, when linguistic-based approaches were carried over into star studies, terms and concepts that could facilitate understanding of screen performance were still missing. As a consequence, scholarship generally focused on stars as "signs" that embodied cultural ideals, instead of exploring performances in terms of "signifiers . . . that are patterned into structures that have meaning for the spectator."[8] As Paul McDonald points out, focusing on a star's unified body as a single sign necessarily obscures insights that derive from the actor's varied "movements through space and time," which in turn demonstrate how a star's "body produces meaning precisely through doing."[9] Thus, alongside fictional characters and actors, star images belong to the list of categories that must be distinguished from performance elements before productive analysis of screen performance can occur.

Audience interpretations of star performances are most certainly influenced by publicity and an actor's work in a series of films. For instance, by the time Rudolph Valentino died in 1926 at the age of thirty-one, his films had become occasions for fans to commune with the cultural image he had portrayed in films such as *The Sheik* (1921) and *Blood and Sand* (1922).[10] While gestures and expressions crafted into filmic representations provide much of the evidence audiences use to construct ideas about stars, and thus in some measure cause or create impressions about star images, fans generally presume that the star's personality is the source of those gestures and expressions. But acting is misconstrued when causal relationships between star images and performance elements are inverted, as when the details of a star's performances, which create the cultural image, are discussed as if they were tangible signs of the star's actual personality.[11]

The presumption that performances arise from star personalities stems from the notion that cameras capture natural behavior, in this case the natural behavior of idealized individuals. But star images that figuratively embody culturally constructed concepts such as "the man of action," "the seductress," "the amusing sidekick," or "the innocent beauty," do not create the gestures and expressions on screen any more than fictional characters do. Impressions conveyed by performance details owe their existence to the training, experience, preparation, and collaboration of actors, directors, makeup artists, costume designers, cinematographers, stunt doubles, and others. Audiences then assemble ideas about a star image from the selection and combination of performance elements that they observe in a series of films.

No doubt the dominant position of Hollywood cinema and the increasing number of media venues have made it especially complicated to analyze performance elements in those cases when an actor is also a celebrity or a star closely linked with a certain genre or type of character. Thus, along with the confused equation between performance details and fictional characters or between acting choices and actors, the more visible effects of marketing and publicity also tend to obscure the role that performance elements play in filmic representation. The emotive and cognitive effect of gestures and expressions in film is what this volume seeks to demonstrate, for scholars have already outlined ways that audience responses are conditioned by a star's appearance in other films and by stories circulated in the press.

For example, in regard to media celebrities, Christine Geraghty explains that film appearances are often just another means of accessing the celebrity's personality. Noting that female stars "are particularly likely to be seen as celebrities whose working life is of less interest and worth than their personal life," Geraghty points out that for Liz Hurley, her "work as a model and actress . . . contributed less to her celebrity status than her Versace dresses and an errant boyfriend."[12] Regarding genre stars, Geraghty observes that "it is quite possible to understand and enjoy the meaning of [their work] without the interdiscursive knowledge which the star-as-celebrity relies on."[13] For these stars, who are closely identified with particular types of roles, performances are valued only insofar as they meet expectations generated by portrayals in previous films. For example, after Sylvester Stallone appeared in films such as *Rocky* (1976) and *First Blood* (1982), his successes were confined to his action-adventure movies. As Geraghty explains, deviating from an "established star image may lead to disappointment for the intended audience."[14] With the cultural image of the celebrity or genre star defined well in advance, fans enjoy a particular performance because it meets their expectations, while critics often dismiss performances by celebrities and genre stars as instances of personification, when performers simply play themselves.

In contrast, performances by a select group of actors are usually seen as examples of impersonation, when actors craft portrayals of characters that are separate from themselves.[15] Yet expectations about the work of legitimate actors is also shaped by the press and an actor's appearance in a series of films. Actors in this category are often closely associated with auteur directors or with leading roles in films that are considered of high quality. Approaching legitimized acting differently than appearances by celebrities and genre stars, audiences enjoy performances by actors such as Robert De Niro and Meryl Streep insofar as they satisfy audience expectations, in this case, that the performances will create memorable characters.

In short, analyses of screen acting are complicated by the fact that extratextual information colors audience responses to performances. Even so, viewers do reckon with the performance details that help to create and sustain their impressions about characters and star images. As later chapters will show, there are terms and concepts for analyzing acting in cinema. For example, craft terminology from the training systems of Delsarte, Stanislavsky, and Laban help one identify the qualities of physical and vocal gestures and the performative rhythms that make performances integral to films. As the study of *Training Day* (Antoine Fuqua, 2001) demonstrates, Laban Movement Analysis contains a storehouse of terminology for describing how gesture and expression reveal character. It facilitates seeing how Denzel Washington uses bound, tightly controlled movements to portray a character continually on guard, while Ethan Hawke works in counterpoint, using light and free-flowing movements to portray a character open to experience (see chapter 8). By using vocabulary designed to describe performance elements, their role in filmic expression becomes more visible.

CLARIFYING DISTINCTIONS AMONG PERFORMANCE ELEMENTS, CHARACTERS, ACTORS, AND STARS

Taxonomies developed by literary scholar Gérard Genette, film theorist Stephen Heath, and performance studies scholar David Graver also illuminate the place of gestures and expressions in performing art. For instance, Genette's observations on the distinction between "story" and "discourse" affirm the difference between characters in a fictional story and performance elements in the material realm of filmic representation.[16] His categories for analyzing narrative discourse are akin to nomenclature used to analyze human movement in the performing arts (see chapter 8). His view that narrative elements such as order, duration, frequency, mood, and voice operate in concert and with no fixed relations among them, is comparable to Prague school perspectives on interactions among the qualitative details of movements, gestures, and expressions (see chapter 4).

Stephen Heath has provided an elegant argument for gestures' and expressions' presence in film by outlining categories that clarify distinctions between performance details and related aspects of mainstream narrative cinema. While Heath's taxonomy reiterates some distinctions outlined in the previous section, it warrants consideration because his better-known work in ideology, psychoanalysis, and film semiotics gives his analysis depth and breadth, and it provides a point of access for scholars coming to the study of performance from work in those areas of research.[17] The following list outlines Heath's discussion of the multidimensional "presence of people" in mainstream narrative film.[18]

1. *Agent.* Fulfills narrative roles or functions, often organized into pairs of oppositions
2. *Character.* Can be an agent, belong to subplots, or contribute to mood and theme
3. *Person.* Actor or nonprofessional whose performance represents an agent or character
4. *Image.* Can influence the way characters and narratives are designed and perceived in commercial films
5. *Figure.* An instance in which star image, narrative design, and performance details combine to create open-ended meaning, often filled in by viewers' knowledge of film history
6. *Idea.* An instance in which people are cast to represent social types or convey points in an intellectual argument

7. *Moments, intensities.* Gestures and expressions present in film representations, evocative in themselves

These seven categories accommodate the cultural reality that audiences approach screen performances as material that "combines different sources or forms of meaning."[19] As noted earlier, some meaning generally comes from outside a film itself, with audiences often approaching performances by celebrities, genre stars, and legitimate actors with rather different expectations. Importantly, however, Heath's categories give recognition to performance elements as one source of meaning. As Paul McDonald notes, Heath "usefully identifies that it is through the small details of the actor's speech and movement that interpretations" of characters and films are formed.[20] Heath is able to see the evocative power of gestures and expressions for several reasons. First, he does not confuse performance details with the actions of agents and characters in a narrative. Second, he understands that "the presentation and effects" of a film actor's body and voice should not be analyzed "under the heading of person" because the person or actor exists outside of the film.[21] Third, he recognizes the profound contrast between performance details, which exist only within a film, and star images, figures, and ideas that are formed in large measure by publicity, events, and social conventions outside of films.

Heath creates a conceptual space for performance details as a source of meaning by first identifying aspects of mainstream narrative cinema that are distinct from but intimately related to gestures and expressions found in films. For example, drawing on work by Vladimir Propp and A. J. Greimas, Heath begins by discussing narrative agents that tend to fall into "six fundamental roles organized in three pairs of oppositions: subject/object, sender/receiver, helper/opponent."[22] He then turns to characters who can be agents or belong to subplots "detached from the movement of the [main] narrative" that contribute to "thematic or symbolic or symptomatic resonances for the film overall."[23] Heath reserves the category of person for the living human being and calls attention to the ability of the professional actor who uses technique to empty "his or her body to fill it with meaning."[24] Recognizing the impact of cultural associations bound into a star image, Heath notes the distinction between a person/actor who exists in daily life and a star image that reflects and shapes audience expectations about a movie star's on-screen appearances.

The Player (Robert Altman, 1992) nicely illustrates distinctions between agent, character, person, and star image, and thus helps to clarify how these factors are also different from intensities (performance details). Re-creating the dystopic view of Hollywood ambition generated by films like *Sunset Boulevard* (Billy Wilder, 1950), *The Player* tells the story of studio executive Griffin Mill (Tim Robbins), who accidentally kills a writer he thinks is sending him threatening postcards. Griffin not only gets away with the murder, but also marries the writer's girlfriend and becomes head of the studio. While the film highlights the characters' lack of moral sense, its tone is far from dismal. It pokes fun at the star system and, at the same time, pays homage to actors for their contributions to cinema. Moreover, it playfully engages audiences by offering several layers of almost interactive entertainment. For example, cameos by more than sixty stars draw attention away from the fiction as one tries to identify them in their brief moments on screen.

The intensities present in the film contribute to audiences' understanding of the characters, some of whom function as agents in the narrative. Consisting of connotatively rich gestures and expressions, they are entirely different from narrative agents, and thus require different terms and concepts than those used to analyze agents. For example, structural analysis of the narrative can reveal that Griffin Mill is a key agent, paired in subject/object relationships with David Kahane (Vincent D'Onofrio), the writer he murders, and June Gudmundsdottir (Greta Scacchi), the writer's girlfriend. Griffin is also paired with helpers like story editor Bonnie Sherow (Cynthia Stevenson) and entertainment lawyer Dick Mellen (Sydney Pollock), and with opponents like rival studio executive Larry Levy (Peter Gallagher) and Detectives Avery and DeLongpre (Whoopi Goldberg and Lyle Lovett). Terms from structural studies of literature are not designed, of course, to analyze the performance details that illuminate Mill's differing relationships with Kahane and Pollock, for instance. To do that, one might turn to Laban Movement Analysis to identify the constricted or bound quality of Robbins's gestures in scenes opposite D'Onofrio versus the more relaxed, free-flowing quality of his vocal and physical expression when interacting with Pollock.

Intensities also contribute to audience impressions about the characters in *The Player* that are not pivotal agents in the narrative. Here again, terms to describe gestures and expressions differ from those used to analyze fictional characters. For example, narrative analysis sheds light on the way studio security exec Walter Stuckel (Fred Ward) contributes to the thematic and symbolic resonances of the film. It leads one to see that Stuckel has the first lines of the film but that they are incidental to narrative development, serving primarily to bring audiences into the story's fictional world. In a similar fashion, writer-producer teams like Tom Oakley (Richard E. Grant) and Andy Civella (Dean Stockwell) are not crucial to the murder story, but they are integral to the film's anthropological examination of societal types that belong to the Hollywood ethos.[25] To describe performance details that provide evidence about these characters, one would work outside of narrative analysis. For instance, to clarify the difference between Stuckel, one of the sure winners in the studio game, and Oakley and Civella, who struggle to become studio insiders, one could draw on Laban taxonomies, which can illuminate the contrast between the light but direct gliding effort that characterizes Ward's portrayal of Stuckel and the intense but nonfocused wringing effort underlying many of Grant's and Stockwell's movements, gestures, and facial or vocal expressions.

Attention to performative intensities can also enhance insight into the cameo appearances that mobilize star images. Tacitly commenting on stardom itself, the film ironically portrays movie stars as a social type, as when celebrities arriving for the gala organized by Griffin's studio are described in the voice-over as "all household names." It also plays on individual star images, for this scene includes Cher costumed in a flame-red gown for the strictly black-and-white attire event. At the same time, with movie stars consistently serving as extras who lend verisimilitude to the narrative setting, *The Player* also allows audiences to see them as collaborative players unencumbered by huge egos. By turning attention to performance details, which influence audience impressions about the cameo appearances, the film's understated celebration of famous actors' contributions to Hollywood cinema becomes apparent: in contrast to the tense, sometimes overwrought physical and vocal choices that Tim Robbins and Peter Gallagher use to portray the competing executive power players, the performances by the stars in bit parts have an experienced, improvisational feel because they tend to move with a refreshed, easy grace.

The Player's combination of actors portraying characters and movie-star extras can also illuminate the unique category of person. Scenes with stars in the background include evidence of the actor as a person, who exists independent of the star image or characters portrayed. For instance, at the cocktail party hosted by entertainment attorney Dick Mellen, Jack Lemmon can be seen playing the piano in the background. Because he appears several times throughout the scene, we are given more than a moment to identify him as Jack Lemmon. Yet he is not integrated into the scene as a character, nor is his appearance linked to his characterizations in films ranging from *Days of Wine and Roses* (Blake Edward, 1962) to *Missing* (Constantin

Jack Lemmon in *The Player:* the actor/person, as distinct from the star or character

Costa-Gravas, 1982). Unencumbered in this way, Lemmon becomes visible as a person. As with other cameos in the film, performance details, such as his relaxed pose at the piano, allow one to contemplate the actor's independent existence outside of this film and others.

In addition to showing that intensities stand apart from agents, characters, persons, and star images, Heath's taxonomy also allows one to see that gestures and expressions themselves are distinct from but contribute to instances in which complex, open-ended figures arise in films. While films often mobilize star images that require awareness of popular culture (consider Cher's appearance in *The Player*), some films appeal to viewers' sense of film history and the aesthetic, economic, and political forces that have influenced films and shaped the lives of filmmakers. Establishing a separate category for these occasions, Heath calls attention to scenes that feature the "circulation between agent, character, person, and image, none of which is able simply and uniquely to contain, to *settle* that circulation."[26] He suggests that moments in *Touch of Evil* (Orson Welles, 1958) exemplify instances in which intensities, narrative design, and star images combine to create multilayered meaning. For Heath, "the scenes between Quinlan and Tanya, Orson Welles and Marlene Dietrich, make up a complex figure that [involves] a minimum of narrative agency; little establishment of character for Tanya [with] Dietrich almost quoted here from a von Sternberg movie, hung with ornament and jewelery."[27] Speaking as a cinephile, Heath explains that the film prompts one to see Welles and Dietrich as "persons with a history which is also that of cinema and other films, [and] *Touch of Evil* as Welles's return to Hollywood, [with] Welles and Dietrich together again now in a memory of the past."[28]

A brief look at the Welles-Dietrich scenes suggests how that dense impression is created. Set in a run-down brothel in a desolate part of a cheap Mexican border town, the scenes with Quinlan, the maverick, has-been detective, and Tanya, the aging but still exotic madam, highlight the film's allusions and the actors' status as individuals whose work signifies pivotal developments in cinema. First, the film stars do not fit the locale: the impoverished setting clashes completely with the grandiose dimensions of their established public images: Welles, the wunderkind responsible for *Citizen Kane* (1941) and iconoclast forever at odds with the studio system; Dietrich, the international film star whose work in Josef von Sternberg films such as *Blonde Venus* (1932) came to symbolize sophisticated filmic spectacle. Second, the narrative actually plays on the obvious parallels between the maverick detective and the maverick director, and those between the aging madam and the aging film star. Third, with the stars brought together as foreigners in an isolated town, the film mobilizes additional aspects of their biographies: cinephiles might recall that both stars had spent a good deal of time in exile, with Dietrich leaving Nazi Germany and Welles leaving Hollywood to avoid executives and anti-Communists. Given the multiple links between the stars and their characters, in their last exchange, when Tanya conveys her protective concern by suggesting Quinlan go home, Tanya's advice to Quinlan resonates as advice that the glamorous, world-weary exile might give the maverick director himself.

Performance details also convey the stars' common history and personal bond, for in the scenes between Welles and Dietrich performative intensities suggest an emotional intimacy. For example, late in the film when Quinlan returns to Tanya's seeking solace in the wake of his investigation gone wrong, Dietrich's impassive physical choices initially allow Quinlan/Welles to take center stage. As Welles plods into the room, one can see that even though Quinlan is drunk, he quickly discerns he has come to the right place when he sees that Tanya has been casting tarot readings, presumably to foretell how he will fare. One soon gathers that the cards have spelled doom, for Dietrich remains unemotional as Tanya tries to deflect Quinlan's questions about the readings. When he insists on knowing what the cards have foretold, she is honest, quietly telling him he does not have a future. At first, Welles had seemed threatening, towering above Dietrich, his gravelly voice

Marlene Dietrich in *Touch of Evil:* a moment when performance details have greater resonance for audiences steeped in film history

pressing out commands. But because Dietrich maintains a slow, measured pace as she smokes her cigarette and a calm, open facial expression as she looks toward Welles, she illuminates the fragility belied by Welles's jerky gestures and off-balance stance. As the scene evolves, Dietrich's understated physical and vocal choices become the more imposing intensities; when Quinlan protests his fate, Dietrich uses a soft but firm voice to say that his "future is all used up." With her low voice creating a character of depth and substance, Dietrich conveys the profound affectation that Tanya/Dietrich feels for Quinlan/Welles through suppressing emotional expression: the only sign of the character's/star's feelings is a tear that glistens in her eye as the scene draws to close.

Performance details also contribute to impressions about characters in cases that exemplify "the use of people in films as ideas, *elements of an intellectual argument.*"[29] As noted earlier, one example of this approach is Sergei Eisenstein's use of *typage,* which involves casting that illustrates idea more than character, "social exposition rather than psychological revelation."[30] As Heath points out, another approach is Jean-Luc Godard's "strategy of personification" in which people are presented and "deployed in a film for typicality [to create] an entirely social or social-sexual recognition."[31] Here, social type and individual interweave because the performances and

Chantal Goya in *Masculine, Feminine: typage* that illuminates social and psychological dimensions of experience

characterizations illuminate the operations of social ideology and human psychology.

Godard's *Masculine, Feminine: In 15 Acts* (1966) reveals the multiple dimensions of his Marxist-Freudian approach to "type" casting. Madeleine is played by sixties pop star Chantal Goya, whose appearance and public image made it possible for her character to represent a generation of French youth shaped by postwar consumer culture. Goya's *yé-yé* music (which shows the influence of simple, verse-repeating songs in the French chanson tradition as well as conventions popularized by the Beatles and American girl groups) is also used throughout the film to suggest British-American pop culture's impact on midcentury French society. Madeleine is a simple object of infatuation for Paul (played by Jean-Pierre Léaud, an icon of the French New Wave who appeared in seven Godard films in the 1960s). However, as embodied by Goya, Madeleine also represents the disruptive influence of British and American consumer culture.

As the film ends, it appears that Paul has met an accidental death just as Madeleine has discovered she is pregnant with Paul's child. The film's central point about the deleterious effect of imported pop culture is revealed by the complex emotions that play across Goya's face in the closing moments. Pensive, speaking quietly, and gently drawing her hand along the hair at the side of her face as if trying to cradle and comfort herself, her gestures and expressions suggest that Madeleine is more than a mere social type with no inner life. In fact, one might argue that it is Goya's performance at this moment that powerfully conveys the idea that consumer culture does not and cannot adequately address the lived experiences of the young people who embrace it.

With the place of actors, characters, and extratextual associations clarified, Heath turns to performance elements: the "moments, intensities, outside a simple constant unity of the body as a whole [or] as the property of some *one*."[32] These gestures, expressions, intonations, and inflections have an impact on audience interpretations. One need not see a performance detail as a nonprofessional's "natural" behavior or as "the stressed attraction of a star in this or that part of the body."[33] Rather, by recognizing that "the momentary sweep of an arm" carries connotations, one can begin to identify intensities' coordinated relationship with other aspects of filmic representation such as framing, editing, and sound design.[34] Because performance elements belong to cinematic discourse, "films are full of fragments, bits of bodies, gestures, desirable traces, fetish points" just as they are full of lighting choices, editing patterns, musical motifs, and framing selections.[35]

Heath proposes that for each of us, there are certain moments, certain gestures in films that are especially memorable. *Personal Velocity* (Rebecca Miller, 2002), the 2002 Sundance Grand Jury Prize winner, offers many such moments, as suggested by a scene in the first of the film's three stories. The short narrative is about Delia Shunt (Kyra Sedgwick), who leaves her abusive husband after a night when she cannot answer her daughters' cries for help because he has locked her in their basement after smashing her face on the kitchen table. Resolved to protect her children, Delia moves to a new town, finds a place to live, a job as a waitress, and a school for her children. She accomplishes this quickly, held together by will and determination. But one early morning, watching her children asleep in the small, remodeled garage that is their temporary home, Delia has a moment to reflect on the events that have brought them here. As the scene opens, Sedgwick leans against a window as soft, hazy light filters in. Suddenly, she winces and begins to cry. Grabbing a sweater and dashing outside, Sedgwick first clamps one hand and then the other over her mouth.

Sobbing, she drops to her knees. Bending forward, she keeps one hand over her mouth and the other tight against her face. Sedgwick's stifled wailing and the way she presses her hands over her mouth and against her face convey Delia's emotional intensity: these performance choices convey the intense effort Delia expends to hold in her sense of loss. Later, as the scene

Kyra Sedgwick in *Personal Velocity:* a scene grounded in the actor's work

ends, Sedgwick is sitting back on her knees, looking around, her face drained but calm. With her weeping just before inviting special attention to Sedgwick's powerful gestures and expressions, these quieter intensities can also draw one's attention. Thus, performance details are crucial here, with the depth and intensity of the character's feelings conveyed largely by Sedgwick's selection and combination of physical gestures and vocal expressions.

This process, of selection and combination of elements within a system of representation, is common to all categories linked to cinema and performance. Heath notes that performance itself involves the selection and combination of details and that gestures and expressions are encountered within "systems of representation," namely, the material, intratextual enunciations of filmic discourse.[36] In a similar but entirely distinct fashion, agents and characters function within narrative systems of representation. Cultural systems of representation define star images. Cinematic figures mobilize extratextual narratives or systems of representation about actors, stars, and film history. Different forms of *typage* rely on ideas embedded in cultural systems of representation.

Heath's insight that intensities are present *in* films creates an alternative to the entrenched opposition between "present" stage actors and "absent" screen actors because it clarifies that in the cinema *performance details are present to audiences,* just as lighting, framing, and editing choices are present to audiences. By comparison, viewers recognize that agents and characters exist in the film's fictional world. They understand that actors have an existence outside of films. They know that extratextual information contributes to their impressions about stars, scenes that generate figures, and instances in which performers are used to embody social types. By disentangling intensities from these other aspects of mainstream narrative film, Heath shows that in film, images of human gestures and sounds of human voices are not "absent," emerging only through a viewer's synthesis of narrative and cinematic strategies. Rather, material performance elements in cinematic representation contribute to a viewer's impressions about the meaning and significance of individual scenes and entire films.

David Graver also considers the tangible details of gestures and expressions as important in his analysis of the "seven ontologically distinct bodies" found in theatrical productions: character, performer, commentator, personage, group representative, flesh, and sensation.[37] His 1997 taxonomy of performance in theatrical venues identifies essentially the same categories as Heath does in his study of film performance published in 1980, but it has a slightly different emphasis. Graver subsumes agent into his discussion of character, while Heath makes a distinction between them. Graver also distinguishes between flesh and sensation, while Heath considers these aspects together in his discussion of gestures. Both studies, however, clarify the multiple registers or aspects of performance. They show that questions about who performs and where actors perform are separate from questions about *what audiences watch when they encounter performances.*

Taxonomies like Heath's and Graver's resolve the confusion between absent actors and present performance elements that has been sustained by linguistic-based approaches. Clarifying the fact that actors, who attend workshops and go to auditions, do not appear in films any more than gaffers or camera operators do, their work shows that performance details are present to stage and screen audiences. The overviews also remedy the focus on narrative operations that once made the contributions of film actors seem incidental. Still recognizing that narrative design influences the way audiences interpret gestures and expressions, Heath and Graver show why performance elements per se are not the result of narrative devices alone. Their work also clarifies that star images can affect interpretations of performances, but that the gestures and expressions of a person, not a star image, belong to stage or screen representations. Together, their taxonomies also illuminate vital connections between theatrical and filmic performance.

A CONTINUUM OF PERFORMANCE FROM NOT-ACTING TO ACTING

Those connections also come to light when one reexamines assumptions about what constitutes acting. As noted before, "true" acting has been identified with stage acting based on actors sharing the theatrical space with their audiences (see chapter 1). Yet even stage performances exist on a continuum that ranges from not-acting to acting. Because shared theatrical space does not guarantee acting, it is not an activity defined by locale. However, acting can be seen as discernable human actions that are infused with connotations conveyed by the quality of actors' gestures and expressions. The not-acting/acting continuum first outlined by scholar-practitioner Michael Kirby in 1972 offers a useful framework for understanding the distinguishing features of acting.

At one end of the continuum, a performance that involves no intention to portray a fictionalized character can be deemed "not-acting." Kirby refers to this as "nonmatrixed performing," unembedded "in matrices of pretended or represented character, situation, place, and time."[38] These are occasions when performers do not impersonate characters but instead perform tasks without reference to fictional information or character identity. To illustrate this category, Kirby uses the example of Kabuki or Noh stage attendants, who shift the set for other actors who do impersonate characters.

In film, "nonmatrixed performing" can be found in some instances of voice-over narration. While sometimes presented as commentary by a character in the story (as in *Sunset Boulevard*, Billy Wilder's cynical satire) or as pronouncements by an unidentified "voice of authority" (as in studio-era newsreels), there are times when voice-over narration does not carry connotations suggestive of any particular character, situation, place, or time. For example, in *Personal Velocity*, John Ventimiglia's delivery of the voice-over narration seems unconnected to the characters in the stories. Instead, his lines simply facilitate the flow of information. Similarly, while some audience members might recognize Ventimiglia's voice from his appearances as Artie Bucco in *The Sopranos*, as performed and presented by the film, his narration does not activate any extratextual associations. It is, in short, "nonmatrixed performing."

Outlining a next step toward acting, Kirby describes "nonmatrixed representation" or, as he puts it in the 2002 reprint of the essay, performance generated from "a symbolized matrix."[39] In these instances, something that frames the performer, such as a costume, suggests the representation of something or someone. However, performers themselves do not do anything to portray characters. There is still no intention to act; performers do not limn the thoughts or feelings of a fictional character. Instead, character traits arise because "referential elements are applied *to* the performer."[40] Kirby finds nonmatrixed representation within a symbolized matrix in some performance art pieces, where audiences encounter "a person, not an actor."[41] Andy Warhol's *Sleep* (1963), *Eat* (1963), and *Kiss* (1963) offer examples of nonmatrixed representation in film, where audiences are presented with a person, not an actor performing the thoughts and feelings of a character. Peter Greenaway's structuralist films include nonmatrixed representation with "referential elements" eventually depicting minimalist characters. For example, snippets of faux-documentary sequences in *The Falls* (1980) create simple characters through costuming, voice-over narration, and conventional "interview" framing.

The next step on the continuum toward acting involves "received acting," in which a person does something that accrues meaning from its context. In this case, much like performances that derive meaning from a "symbolic matrix," the performer's behavior seems imbued with meaning because it takes place within an already defined theatrical event. Consider performances by extras that provide background action to foregrounded events. As Kirby points out, when the matrices of character, situation, place, and time "are strong, persistent, and reinforce each other, we see an actor, no matter how ordinary the behavior."[42]

Kirby proposes that while these first three points on the continuum are cases of not-acting, the next step to "simple acting" marks a shift into the realm of acting because the performer "does something to simulate, represent [or] impersonate" a character or engages in a process of selection and projection to present his or her beliefs or emotions to an audience.[43] In these instances, there is an intention to act on the part of the performer, but "no emotion needs to be involved."[44] As Kirby points out, simple acting can involve an emotion that is "created to fit an acting situation" or simply drawn from one's own experience.[45] While the transition from not-acting to acting might seem to be a sharp division, examples from cinema show that "received acting" and "simple acting" lie close to one another on the continuum. In the earliest films produced, one finds "received acting" of different degrees, "simple acting," and "complex acting."

Beginning with "simple acting," in Lumière actualities such as *Photograph* (1895) and *The Sprinkler Sprinkled* (1895), both one-minute, single-take films with coherent scenarios, performers indeed use physical gestures and facial expressions to "simulate, represent [or] impersonate" characters who are distinct from the individuals who portray them. *Photograph* presents the difficulties of a photographer trying to set up a portrait shot. *The Sprinkler Sprinkled* follows the stages of a prank that ends with the unsuspecting gardener being sprayed in the face with a hose.

Performances in other Lumière actualities feature various degrees of "received acting," while some approximate "simple acting." In *Leaving the Lumière Factory* (1895), "most of the workers exit the factory gate and proceed on their way without disturbing 'the picture' and without breaking from their stage business of being engaged in quotidian behavior."[46] But in addition to those rather clear instances of "received acting," there are also a few individuals who engage in "simple acting" or a more intentional form of "received acting." For example, "one man catches audience attention by chasing a dog through the crowd toward the camera, while another man clowns around as he pushes a child on a bicycle out the gate, through the crowd, toward and past the camera."[47] Some might argue that chasing a dog and pushing a child on a bicycle do not qualify as "simple acting" because the performances do not involve representing or impersonating characters. Yet the performances of the two men are distinct from the received acting of the other people in the crowd and thus belong closer to the acting end of the continuum. Moreover, even though *Leaving the Lumière Factory* lasts less than a minute, the performances of the two men convey the idea that they (or their characters) are pranksters aiming to provoke a good laugh.

Similar combinations of "received" and "simple acting" or, if one prefers, different degrees of "received acting," occur in other Lumière actualities. For example, in *The Snowball Fight* (1896), the scene is staged so that "the most defined 'performance' [is] given by the man on the bicycle, who occupies the center of the frame for most of the scene."[48] In *Children Fishing for Shrimp* (1895), "the girl who consistently occupies the center of the frame carries out the most directed action, as she moves from foreground to middle ground and back."[49] She also becomes distinct from the other people in the film because she glances several times at the camera, a gesture that seems to suggest a certain anxiety about performing the scene properly. Actualities such as these highlight the point that performances are best understood as belonging on a continuum, rather than to opposing categories of acting and not-acting.

Kirby finds that the simplest acting involves "only one element or dimension of acting," while the next step on the continuum involves complexity both within individual aspects of acting and in the number of aspects in play at the same time. In complex acting, the portrayal of emotion now becomes "specific, modulating and changing frequently within a given period of time."[50] Moreover, "more and more elements are incorporated into the pretense."[51] Thus, the actor might draw upon "emotion (fear, let us say), physical characteristics (the person is portrayed as old), place (there is bright sun) . . . simultaneously or in close proximity to each other," and so on.[52]

Just as the Lumière actualities featured "simple acting" and different degrees of "received acting," *Kid's Auto Race* (Henry Lehrman, 1914) includes "simple acting," "received acting," and "complex acting." James Naremore has shown that the film features various types or degrees of acting.[53] Sequences of "complex acting" can be found in Chaplin's performance as the brazen little tramp because the portrayal of emotion is "specific, modulating and changing frequently within a given period of time."[54] By comparison, Henry Lehrman's performance as the impatient newsreel director is best understood as "simple acting," while "received acting" best describes the performances of people in the crowd who fulfill "their role as the anonymous masses in a newsreel."[55]

Chaplin's performance over the course of this four-minute film shows how the Tramp becomes more "determined to ignore the director" as the story develops.[56] It also serves to portray a character who is sometimes "ostentatiously oblivious" of the people around him and, at other moments, inspired by attention from onlookers in the grandstand to perform (for people in the film and in the film's audience).[57] Thus, the Tramp/Chaplin "lights his cigarette, shakes out the match, flicks it over his shoulder, and does a little dance kick with his heel, bouncing the dead match away before it hits the road."[58] In brief, Chaplin's performance develops over time and utilizes multiple strategies, as do other instances of "complex acting."

While Chaplin's performance in this short film might not seem like an ideal example of "complex acting," other film performances are. As suggested by the brief look at scenes in *A Woman Under the Influence* and *Far From Heaven* (see chapter 2), the performances by Gena Rowlands, Julianne Moore, and Viola Davis epitomize "complex acting" because they create the impression of "many things taking place simultaneously in the work of a single actor."[59] The examples from *The Rules of the Game* and *Matewan* also show that films can feature complex acting that arises from the work of the actors.

Kirby's not-acting and acting continuum suggests a range of performance comparable to the one illustrated by Richard Maltby's discussion of autonomous and integrated performance in Hollywood cinema. Also noting that film performances are best understood as exemplifying points on a continuum, Maltby explains that "any individual performative act in a Hollywood movie can be seen as operating somewhere between the poles of integration into the narrative and autonomy from it."[60] With most Hollywood movies featuring both integrated and autonomous performance, the two tendencies are emphasized at different moments or become "characteristic of particular performers."[61] Autonomous performances (often seen as instances of not-acting) belong to scenes that highlight the nonnarrative thrill of cinema; they generally feature display, spectacle, and technical skill. By comparison, integrated performances (sometimes identified with complex acting) are more closely linked to narrative development and character psychology.

Kirby's continuum complements Maltby's approach by articulating objective features of acting. As Kirby observes, at base acting is "active—it refers to feigning, simulation, and so forth, that is *done* by a performer."[62] Second, acting is "something that is done by a performer, rather than something that is done for or to him."[63] Third, as Kirby notes, "It may be merely the 'use' and projection of emotion that distinguishes acting from not-acting."[64] In simple acting, such as Lehrman's portrayal of the newsreel director, performance details communicate ideas, beliefs, or emotions. In complex acting, such as Chaplin's characterization of the Tramp, acting choices convey the continually changing emotional experiences of clearly delineated characters. Gestures and expressions that reveal feigning, action, and the projection of emotion can be found in essentially all narrative films.

In "On Acting and Not-Acting," Kirby makes a passing observation that "simple acting" is found in films that feature a simple type of realism. Without any reference to specific films or to his later category of "complex" acting, he writes: "there are many approaches to realism; some—such as those used in many films—ask very little of the actor and would be considered relatively simple."[65] It is not clear what films Kirby has in mind or if he recognizes the complexity of much film acting. Still, one might note that he places the film performances he does consider in the domain of acting rather than not-acting.

By comparison, some observers still imagine *(a)* that film actors are not active; *(b)* that they do not act but instead have performances created for them; and *(c)* that they do not use or project emotion. For example, revising Kirby's terms to suit his own argument, Philip Auslander proposes that "film acting [in general] seems to be a good example of nonmatrixed representation."[66] In other words, according to Auslander, all screen performances are instances in which "referential elements are applied *to* the performer."[67] They are all comparable to performance art pieces in which audiences encounter "a person, not an actor."[68] In this view, there is no difference between the images of the man sleeping in *Sleep* and Gena Rowlands's portrayal of Mabel Longhetti in *A Woman Under the Influence.*

Auslander's suggestion that film performance does not involve acting of any sort (complex, simple, or even received) is, of course, untenable. It ignores the differences between films like *Pickpocket* and *The Rules of the Game.* It fails to recognize that film audiences generally encounter performances that involve the simulation or representation of fictional characters. It also elides the fact that dramatic context and theatrical design elements contribute to the way performances on stage are understood, and, to paraphrase Kirby, that stage actors sometimes do very little while the physical and informational context does the acting. While theatrical productions, like films, involve the selection and combination of performance and nonperformance elements, critics do not, as they sometimes do for film, see all stage performances as instances of not-acting.

The complex interaction between performance and other cinematic elements does not require us to define screen acting in a monolithic way or in opposition to acting on stage. As Kuleshov might note, just as theatrical production reveals the preparation, training, and experience of its cast members, performance elements in a film will often reflect the preparation, training, and experience of the actors involved. Moreover, the degree of agency in any performance would appear to depend less on the medium than on the production circumstances. Consider differences found in community versus professional theater, understudy versus star, or spear carrier versus lead character.

CONCLUSIONS

While there are exceptions (cel animation, puppets, and computer-generated characters), stage *and* screen performances use human gesture and voice as the primary means of expression. Theater scholar Eli Rozik explains that acting depends on human beings who "imprint images of fictional worlds upon their own bodies."[69] As we have explained, because acting involves use of a performer's body and voice, crafted gestures and expressions are sometimes confused with captured, natural behavior. This confusion reaches its murkiest when actors use quotidian gestures such as handshakes and smiles and expressions of intense emotion (see chapters 4 and 7). Yet actors consistently "fill [their bodies] with meaning" by turning audience attention away from themselves as persons and toward the characters they embody.[70] Playing societal roles in everyday life, however consciously performed, remains a self-expressive activity, whereas performances in fictional narratives are not instances of self-expression.[71] Acting in dramatic contexts is distinct from actions in daily life, however performative they might seem, for when people are acting on stage or screen, "they are genuinely and professedly enacting characters distinct from themselves."[72]

Taxonomies like those outlined by Heath and Graver provide an antidote to the notion that because actors are absent from films, performance details have little if any efficacy. Setting aside linguistic-based approaches that are not equipped to address the performative aspect of cinema, one can see that actors' gestures and expressions are very much a part of a film and that they are not created by characters, star images, or other cinematic elements. Far from inert bits of matter, performance details can indeed project intention and emotion. They are a concrete component of film that requires analysis, if one wants to gain a better understanding of an individual film or film practice in general.

Kirby's continuum also dispels assumptions that have relegated all film acting to the domain of not-acting. As his outline reveals, acting is not defined by the performer's presence on stage but instead by the complexity of the actor's gestures and expressions, and the degree to which the performance establishes a character distinct from the player. Attendants in Kabuki productions are present to audiences, but their performances are instances of not-acting in that they do not simulate characters. By comparison, gestures and expressions in fiction films generally do function as acting elements. Not only are these present to audiences, they have an efficacy confirmed by mirror neuron research, which refutes the presumed difference between responses to actions observed in the same space and actions observed on screen (see chapter 2).[73]

Acting in the cinema can be as simple as the antics in *The Sprinkler Sprinkled* and as complex as Julianne Moore's portrayal in *Far From Heaven.* While some might insist that "true" acting involves the portrayal of lifelike characters in a theatrical space shared by actors and audience members, analyzing performances in light of a continuum from not-acting to acting reveals that simple and complex acting is distinguished essentially by the *discernable actions that are colored by connotations suggested through the specific qualitative aspects of gestures and expressions.*

PART TWO

PERFORMANCE ELEMENTS, CINEMATIC CONVENTIONS, AND CULTURAL TRADITIONS

CHAPTER FOUR

OSTENSIVE SIGNS AND PERFORMANCE MONTAGE

Chapters in part 1 suggest that performance elements are a component of cinematic representation, rather than evidence of natural behavior captured and projected on screen. They emphasize that gestures and expressions carry connotations even before they "are patterned into structures that have meaning for the spectator."[1] They see film acting as "composed of signifiers such as bodily gestures and facial expressions."[2] Discussions in part 2 build on Prague school semiotics to elucidate the interplay among performance details, social gestures, aesthetic conventions, and non-performance elements in films from different eras and cultural traditions. Chapter 4 employs Prague taxonomies to describe the complex interaction between aspects of Chaplin's performance in *City Lights* (Charles Chaplin, 1931) and thus provides vocabulary for analyzing the selection and combination of elements within what might be called "performance montage."

As should become clear, Prague theorists effectively address the performative aspect of film. Their view, that structure involves dynamic relationships of subordination, equilibrium, and domination, offers a simple and elegant way of considering relationships between performance elements and among the various aspects of narrative cinema. In addition, by theorizing the operation and function of "ostensive signs," Prague theorists are able to examine forms of representation not considered by Charles Sanders Peirce or Ferdinand de Saussure.[3] Finally, the Prague school's distinction between "gesture-signs" (conventional gestures such as handshakes) and "gesture-expressions" (individual uses of those gestures) leads to terms and concepts for analyzing the way a particular detail of performance sustains, amplifies, or contradicts the thought or feeling usually conveyed by such social expressions as greeting, farewell, apology, concern, condolence, and so on.

PRAGUE SCHOOL SEMIOTICS

The Prague Linguistic Circle (1926–48) was a loose association of Czech, Russian, German, and British scholars with an interest in linguistics, aesthetics, dramatic art, film, literature, ethnography, and musicology. In 1929, key insights of the group were published in a work entitled *Travaux de Cercle Linguistique de Prague*. The publication included essays by Jan Mukařovský, Vilém Mathesius, Roman Jakobson, and B. Havránek. After Otakar Zich's *The Aesthetics of Dramatic Art* was published in 1931, "the semiotics of theatre and drama . . . constituted a primary area of inquiry for Prague School writers."[4] Prague theorists whose work focused on the composite arts of theater and film include Mukařovský, Petr Bogatyrev, Jiri Veltruský, and Ivo Osolsobe.

Prague structuralism can be seen as "both a continuation and a reassessment" of Russian formalism, an important school of literary criticism in the Soviet Union in the 1920s.[5] Departing from the formalist focus on artworks' quintessential features, Prague school writers envisioned the work of art as an artifact that functions as "an intermediary between the creator and the community [and is thus] capable of meaningful interpretation."[6] Mediating between individuals and audiences, works of art are not statements of fact; they do not acquire meaning by a relationship to some external reality. Instead, they mediate between individuals and audiences by raising questions, by being open to readings influenced by conventions that shape audience encounters with the work of art.

Prague school aesthetics sought to explain how an "artifact or text remains virtually the same in the course of time (or undergoes the changes due to merely the aging of matter)" while norms and rules governing interpretations "may change quite substantially."[7] Prague school writers were concerned with the internal organization of aesthetic forms as well as the changing aesthetic traditions against and within which works of art are perceived and assessed.[8]

Their approach to the analysis of art did build on the Russian formalist notion of "making strange" but their formulation of "deautomatization," in which "one element (or group of elements) becomes dominant and subordinates all the others" was heuristic rather than definitional.[9] It provided a concept for analyzing the systematic internal organization of artworks in which "elements are subordinated and superordinated to each other."[10] Michael Quinn argues that Prague theorists made a "clear break" with Russian formalism because they did not "attempt to find in each object [or art form] a single, dominant component" but instead developed "a sociologically sensitive concept of semiotic function" that avoided fixed definitions of artworks or art forms and opened up analysis of changing patterns within an individual production and in the norms and values shaping art forms and audience responses.[11]

Besides drawing upon and revising models provided by Russian formalism, in the early 1930s Prague writers also borrowed from "Peirce's *semiotic* and Saussure's *semiology*" to develop what has come to be known as Prague structuralism.[12] Prague theorists extended Peirce's work and developed a distinctly different focus from Saussure. Ladislav Matejka points out that the Prague school "kept its methodological distance from those followers of Saussure who regarded only the abstract system [of language or culture as] worthy of scientific scrutiny."[13] Starting instead from the premise that "the signifier and the system of signification [form] an indissoluble opposition," Prague writers focused their studies on "the very interaction of the 'two objects.'"[14]

While Prague writers departed from Russian formalism, Peirce's semiotics, and Saussure's semiology, they incorporated other influences as they developed their own functionalist structuralism. As Matejka notes, Prague theorists were greatly influenced by "Karl Bühler's model of the bond between *Sprechakt* (speech act) and *Sprachgebilde* (language structure)."[15] They built on perspectives outlined by Johann Herbart, whose interest in "apperception," the way related ideas reinforce one another, led to work in aesthetics that considered the relations of elements to be the source of beauty.[16] Prague school theorists drew on writings by Tomás Masaryk, who was not only a "well-informed observer of the [Prague structualist] movement and the [Prague Linguistic] Circle's generous benefactor," but also the Republic of Czechoslovakia's first president, serving from 1918 to 1935.[17] Inspired by Masaryk's interest in "static and dynamic linguistics," they considered "general regularities" but argued energetically "against excessive, mechanistic simplifications" of linguistic and aesthetic phenomenon.[18]

Another important influence was Otakar Zich's work on the "mutual interrelationship and interaction of heterogeneous systems" in theater, which led Prague writers to analyze other cultural forms in those terms as well.[19] Zich's interest in "the material substratum" in poetry and in the way things represent other things in theater provided the foundation for Prague work on "ostensive signs."[20] Prague theorists recognized that while "no work of art could be reduced to its sensorily perceptible substratum" and that there were art forms, such as literature, that did not have a sensorial or performative dimension, there are indeed occasions when "the material make-up of the sign" warrants close analysis.[21] For example, "a gold coin and a paper bank-note may signify the same value [but] there is a quality inherent in the sign material that creates an important difference in their significance."[22]

By recognizing the sensorial aspect of some art forms, Prague theorists developed a conceptual framework for analyzing film that is entirely distinct. Compare, for example, the approach taken by Christian Metz, who set out to show that "film selects and combines images and sounds" in the same way that language "selects and combines phonemes and morphemes to form sentences."[23] Metz not only tried to equate cinematic images and sounds with linguistic components, his Grand Syntagmatique "constitutes a typology of the diverse ways that time and space can be ordered through editing within segments of the narrative film."[24]

By comparison, Prague school semiotics is not language-based and its studies of art forms do not take language as a model. Moving beyond studies of literature, Prague writers explored "the principle of deautomatization in other arts as well."[25] Mukařovský 1931 paper on Chaplin's performance in *City Lights*, the foundation for the case study later in this chapter, illustrates the process of deautomatization in composite art forms like film and theater by showing that Chaplin's gestures, poses, and facial expressions film dominate *(a)* other aspects of performance, *(b)* other performances in the film, *(c)* framing and editing choices, *(d)* plot design, and *(e)* sometimes even the disclosure of character. Mukařovský's essay reveals the contrast between Metz and Prague school theorists because its analysis of cinema does not attempt to isolate elements of "film language" or prove that editing is the art form's dominant and defining feature. Instead, Mukařovský illuminates the distinction between actors and performance elements that he thought "more readily discernable" in film than in theater.[26]

Prague theorists proposed that "structure need not imply inflexible permanence."[27] Instead, any structure features "a collection of elements whose intrinsic organization is contradictory, causing the permanent movement of the whole."[28] For Prague theorists, structure emerges from the mutual subordination and domination of elements that appear at particular moments to be organized into hierarchical arrangements.[29] For Mukařovský and other Prague writers, structures are processes, "dynamic wholes whose elements are charged with energy and interlocked in an ongoing struggle for domination."[30]

The Prague school developed terms and concepts for analyzing ongoing processes of *simultaneity, redundancy,* and *contradiction,* and relationships marked by *subordination, domination, equilibrium,* and *parallelism,* regardless of the elements considered. Quinn proposes that by describing the way various "semiotic systems combine, complement, and conflict with one another" in film and theater, Prague theorists "allowed problems like simultaneity, redundance [*sic*] and contradiction in signification to be recognized and analyzed, in some cases for the first time."[31] Their intervention was possible because they focused on relationships between elements in "sign-complexes"; they did not isolate "signs into fundamental units of meaning—a method that tends to work well only when a single code or single string of information, like written language, is studied at a time."[32] Prague school work on sign-complexes is particularly useful for studies of film, which features "combinations of signs that change concurrently," for example, moments when a vocal inflection, a head movement, a change in music, and a camera move all occur as a cluster of signs operating in concert.[33]

Like other Prague writers, Mukařovský also "went beyond Formalist aestheticism [by insisting] on the social and institutional dimensions of art and its strong imbrication with 'historical series.'"[34] Prague school theorists consistently rejected the notion that language or art could be studied in isolation from other cultural phenomena. They proposed that the aesthetic function of an object manifests itself only in a certain social context and that "as soon as we change our perspective in time, space, or even from one social grouping to another . . . we find a change in the distribution of the aesthetic function and its boundaries."[35] They also recognized that expectations about and violations of aesthetic norms were social processes, and that societies create institutions that influence aesthetic value through the regulation and evaluation of art works.

In their studies of dramatic art, Prague theorists analyzed relationships of mutual interaction among dialogue, "pantomime, music, lighting, architecture . . . dance" and other presentational elements.[36] They also developed "a highly original theory of acting signification" that does not reduce the performative aspect of theater and film to representation that involves the sign systems outlined by Peirce and Saussure.[37] Prague writers recognized that composite art forms do use iconic signs (such as portraits) that represent things by means of resemblance. They acknowledged that theater and film productions also use indexical signs (such as weather vanes) that have a causal link with what they are representing. Emblematic of their focus on interaction between elements, Prague theorists examined the way these two sign systems functioned in relationship to theater's and film's symbolic signs (such as spoken and written language) that depend on convention. They also developed a category of signs that would come to be known as "ostensive." Analyzed most fully in work by Ivo Osolsobe first published in the 1970s, ostensive signs are "essentially theatrical" in that "things stand for themselves."[38] Use of these signs involves selection and presentation, of course, but when employed, an ostensive sign "simply represents itself or something which is, for all practical purposes, just like it."[39]

The distinction between ostensive signs and other, more familiar semiotic signs becomes clear when one considers how the same thing can be represented by means of the various types of signs. For example, in a scene (on stage or screen) that includes the painting or photograph of an old straight-backed wooden school chair, there would be a discernable difference between the picture and an actual chair placed in the scenic space. The material, three-dimensional chair in the scene could also be distinguished from an indexical sign of the chair, which might take the form of an actor pantomiming the process of sitting down on the hard wooden seat of an imaginary chair. In addition, the ostensive sign of the chair in the scene would be distinct from a symbolic sign of the chair, which might take the form of a banner with the words "old wooden school chair" printed on it or some line of dialogue or narration that makes reference to "the old wooden school chair" that audiences are supposed to imagine is in the scene.

The unique operation of ostensive signs becomes apparent when one considers something like the cane that belongs to Chaplin's costume as the Tramp. The cane itself could be represented through iconic signs. However, a picture of the cane alone would convey little information about the Tramp, whereas a single image of Chaplin striking a pose with the cane could convey a particular attitude or mental state. For example, imagine a painting or photograph of Chaplin with his left palm resting on the top of his cane. However, if one then imagines a framed picture of this pose in a scene that features Chaplin moving into position to rest his hand on the cane, the existential difference between the two types of signs comes into view.

Certainly, in dramatic art, narrative information does contribute to impressions about performances. But even in experimental, nonnarrative productions, and autonomous scenes not integrated into the narrative, impressions about performance details are affected by poses, gestures, and expressions just before and after those details. Thus, when we encounter Chaplin's pose with the cane as an ostensive sign, that is, as a spatial, temporal, dramatic sign in *City Lights,* impressions of the qualities that infuse Chaplin's pose with the cane are shaped by his movement leading into the pose and his movement coming out of it. Illustrating Kuleshov's study of single images and combined images, the contrast between the iconic sign of Chaplin posing and the ostensive sign of Chaplin assuming the pose demonstrates that impressions created by a single image can be quite different from those prompted by the performed gesture. As a close look at *City Lights* will reveal, the ostensive sign of Chaplin leaning on his cane when he contemplates the sculpture of the female nude conveys impressions not captured by the static image of that pose. The ostensive sign generates different, perhaps more complex connotations. By itself, the painting or photograph of Chaplin leaning on his cane might suggest a moment of calm, nonchalant repose. But when we see how Chaplin moves into that pose, pressing his hand down on the cane as if to establish some sort of control, and we see that the pose is a momentary pause before he quickly lifts his hand in a gesture of energized resolve, the pose becomes an instance in which the Tramp is intensely focused, and far from a moment of casual repose.

The contrast between the cane as an indexical sign and as an ostensive sign comes to light when one imagines a static image of Chaplin pantomiming the act of leaning on an imaginary cane. Here again, different connotations are conveyed by the indexical sign and the full-fledged spatial and temporal gesture in the ostensive sign. Similarly, the contrast between symbolic and ostensive signs comes into clear view when one considers the possible impact created by verbal or written descriptions of Chaplin leaning on the cane. A description of the cane itself would likely convey little information about the Tramp, but description of a particular pose with the cane might characterize a single attitude. A verbal description of a series of gestures might even begin to evoke the meaning conveyed by Chaplin's performance in scene. However, placing a page with this description within the actual scene would underline the obvious difference between the pose as described and the pose as performed. More to the point, while descriptions of the pose allow one to understand what has taken place, seeing Chaplin perform the gesture allows for insight into the character, delight in the skill of the performer, and the opportunity to see the psychological experience acted out.

The evocative power of ostensive signs is what prompts Stephen Heath to see performed gestures as intensities, desirable traces, and fetish points.

Functioning in ways distinct from iconic, indexical, or symbolic signs, ostensive signs are also unique because of their density and richness.

Prague semiotics reminds one to consider the multiple uses of signs in the cinema. Films do use iconic signs (such as portraits) to represent things by means of resemblance. Paintings or posters in the background of scenes sustain impressions of verisimilitude or, as in the case of *The Player*, provide commentary on the events in the scene. Films do employ indexical signs (such as weather vanes), which have a causal link with what they are representing. For example, audiences might deduce that characters have been out in the rain when they see images of actors' wet hair, clothes, and shoes. Films do feature symbolic signs (spoken and written language), which depend on convention; consider dialogue, song lyrics, silent-film title cards, store signs, and letters discovered at inopportune times.

But what distinguishes film and theater is their use of ostensive signs. In contrast to painting, sculpture, architecture, music, poetry, and literature, dramatic arts use objects and people to represent "things just like themselves." The iconic picture of a woman's shoulder pressed against a young girl's face could indeed carry powerful connotations. The indexical sign used by an actress who seems to grasp an imaginary figure in theatrical or cinematic space could also convey powerful emotions. Dialogue or narration could function as symbolic signs that allow audiences to imagine an evocative moment in which a mother embraces her daughter. Yet these signs all function differently from ostensive signs; consider the moment in *The Horse Whisperer* (Robert Redford, 1998) when Annie (Kristin Scott Thomas) holds Grace (Scarlet Johansson) in her arms after the girl has failed in her first attempt to ride after the accident in which she lost a leg; the image of the girl's face pressed into the woman's shoulder conveys impressions that emerge from the spatial and temporal expression of recognizable human gestures. The possible effects of this ostensive sign are distinct from those conveyed by other types of signs because perceptible clusters of details in the actors' gestures and expressions represent the gestures and expressions of fictional characters and convey the complex and shifting emotional experiences of the two characters.

Impressions created by an ostensive sign such as this are sustained and enhanced by the surrounding details in the narrative and in the cinematic representation. As Mukařovský notes, gestures and expressions in performance become unambiguous within "the total structure of the dramatic work."[40] But even as fragments taken out of the narrative, an ostensive sign performed in dramatic art can carry dense connotations. The surrounding cinematic or theatrical elements *do not infuse the gestures with meaning.* Instead, they *help to delimit the possible meanings conveyed by evocative ostensive signs.*

Prague semiotics facilitates analysis not only of acting in film but of cinematic representation in general. Its vision of structure as a process suggests that gestures, frame selections, costumes, editing patterns, lighting choices, vocal inflections, sound effects, and camera movements can be analyzed as sign-complexes. Its focus on the interaction between signifier and system of signification even suggests that all aspects of filmic representation can be seen as components of a film's overarching, multifaceted performance.[41] Prague work on ostensive signs clarifies why film "language" cannot be reduced to representational processes specific to iconic, indexical, and symbolic signs.

CITY LIGHTS IN CONTEXT

Mukařovský's analysis of Chaplin's performance in *City Lights* illuminates recognizable patterns in film practice. Highlighting the range of aesthetic practice exemplified by the contrast between Bresson or Antonioni films on the one side, and Renoir or Cassavetes films on the other (see chapter 2), Mukařovský notes that framing and editing dominate some films, while performance dominates others. Identifying the same distinction Kuleshov made between films (like Bresson's) that use montage to create meaning and films (like Renoir's) that depend on the work of actors, Mukařovský shows that framing and editing play a passive role in *City Lights,* even as he acknowledges "the active role of the camera in Russian films where the changeability of standpoints and perspectives plays the dominant role in the structure of the work."[42] Thus, he recognizes that examining film performance involves analyzing cinematic techniques, even when he analyzes gesture as a cinematic element that may dominate or be subordinated to camera movement, shot composition, and editing patterns. Seeing performances as existing in cinematic space and in cinematic time, Mukařovský proposes that performance details should be discussed in terms of *selection* and *combination,* terms often used to discuss framing and editing.

Mukařovský also incorporates the distinction between autonomous and integrated performances (see chapter 3) into his discussion of *City Lights.*[43] He observes that expressions, gestures, and poses are often subordinated to the narrative, with performances serving primarily to communicate information about the thoughts and feelings of fictional characters. However, he notes, *City Lights* is also distinguished by its many scenes of autonomous performance with the narrative subordinated to Chaplin's performance; in these instances "a series of events [is] linked by a weak thread" with "divisions between individual events [serving] only to provide pauses in the sequence of gestures."[44] As we will see, sometimes the narrative in *City Lights* dominates and Chaplin's gestures serve primarily to reveal character. Sometimes, Chaplin's work has the dual function of revealing character and the performer's skill. And at other times, his performance is barely integrated into the narrative, functioning instead as commentary or direct address.

Mukařovský's essay also emphasizes the distinctions Heath makes between characters, actors, and performance elements (see chapter 3). Drawing on Otakar Zich's work, Mukařovský highlights the distinction between actors and performance elements. Zich and Mukařovský refer to performance elements as the "material vehicle" of dramatic representation or as "the dramatic figure" in representation. Note that Zich's view of the material, intratexual "dramatic figure" should not be confused with Heath's notion of the multifaceted "figure" mobilized in part by viewers' knowledge of film history. For Zich and Mukařovský, "the dramatic figure is the sensorily perceptible substratum (material vehicle)" that provides evidence for impressions about "the dramatic character" which is "the immaterial referent of [the material] vehicle."[45] In other words, there is no direct connection between the character in the story and the actor, who has an existence outside the fictional story and outside of any individual stage or screen production. Instead, audiences glean information about dramatic characters by attending to "the material aspect of acting" presented in any production.[46] In Mukařovský's essay on Chaplin, the distinction between character, performance element, and actor allows him to set aside questions that pertain to "the Tramp" or to Chaplin as an international film star. Focusing on the perceptible details of the performance, Mukařovský analyzes what Heath calls the intensities of gesture in performance. He presents his study of the material performance elements in *City Lights* as an analysis of performance phenomena in theater and film.[47]

Mukařovský observations about the *internal structure of performances* highlight considerations pertinent to any study of performance. While basic and perhaps self-evident, his delineations warrant review because they allow one to pinpoint expressive details within an individual performance and illuminate distinctions among films, distinctions that might otherwise go unnoticed. He begins by noting that the components of the internal structure of performance "are many and varied."[48] The first group, vocal components, is "quite complex [because it includes] the pitch of the voice and its melodic undulation, the intensity and tone of the voice, tempo" and so on.[49] The "second group cannot be identified otherwise than by the triple designation: facial expressions, gestures, poses"; however, one can "simply call them gestures and thus extend this term to facial expressions and poses without undue distortion."[50] The third group is "composed of those movements of the body by which the actor's relation to the [cinematic] stage space is expressed and carried."[51] He distinguishes between movements in cinematic space and gestures that express a character's mental state and emotions.[52]

While simple, these distinctions make it possible to identify differences in the way acting choices are used in films. For example, focusing on questions of gesture and movement, one can see the difference between autonomous sequences in *City Lights* and autonomous sequences choreographed by Busby Berkeley in a film like *Gold Diggers of 1933* (Mervyn LeRoy, 1933). In *City Lights,* facial expressions and small gestures display the performer's skill, while in the Busby Berkeley numbers, the expressions, gestures, and poses of individual performers are subordinated to the dynamic movement of an ensemble. In a similar fashion, the complex interplay of Chaplin's facial expressions, gestures, and poses makes *City Lights* different from a film such as *Top Hat* (Mark Sandrich, 1934). While *Top Hat* features the individualized performances of Fred Astaire and Ginger Rogers, the film depends far more on the actors' graceful movement through cinematic space than *City Lights* does.

Mukařovský points out that Chaplin "does not move too much (his immobility is even stressed by an organic defect in his feet)."[53] In fact, one of the most salient ways Chaplin creates meaning is by assuming momentary poses and by pausing to present tableaux in which facial expression and small gesture dominate.[54] That intense use of facial and gestural expression makes Chaplin's performance in *City Lights* entirely different, for example, from Tom Mix's performance in *Riders of the Purple Sage* (1925), one of the many Tom Mix Westerns that featured exciting action and daredevil stunts in picturesque locales. Like action adventure films today, these Westerns were prized for the display of spectacular movement in cinematic space, not the static moments of expressive tableaux featured in *City Lights.*

Mukařovský's simple outline of vocal, gestural, and movement elements enhances insight into other patterns in narrative films. He notes, for example, that with the arrival of sound films, spoken dialogue often took a dominant role, with gestures serving to support the content of the dialogue. Thus, even though *City Lights* and a film like *Duck Soup* (Leo McCarey, 1933) are comparable because performance dominates plot and framing and editing choices, in the Marx Brothers' film verbal comedy dominates all else. With the arrival of sound cinema, an actor's gestures could also be subordinated to the intonation, rhythm, tone, pitch, and volume of his or her vocal expressions. Thus, *Dinner at Eight* (George Cukor, 1933) uses actors' intonations and inflections to provide glimpses into the characters' carefully guarded emotional experiences. However, unlike *City Lights* and *Duck Soup,* the performances in *Dinner at Eight* are fully integrated into the narrative, even though John Barrymore's bravura performances in *Dr. Jekyll and Mr. Hyde* (John S. Robertson, 1921) and his 1920s theatrical productions of *Richard III* and *Hamlet* might have invited some members of the film's contemporary audience to see his death scene as one that featured the performer's skill.

By examining the internal structure of performance, one can identify and describe the contrast between *City Lights* and a film such as *Grand Hotel* (Edmund Goulding, 1932). In Goulding's film, performance dominates framing and editing. However, no one character or actor dominates the film, and vocal and gestural components are balanced within individual performances. Here, acting choices by John Barrymore, Greta Garbo, Lionel Barrymore, Joan Crawford, and Wallace Berry not only balance voice and gesture; they also balance the interplay between characters and actors, for their performances often serve the dual function of revealing character and presenting moments that can be enjoyed as displays of spectacle. With the actors' work fulfilling autonomous and integrated aspects of performance, as when the ballerina/Garbo flits about in delight after being courted by the con-artist/John Barrymore, the expressive clarity of vocal and gestural components, the scene's place in the narrative, its highly theatrical qualities, and associations made possible by Garbo's and Barrymore's extratextual star images combine to create emotional resonance.

GESTURE AND EXPRESSION IN *CITY LIGHTS*

While *Grand Hotel* and the other films effectively illustrate discernable patterns in cinematic representation, *City Lights* offers especially useful material for analyzing performance because the simultaneous and successive interactions between a single actor's facial expressions, gestures, and poses are the most significant relationships in the film. Chaplin's expressions, gestures, and poses are not subordinated to cinematic technique, narrative demands, the performances of other players, vocal components, or even movements in cinematic space, but instead "are charged to the utmost with the function of gestures (Chaplin's walk sensitively reflects every change in [the Tramp's] mental state)."[55]

In any performance, facial expressions, gestures, and poses "can parallel one another, but they can also diverge so that their interaction is felt to be an interference (an effective comic means)."[56] As Mukařovský notes, "one of them can subordinate the other to itself or, conversely, all of them can be in equilibrium."[57] The salient feature of facial expressions, gestures, and poses is that "they are felt to be expressive, to be an expression of the character's mental state, especially his emotions," even in moments that are not integrated into the narrative.[58] For Mukařovský, one of the distinguishing features of Chaplin's performance in *City Lights* is that "none of the three elements (facial expressions, gestures, poses) prevails over the others but [rather] assert themselves equally."[59]

The perceptible elements of Chaplin's performance can be seen as a series of interferences or disparities between Chaplin's facial expressions, gestures, and poses. The disparities among these elements make the performance visually and intellectually intriguing. They have the potential to engage audience attention because they confound expectations established by daily life; Chaplin's gesture of tipping his bowler in apology might be followed immediately by a twirl of his cane that indicates defiance. These moments of gestural contradiction display Chaplin's skill as a performer and can imaginatively express meanings bound into familiar axioms, quips, and witticisms.

One of the first scenes in *City Lights* features a remarkable display of disparities within the internal structure of Chaplin's performance. The scene begins with a wide shot of a crowd waiting for the unveiling of a new monument to "Peace and Prosperity." City leaders briefly address the crowd, with the sound of a kazoo substituting for their words. The curtain over the monument rises to reveal the Tramp asleep, cradled by the central figure of blind justice. The moment presents audiences with a wry comment: only blind justice offers comfort to the disenfranchised. Having performed the statement that monuments to peace and prosperity do not alleviate poverty, Chaplin moves out of the tableau. He scratches his head and stretches a leg. Finally aware of the crowd, the Tramp tips his bowler in apology and starts to descend from the statue of blind justice. As he reaches the bottom of this central figure, Chaplin's baggy pants get caught on the raised sword of the reclining statue that is screen right. With the sword slipping up and through the back of his pants, the Tramp becomes impaled on

Chaplin in *City Lights,* at attention but impaled on the sword of justice: commentary created by disparities within the actor's performance montage

the sword of justice. Discovering his situation, the Tramp expresses surprise and tips his hat in apology to the crowd. Suddenly, a band begins to play the national anthem. Officials standing at the foot of the monument immediately come to attention; placing his bowler over his heart, the Tramp also stands at attention, still impaled on the sword of justice. A couple of flailing slips incorporated into this performative segment highlight the absurdity of the Tramp, standing at attention, dutiful, while he is getting it from behind, not from some conventionally nefarious figure but from the sword of American justice.

When the musical passage from the national anthem ends, Chaplin moves out of this second tableau that critiques the government's misuse of citizens. He wiggles off the sword and then casually but defiantly plops himself onto the sword of justice statue's face. Tipping his hat to the crowd, he gets up and then turns to tip his hat in farewell to the reclining statue. Still not finished with his public display of civil disobedience, the Tramp proceeds to the third statue in the monument, a figure that represents the right hand of justice. He places his foot in the outstretched palm of the statue and reties one of his shoes. Stepping up on the knee of the statue, he reties his other shoe. Then he removes his hat and places his nose so that it touches the thumb of the statue's right hand. Sticking out his arms as he holds his nose to the statue's thumb, Chaplin finds a comical way to thumb his nose at civil affairs, social norms, and the pretensions of justice. With this final tableau completed, the Tramp leaves the monument, tipping his hat as he exits.

The expressive incongruities in this two-minute scene offer audiences a remarkable display of showmanship. More importantly perhaps, Chaplin's interaction with the figures in the monument requires audiences to pay close attention to make sense of moments that are recognizable but unexpected. The combination of elements in each of the three tableaux, the Tramp cradled by blind justice, impaled by the sword of justice, and thumbing his nose at the right hand of justice, are comparable to a series of shots that would create "intellectual montage" in the films of Sergei Eisenstein. For example, the "performance montage" of Chaplin at attention with the sword up the back of his trousers operates in much the same way that the three images of the lion statues (asleep, head up, and sitting up) do in *October* (1927).[60] The only difference is that in *City Lights,* the montage features performance elements presented together in a single shot, while *October* depends on the ostensive signs of different statues presented in a series of shots. In both cases, interplay between perceptible elements of cinematic representation offers social commentary.

Chaplin's performance calls attention to the role of cultural norms because there are moments when his choices glaringly diverge from social conventions.[61] The disparity between expected behavior and what Chaplin delivers points to the dynamic relationship between conventional social gestures and the individual nuance of gestural expressions. Throughout *City Lights,* Chaplin's performance features a "tension between codified gestures and personal uses of those gestures."[62] It thus reveals a great deal about "gesture-signs" (social gestures, like bows or handshakes, recognizable within specific milieus and social contexts) and individual "gesture-expressions" (social gestures that are colored by human feeling).

Mukařovský explains that gestures can be seen as "immediate and individual," and can serve as an "expression of the character's mental state, especially his emotions"; at the same time, a gesture can "also acquire a supra-individual validity" and thus become "a conventional sign, universally comprehensible (either in general or in a certain milieu)."[63] For example, ritual gestures and social gestures function as "signs which conventionally—like words—signal certain emotions or mental states, for instance, sincere emotional participation, willingness, or respect."[64] However, while social gestures are easily recognized signs of certain emotions or mental states, "there is no guarantee that the mental state of the person who uses the [social] gesture corresponds to the mood of which the gesture is a sign."[65] The truth or sincerity of gesture-signs can only be confirmed or refuted if and when the individual gesture-expression dominates and personal expression significantly colors the conventional sign of greeting, respect, concern, farewell, and so on.

In *City Lights,* scenes of autonomous performance feature moments when the Tramp's mental or emotional attitude does not coincide at all with the mood generally indicated by a gesture-sign. For example, when the Tramp first tips his bowler in the scene at the monument to "Peace and Prosperity," it seems to be a straightforward sign of apology. However, as the scene develops, Chaplin undermines the appeasing message of that gesture-sign as the Tramp begins to tip his hat with a bit of bravura, so that instead of apologizing he seems to be taking a bow for the crowd.

The Tramp's use of convention and his deviation from the gesture-sign's conciliatory meaning is sometimes simultaneous: the disparity between the gesture-sign's conventional meaning of apology and the brazenness of Tramp's gesture-expression arises because his gesture is larger and more excessive than conventions of apologetic hat-tipping. However, the mismatch between the Tramp's arrogant attitude and the conciliatory mood associated with tipping one's hat is also conveyed by successive discrepancies: as the Tramp makes his circuitous exit from the statue, he tips his bowler as if to apologize and then immediately acts out in obvious defiance by placing the seat of his pants on the face of the statue that holds the sword of justice; he tips his hat as if in apology and then casually pauses to tie his shoe with his foot placed in the open palm of the figure that represents the right hand of justice. To add to the confusion, and humor, the Tramp confounds expectations by tipping his hat in greeting and farewell to figures in the monument, "mistakenly" using social gestures to address inanimate objects.

In sharp contrast to the Tramp's display on the monument, the use of social gestures in everyday life usually follows established expectations. Individual gesture-expressions are often subordinated to or in equilibrium with gesture-signs. For example, a handshake generally reflects the circumstances of the social encounter as much or more than the individuals' mood or even feeling about seeing or meeting the other person. But in *City Lights*, Chaplin's performance calls attention to the norms underlying conventional gesture-signs because the Tramp's use of gesture-signs is so often and so deeply colored by his mental or emotional state. In these cases, convention is exposed by Chaplin's flamboyant gesture-expressions. Audiences are allowed to assess and enjoy discrepancies between the mood generally conveyed by an established gesture-sign and the feeling communicated by Chaplin's individual gesture-expression.

The conflict between "conventional, socially coded gestures and personal gestures that express the mental state of the character" is especially clear in another scene of autonomous performance, this time the Tramp's encounter with a statue of a female nude in a window display.[66] Like the scene with the monument to "Peace and Prosperity," Chaplin's performance again provides incisive social commentary. This scene highlights the fact that social gestures sometimes function to signal "good breeding" and thus "regulate social encounters among members of a collective."[67] It makes the pointed statement that social gestures used to designate "good breeding" often suppress "the originally spontaneous expressiveness" of human gestures.[68]

The scene begins with the Tramp walking down the sidewalk of a city street and passing a sign that says "Danger." In the next instant, he notices a window display that features a sculpture of a female nude. He stops and begins to study the breasts and pelvis of the unclothed figure, but he attempts to mask his erotic, antisocial impulse by making a pretense of admiring the sculpture of a horse that can be seen in the lower, right corner of the frame. Leaning down as if to look more closely at the horse sculpture, Chaplin scratches the left side of his head so that he has a legitimate reason to turn his head and look over at the nude sculpture. Carrying the act of good breeding one step farther, Chaplin stands erect, his chin down, his hand pressing down on the top of his cane as he leans on it to assess the nude statue. Expanding on that, he steps back and assesses the nude object of art by placing one hand in front of his eyes as if looking through a director's or photographer's viewfinder.

A new element of danger is added to the scene when Chaplin walks forward to get closer to the window display; an industrial lift is suddenly lowered to create a rectangular hole in the sidewalk in exactly the place he had been standing. Now close to the window, the Tramp still tries to demonstrate good breeding. Calmly glancing back and forth between the nude statue and the sculpture of the horse, Chaplin holds his hand over his mouth as he coughs and politely clears his throat. Then, just as the lift rises to become level with the sidewalk, Chaplin steps back. Tilted back with his right leg held up off the ground and his hand on his hip, the Tramp's sexual excitement starts to dominate the dignified mood of the gesture-signs he has been using to assess the art.

Chaplin walks forward to the window display once more and again glances at the sculptures of the female nude and the horse by turn. The lift opens behind him and he steps back, but only half way. Impervious to the fact that he could easily fall into the storeroom below, the Tramp gives in to spontaneous expressiveness. Perched on the edge of the precipice, Chaplin stands gawking at the nude female, his cane up on his shoulder, his hand on his hip, which is slung wildly to the side. After holding this outlandish pose, Chaplin steps back and around just as the life rises to become level with the sidewalk. With the Tramp still transfixed by the nude statue, the lift begins to lower with Chaplin standing on it. He awkwardly climbs up and out onto the sidewalk. But he quickly returns to using social gestures that suggest good breeding as he leans down to scold the person who disturbed his artistic contemplation. He soon loses the upper hand, however, for as the lift rises it brings with it a fellow who is two feet taller than the Tramp and twice his weight. Now in danger of physical injury, the Tramp scurries off, his pretense at good breeding and his moment of erotic abandon quickly subordinated to his need to survive on the streets.

One of the thrills of watching the window display scene is that the performer is not required to conform to social norms. As Mukařovský points out, in dramatic art "the gesture is an artistic fact with a dominant aesthetic function and consequently free of any context involving social relationships."[69] There can be "more freedom for alterations of gestures" in dramatic performances. Rather than conform to social norms, dramatic performances can thus comment on the way social gestures consistently suppress the spontaneous expression of individual experience.[70] The selection and combination of gestures in dramatic performances can also, perhaps inadvertently, affect choices about gestures used in daily life. Discussing the rising influence of film in the 1930s, Mukařovský notes that "in the space of a

The Tramp dispassionately assesses the sculpture of the horse: his improper gesture-expression remains subordinated to a proper, conventional gesture-sign

The Tramp's lusty enthusiasm for the female nude: his indecent gesture-expressions eventually overtake socially acceptable gesture-signs for observing art

few years this influence has manifested itself . . . in the entire system of gesticulation, from ambulatory gait to the most detailed motions such as opening a powder-box or the play of facial muscles."[71] One wonders if the ostensive sign of Chaplin with his hip slung to the side is linked in some way to gestures that later found their way into daily life and were made famous by Elvis Presley.

Beyond the overt social commentary featured in the scenes of autonomous performance in *City Lights,* there are also more subtle moments when the Tramp's gesture-expressions complicate the usual meanings of gesture-signs. The Tramp's sense of inferiority often colors the social gestures of assurance he uses; at other times his passing feeling of superiority will unexpectedly burst out in a series of social gestures that are supposed to convey subservience. Chaplin represents these character traits through gestural disparities in scenes when the Tramp's behavior is integrated into the narrative and thus serves primarily to reveal character. The disparities between conventional gesture-signs and individual gesture-expressions can transpire within a single unit of dramatic action. For example, in one of the scenes at the mansion, the Millionaire (Harry Myers) has brought the Tramp home to toast him for saving his life. While the eccentric, intoxicated millionaire bumbles around getting champagne and glasses, the Tramp seats himself on the living room sofa. This action causes the millionaire's self-satisfied butler (Allan Garcia) great consternation and he motions for the Tramp to stand. Promptly accommodating him, Chaplin stands up quickly, giggling and wincing in apology. His self-assurance returns, however, once he has finished his drink. Reasserting his place as the millionaire's peer, the Tramp dismisses the butler with a flick of his fingers. Thus, within the space of one minute, Chaplin succinctly contradicts the apology conveyed by his giggling wince with the affront conveyed by the flick of his fingers.

Even when the Tramp's mental state parallels the one typically indicated by a gesture-sign, Chaplin sometimes presents the social gesture in an exaggerated form. For example, when the Tramp brings a bag of groceries to the Blind Girl (Virginia Cherrill), he does not simply place the bag on the kitchen table but instead takes each item out, one by one, with special emphasis on making the neck and wings of the chicken flop about as he pulls it up and out of the bag. Here the disparities that engage audience attention are between social norms and the physical details of Chaplin's expressions, gestures, and poses. The interplay between gesture-sign and individual gesture-expressions in Chaplin's performance engages audience interest, for moments when the Tramp's social gestures deviate from social norms require audiences to consider both the norm and the deviation. The process can illuminate the character's feelings and attitudes. It can also provide insight into the social circumstances that help to define a milieu's norms of interaction. As the film progresses and Chaplin's performance becomes increasingly integrated into the narrative, the "social paradox" of "the beggar with social aspirations" comes more sharply into focus.[72] The Tramp's social and personal predicament becomes the central issue in the closing scenes of the film.

The parallel stories of the Tramp's involvement with the Millionaire and the Blind Girl converge when the Tramp is finally able to give the girl the thousand dollars he has gotten, first as a gift and then by stealing it, from the millionaire. She will be able to have the operation that gives her sight, but the Tramp is imprisoned. While the girl's rebirth is suggested by the ellipsis of nine months, the narrative resumes with the Tramp looking more ragged than before. Heckled by newspaper boys that he had been able to fend off in the past, the Tramp is at a particularly low moment when he turns his head away from the boys only to see the girl in the front window of a flower shop. For a fleeting moment, the Tramp is not encumbered by social norms; instead Chaplin's intent facial expression simply conveys that the Tramp is mesmerized by seeing the woman who had inspired him to assume the role of gracious benefactor.

In this moment, Chaplin holds the stem of a small flower gently between his fingers. One might imagine that this gesture-expression is a play on a conventional gesture-sign, a parody of the traditional social gesture of presenting flowers to a lover. But in the context of the narrative and as performed, the gesture seems to reveal the delicacy of the Tramp's feelings for the woman in the window. In addition, while the Tramp had been entirely comfortable creating offensive tableaux with the statues in the monument to "Peace and Prosperity" and expressing his prurient desires for the statue of the female nude, held by the gaze of a beautiful woman, he is helpless. Chaplin's pensive expression and delicate hold on the flower convey the Tramp's feeling of vulnerability as he becomes visible to the woman he had once tried to impress.

Here, gesture-expression dominates gesture-sign, but instead of the usual disparities between the two, in this case the gesture-sign provides a way to illuminate character and social circumstance. The Tramp is vulnerable because he has been caught unaware by the woman watching him from the shop window. More importantly, it is clear that she belongs to middle-class society and that he is nothing more than an outcast looking in. It mat-

The Tramp caught in the Girl's gaze: his earnest vulnerability illuminated by the coincidence between fleeting gesture-expression and recognizable gesture-sign

ters little that the Tramp had once performed the role of kind benefactor. One look at him and she knows that he is not the man she has been waiting for. As the scene progresses and she determines that the Tramp is in fact the person who had helped when she was blind, Chaplin's smile grows bigger but remains uncertain. Even if one decides that the couple will find happiness, Chaplin's gesture-expression in the film's final moment suggests that the distance between their social circumstances will remain unassailable. As these moments might suggest, Prague school vocabulary can facilitate studies that explore the way "gendered, racial, and sexual meanings are . . . acted in the uses of speaking voices and moving bodies."[73] It can offer terms and concepts for analyzing the nuances of gestures that reveal mental state, emotional attitude, and social category. Work by Prague theorists dovetails with that of Rudolf Laban, another Czechoslovakian whose insights have been largely overlooked in scholarship (see chapter 8).

CONCLUSIONS

The observable patterns in *City Lights* and films of its time illustrate different ways that films combine performance and cinematic elements. Specific moments in Chaplin's performance illuminate both autonomous performance that emphasizes the skill of the performer, and integrated performance in which gestures and expressions are subordinated to the demands of the narrative. The study of Chaplin shows that Prague semiotics offers precise vocabulary for analyzing performance. For example, terms such as "gesture-sign" and "gesture-expression" allow one to describe telling details of screen acting. It also shows that performances convey meaning through the interaction of social and personal expression. Interplay between gesture-signs and gesture-expressions can reveal character, show the performer's skill, and contribute to commentary on social class, time period, and cultural circumstance.

Prague semiotics also provides conceptual models that circumvent the entrenched notion that framing and editing are cinema's defining features, dominant in any film. Looking at cinema through Prague perspectives, films can be seen as composite art forms that feature dynamic relationships between textual and extratextual elements, and between textual elements related to one another in continually evolving organizational structures. Rather than encouraging observers to locate fixed properties of the cinema, Prague theories suggest ways to study relational processes of subordination, equilibrium, and contradiction, and to analyze relationships between various textual and extratextual elements.

Examining filmic discourse as mutual interactions between ostensive signs provides insights into composite forms like film and theater. In contrast to symbolic signs that become filled with meaning as they are assembled into organized structures, ostensive signs are infused with connotations that become delimited and clarified when clustered together. It takes a string of words to convey the abstract idea of an old wooden school chair; to give that chair specificity one would need to add additional strings of words that together could create a more distinct mental image. By comparison, the ostensive sign of an old wooden, straight-backed school chair is a material and specific whole, with its varied connotations brought out by combinations with other, equally dense ostensive signs. For example, bathed in warm, diffuse light, the chair and light might suggest memories of a simpler time; exposed to view in hard, cool light, the chair and light might represent rigid discipline.

Prague semiotics offers simple and elegant terms for analyzing the expressions, gestures, and movements of an actor's "performance montage." It offers useful principles for studying mutual interactions among a film's many textual elements. It also facilitates analysis that considers a film's selection and combination of textual elements in relation to extratextual factors. The next chapter examines interactions between acting choices and other cinematic elements; the chapter that follows looks at interactions between performances and the aesthetic conventions that belong to different cultural traditions.

CHAPTER FIVE

ACTING CHOICES AND CHANGING CINEMATIC CONVENTIONS

Building on discussions in the preceding chapters that position performance elements as legitimate aspects of film and semiotic signs in their own right, this chapter analyzes selected film adaptations of *Romeo and Juliet* and of *Hamlet* to show why performance details are best understood as integral components of cinematic montage. As the case studies will reveal, recognizing that montage involves the selection and combination of *all* cinematic elements affords deeper insights into film and acting.

Filmmakers themselves have emphasized that performance details belong to the larger constellation of montage elements in a film. For example, Sergei Eisenstein, one of the first directors to write extensively about montage, opposed a narrow definition that equated montage with the selection and combination of shots alone. Exploring this more complex vision, he located principles of montage in haiku poetry, Japanese landscape painting, and the novels of Charles Dickens. Attentive to the dynamic elements within a single frame, Eisenstein's writings and films give credence to the connotative power of different textures, tones, and amplitudes. His choreography of human movement within and between shots, scenes, and sequences mobilizes the connotative potential of direct versus flexible movements, sudden versus sustained movements, weighted versus light move- ments, bound versus free-flowing movements.[1]

For Eisenstein, the logic behind selecting and combining images could arise from the images themselves; as he points out, "in rhythmic montage it is movement within the frame that impels the montage movement from frame to frame."[2] It might also be based on the emotional "sound of the pieces": a sequence with a shrill emotional tone might be created by selecting and combining images with "many acutely angled elements"; a subtext or secondary tone could be created by adding visual or audio details to emphasize selected aspects of the tone or meaning established by the principal elements of the sequence.[3] In other words, Eisenstein saw montage as a selection and combination of images based on the tonal and emotional connotations conveyed by the details within individual shots and sound elements.

Eisenstein saw performance details as components of cinema, even though his films have become known for "the active role of the camera . . . where the changeability of standpoints and perspectives plays the dominant role in the structure of the work."[4] While framing and shot-to-shot relations dominate his films, gestures and expressions contribute to the impressions they create. Even when human figures function as graphic design elements, performances contribute to meanings generated by his films. For example, while *The Battleship Potemkin* (1925) is remembered for the often-parodied baby carriage that bounces down the steps amid the massacre of civilians, the emotional impact of the sequence depends, at least in part, on the strong, direct quality of the soldiers' high-stepping legs as they press down the steps in an unbroken line that sharply counterpoints the weak, jerking quality of the victims' movements when they try to flee or protest futilely against the onslaught.[5]

Eisenstein never suggests that film performances are produced by "cinematic" techniques that combine inert matter, meaningless block by meaningless block.[6] When one keeps Prague semiotics in mind, his ideas clearly suggest that cinema is an art form in which collage technique informs the orchestration of all its elements. As the films discussed in this chapter reveal, performance elements are not the product of framing and editing but instead a part of cinematic representation. Actors' gestures and expressions have a mutually interactive relationship with the selection and combination of shots, editing patterns, design elements, and audio choices. Integral links exist between acting choices and filming choices because movements, gestures, and vocal and facial expressions have dynamic force that can and should interact with other aspects of cinematic montage.

VARIATIONS IN ADAPTATIONS OF *ROMEO AND JULIET*

Analyzing gestures and expressions as legitimate components of filmic design allows one to set aside questions about actors' personal styles. The interactions among gestures, expressions, and other cinematic elements are so clear that they are accessible even in introductory cinema and film-acting courses.[7] Different adaptations of the same story show how actors' gestures and expressions join with frame selection, shot duration, sound design, and production design to create meaning in film. Comparisons between the 1936, 1968, and 1996 adaptations of *Romeo and Juliet* bring to light variations in the conventions used to present screen performances and allow one to pinpoint the specific ways in which physical and vocal choices are integrated into the overall design of films.

Romeo and Juliet was first adapted for film in 1900. Since that time, there have been at least twenty film versions, seven television productions, and a series of adaptations that build upon the initial story including films such as *West Side Story* (Robert Wise, Jerome Robbins, 1961). The three adaptations considered in this discussion were produced at intervals that set each of them thirty years apart. Taken together they illustrate three different sets of assumptions about, and conventions for, presenting film performance. In 1936, the approach is consciously theatrical; in 1968 acting choices reflect naturalistic conventions; in 1996 performances are attuned to postmodern collage techniques.

In MGM's 1936 adaptation of *Romeo and Juliet,* acting choices suit framing, editing, production, and sound design selections that create a "theatrical" presentation. This aesthetic intent is articulated in the very opening of film when a tapestry mural rises to reveal an actor on a stage reading Shakespeare's prologue to *Romeo and Juliet* from a scroll. Clearly, the film's aesthetic model is legitimate theater and, more specifically, Shakespearean theater legitimized by four hundred years of production in England. For audiences of the time, this image, together with the production's grandiose sets and lush costumes, could easily suggest that the film adaptation was as good if not better than any theatrical production of Shakespeare could be.

For the last picture Irving Thalberg produced before his death, he assembled a production team that included George Cukor, who had been entrusted to direct other prestige pictures for MGM; Cedric Gibbons, the studio's legendary art director; and William H. Daniels, who had established his reputation as Garbo's cinematographer.[8] The vast and beautifully crafted sets built on one hundred acres of land were created under Gibbons's supervision. The carefully researched design based on Italian Renaissance paintings provided stages for the actors who were costumed with equally lavish care.[9]

The decision to cast forty-two-year-old Leslie Howard as Romeo and thirty-seven-year-old Norma Shearer (Mrs. Thalberg) as Juliet reflects the era's view that great acting depends on great actors' interpretations of great roles.[10] While this casting flies in the face of realism, it discloses Thalberg's view that performances in prestige pictures could and should be seen as comparable to performances on the legitimate stage. That perspective also dovetails with principles of acting central to the studio era, for drama coaches of the period emphasized that acting on stage and screen required the same training and preparation, and that informed, quantitative adjustments allowed actors to move from stage to screen and back. This presumption is one reason that more of Shakespeare's text remains in this filmic adaptation than in the others we are considering. For example, in the scene when Juliet drinks the sleeping potion, only the 1936 film allows the actress to deliver the entire soliloquy.[11]

Given predominant notions of propriety in 1930s Hollywood, the actors' ages also allowed Thalberg to tell Juliet's love story more completely and thus to position Shearer as an actor of equal importance to Howard. Whereas Shakespeare had created a feisty Juliet, more pragmatic than Romeo, and equally willful and sexual, most adaptations in the United States during the early twentieth century expressed the culture's discomfort with the determined Juliet by cutting her lines, especially those of act 3, scene 2 in which she anticipates the consummation of her marriage. In those productions, Juliet plays a subordinate role to her male counterpart. As Stephen M. Buhler explains, "Over the centuries, the character of Juliet has been rewritten in accordance with shifting notions of identity and propriety for young women," either by excising lines with sexual innuendo, hence reducing Juliet's role, or by adjusting Juliet's age "upwards, making the inclusion of such complexities less distasteful."[12] By casting a mature actress to play Juliet, Thalberg could include Juliet's sexually explicit lines. Fostering his wife's career and showcasing her skill as an actor, Thalberg retained "lines that make it possible to establish Juliet's character as very much Romeo's match in assertiveness."[13]

Despite the more explicit lines, however, Juliet's youthful love for Romeo is expressed through a measured performance. Howard's and Shearer's portrayals in previous films allowed audiences of the time to see their characters as lovers made youthful by the purity of their spirit. They had appeared together in the gangster melodrama *Free Soul* (Clarence Brown, 1931). Both had received Oscar nominations, Howard for his work in the romantic fantasy *Berkeley Square* (Frank Lloyd, 1933) and Shearer for her performance as Elisabeth Barrett in love with poet Robert Browning in *The Barrets of Wimpole Street* (Sidney Franklin, 1934). To suggest the youth of their characters in *Romeo and Juliet,* Howard and Shearer use gestures, facial expressions, and vocal styles that could be interpreted by their audiences as childlike. Throughout the film, they fill their performances with soft, gentle, carefully modulated movements, avoiding anything quick, rigid, or angular. Their facial expressions convey openness, hopefulness, and quiet interest. They never frown, glare, or narrow their eyes, and their voices feature melodious tones and wistful lilts, never harsh, angry, or anguished cries.

The film's overall design, distinguished by wide shots and sets of vast scale, complements the soft, ethereal quality of the stars' work. As orchestrated, the long shots and huge sets make Howard and Shearer seem smaller, more vulnerable, and more youthful. Deep-focus cinematography draws viewers into the fantasy world surrounding the lovers. Long takes and long shots create space around the lead actors that helps to convey the sincerity of the characters' lofty sentiments, the purity of their souls, and the elegiac tragedy of their suffering.

Framed by Gibbons's impressive sets and Daniels's deep-focus cinematography, performance details convey the sense that the lovers are graced by purity of spirit. Drawing on the model of traditional proscenium staging, the MGM production allows the actors to take center stage. In the scene when Romeo and Juliet first meet, Shearer enters the ballroom upstage center. Diagonal lines of dancers begin at the outside borders of the frame and end where Shearer enters, marking her as the focal point in both the set and the frame. A long dance sequence, choreographed by Agnes de Mille early in her career, keeps Shearer as the center of attention, with Howard's point-of-view shots following her movements through the room. To suggest the purity of Romeo's gaze, Howard is shown in medium long shots against an empty background that sets off his graceful carriage and delicate, patrician features.

The sequence that begins with Howard entering the ballroom and that ends with him dancing with Shearer is presented in five wide shots. Their initial meeting and private encounter take place in three connected playing areas, all presented in one long take. The choreography of actors and camera takes Howard and Shearer from the public dancing area to the private space of a balcony and then even closer to the audience when the actors stand at the balcony's edge. The sequence ends when Juliet/Shearer asks her nurse for Romeo's name; a long take shows Shearer moving slowly away from both the camera and Romeo down a long hallway as a servant extinguishes the lights behind her one by one.

Throughout the dance sequence that allows Romeo to approach Juliet, the gestures of the lead players and the surrounding figures are stately, mannered, and suited to public performance. Even after Howard and Shearer move away from the other dancers to exchange private words and a kiss, their encounter remains entirely chaste. The actors present audiences with carefully selected pictures of childlike flirtation. Their eyes stay wide open; they seem to float close to one another and then gently pull back. Their melodic voices are lightly expressive. As portrayed by Howard and Shearer, Romeo and Juliet are youthful because they are virginal and inexperienced; their love is romantic in its purity. While their gestures are not sexually suggestive, the almost quivering quality of their movements carries the same suggestion of excitement that is conveyed by the glittering rhinestones on Shearer's head and gown.

With Shakespeare's text largely retained and elegantly spoken, sound design further contributes to impressions created by the film's framing, editing, setting, and performances. The actors' physical gestures and facial expressions never interfere with their line deliveries. Instead, the perfectly balanced tableaux that Howard and Shearer create at each stage of their encounter serves to emphasize the lines they deliver in clear mid-Atlantic accents. Their performances indicate a great deal of control, for Howard and Shearer both speak with a stillness and composure that allows audiences to absorb the ornate language and the impressive picture of their presence in the grand hall. Emblematic of the fact that films feature the coordinated orchestration of numerous elements, the 1936 film presents audiences with lines spoken in a distinctly theatrical space. As we will see, that choice distinguishes it from the 1968 and 1996 films, which feature close miking and postdubbing that give audiences the impression of overhearing the young lovers' most intimate words, breaths, and interior monologues.

While Franco Zeffirelli's lush 1968 adaptation of *Romeo and Juliet* is quite different from MGM's 1936 production, it too provides clear evidence that acting choices are on a par with decisions about other cinematic elements. Here again, the selection and combination of performance details are as important to the film's overall design as the selection and combination of its other components.

The 1968 film does not address an audience of thousands in a grand theater but instead an audience that usually shares an intimate space with the actors. It often presents the actors' performances as if they were overheard conversations, placing audience members in the titillating position of being eavesdroppers on intimate moments. It also offers viewers a curious blend of fantasy and materiality, combining an anachronistic re-creation of Re-

Norma Shearer and Leslie Howard in 1936: wide shots and long takes present innocent gestures in a dazzling and impressive theatrical space

naissance Verona with a concrete world of flesh, solid buildings, and marketplaces. As Peter Holland has observed, "Stage productions of *Romeo and Juliet* can rarely show life in Verona in the way that Zeffirelli did in his 1968 film, the exact and excited depiction of an imaginary Renaissance Italian reality bearing, of course, scant relation to the truth of history but with a verve and energy that was itself convincing."[14]

Zeffirelli's decision to cast seventeen-year-old Olivia Hussey and eighteen-year-old Leonard Whiting shows that a significant change in ideas about acting had occurred since 1936. Hussey and Whiting were quite experienced for their age: Hussey began dramatic training as a child and had appeared in small theater and film roles, while Whiting had been in long-running theatrical productions since the age of twelve. But compared with Shearer and Howard they were unknowns. Rather than feature "great" actors' interpretations, the 1960s film presents audiences with the illusion of "authentic" emotion. Thus, Hussey and Whiting were cast in part because of their physicality.[15]

The casting also reflects the film's overall conception, for Zeffirelli uses Romeo and Juliet to represent the rebellious and idealistic youth of the 1960s.[16] Situated thirty years after the MGM production and nearly thirty years before Baz Luhrman's postmodern extravaganza, Zeffirelli's British-

Italian production is a study in operatic cinéma vérité. In contrast to the ethereal 1936 black-and-white film, Zeffirelli's adaptation is filled with rich colors and sweeping movements. Its aesthetic models do not derive from Broadway theater. Instead, the film's sumptuous design and musically driven dialogue show the influence of opera, which revels in overwhelming production design and emotional waves of music. The film's locations in Tuscania, Pienza, and Gubbio as analogues of Verona also suggest the open-air rock concerts that were part of youth culture in the 1960s. Zeffirelli's visual design overturns the reverence that permeates the 1936 production, offering instead an anthem to the generation that responded to rock operas by The Who that include *Tommy* (Ken Russell, 1975) and *The Kids Are Alright* (Jeff Stein, 1979). Zeffirelli's *Romeo and Juliet* conveys the idealism that infused the civil service strikes in Paris during May 1968 and the worldwide protests against the war in Vietnam. In Zeffirelli's adaptation, the young lovers' intense and purifying sexual desire allows them to move beyond the corrupt divisions established and maintained by their parents' generation. The political rivalries in the sixteenth-century story suggest familiar generational divisions in the 1960s; as Buhler notes, Zeffirelli's film "offered a distinctive 'generation gap' reading of the play."[17]

The Oscar-winning costumes created by Danilo Donati contributed to the young lovers' unearthly beauty and utterly grounded physical presence. As in the 1936 film, the actors in Zeffirelli's adaptation seem to be bound in, supported by, and cloaked in their period costumes. While performances in both films feature gracefulness hidden and enhanced by the layers of clothing, Zeffirelli calls attention to the actors' physicality with tighter framing. The ornate, Oscar-winning cinematography of Pasqualino de Santis creates an environment suited to the histrionic but sensually realistic performances. Compositions select and frame the actors' naturalistic gestures and expressions. In the ballroom sequence, frame selections range from wide shots to extreme close-ups, and the young actors' eyes and faces become isolated momentarily, set off from the colorful and continuous movement of the dancers and onlookers. Subjective point-of-view shots suggest the young lovers' thoughts, and eye-line match shots bring audiences into their developing flirtation. In this film, viewers are allowed to eavesdrop on the lovers' first meeting, brought so close that the intimacy of their furtive connection is conveyed and authenticated by physical signs of deep breathing, flushed cheeks, and quivering hands.

In the sequence that allows audiences to witness Romeo and Juliet's first kiss, shot selection is, for the most part, restricted to medium shots, medium close-ups, close-ups, and extreme close-ups. Frame composition features tight shots of faces and bodies. The audience is pulled into the scene by motivated point-of-view shots. From beginning to end, the searching eyes of the young lovers are almost crowded out by the uninterested figures of the older generation. While the 1936 film uses less than twenty shots to cover the entire scene of the lovers' first meeting, the 1968 film presents their meeting in four sequences, each with about thirty shots: Romeo sees Juliet; Romeo and Juliet exchange glances as participants in the dance; during the ballad, Romeo finds Juliet in the crowd and takes her into a private area behind a pillar; Juliet's nurse intrudes on the lovers. In the MGM film, the scene of the Capulet ball lasts about seven minutes, while Zeffirelli uses eleven minutes to stage the lovers' initial meeting at the ball. Yet in both films, the lovers' intimate exchange takes place within about three minutes.

The ballad sequence at the Capulet ball begins with shots that emphasize Romeo and Juliet's search for one another in the crowd. Images of the lovers' young faces are often framed by older characters placidly watching and listening to the ballad. Short point-of-view shots convey the two lovers' urgent desire to see one another. Once the lovers' finally connect, tight shots of their eyes, faces, and hands convey their impatience and uncertainty as Romeo reaches for Juliet's hand, and the two characters slip behind the curtain. Once they are behind the curtain, a long take that follows them through three units of action helps to create a sense of their intimacy and connectedness. Each phrase of dialogue is like a musical passage that is given its own framing and setting. With the actors gently enclosed within the frame, the pillar that had first separated them now becomes a wall that protects them. While the actors' private space is comparable to the one in the MGM film, their performances are framed in medium shots and medium close-ups that allow audiences to study the actors' young faces more closely.

Production design further enhances impressions created by the acting and framing. The banquet table in the private enclosure that is filled with food, glasses, and bottles of wine emphasizes the soft sensuality of the brief encounter between the new lovers. The golden stained-glass window behind them provides a radiant frame around Hussey's face in the moments before she is kissed, making visual the saintly images of the formal sonnet that the two lovers compose as a prelude to their kiss. When the sequence ends with the lovers' embrace, the tighter framing echoes the intimacy created by the choreography of performance that keeps Hussey's face hidden from view.

Sound design resonates with acting, framing, editing, and production

Olivia Hussey and Leonard Whiting in 1968: medium close-ups and close miking allow audiences to eavesdrop on chaste but passionate expression in filmic space

design. In the 1968 film, the sound track is dense with dialogue, music, and background sound. Whiting's and Hussey's voices are as melodic and mid-Atlantic in accent as those of Howard and Shearer. However, sound design makes the young actors' sensuous gasps carry the same importance as the words they speak. With their wide-open eyes and youthful faces as signs of romantic love, their breath becomes a physical symptom of their desire. Like Shearer and Howard, Hussey and Whiting deliver their lines in trained voices. Their words are clearly articulated. Intonations and inflections serve to clarify the meaning of more arcane terms. Pronunciations bear no trace of specific class or ethnic background. Yet Hussey's and Whiting's measured phrasing gives their speech a musical quality, and their intimate sounds enhance and sometimes replace spoken words. Tighter framing allows for barely whispered lines, and close miking creates an impression of intimate proximity and coherence between choices in acting, framing, and sound design.

Throughout the film, Hussey and Whiting appear more animated than Shearer and Howard. In the 1936 film, blocking and camera movement enhance the languid, dreamlike impression established by the film's performance details. By comparison, in the 1968 film, short takes of tight shots make Hussey and Whiting appear more fervent, with close views of their facial expressions communicating the intensity of their feelings. In the MGM film, full shots that pull back to show Shearer drifting away from the dance reveal Juliet's interest in Romeo. For Zeffirelli, Juliet's curiosity about Romeo also emerges during the dance sequence, as Hussey wanders away from the crowd to look for him. But in the 1968 film, Hussey's small, sharp gasp shown in a close-up is what signals Juliet's interest in Romeo's amorous advances. Then, through Whiting's point-of-view shot, viewers see the series of thoughts that pass through Hussey's eyes and across her face. Her expressions convey Juliet's initial surprise that Romeo has clutched her hand, then her delight, then concern, then curiosity, and finally pleasure in seeing the beautiful young man who is kneeling to hold her hand.

While the 1936 film frames the actors in ways that do not distract attention from the spoken words, the 1968 film makes audiences consider the meaning underlying the spoken and unspoken words. While wide framing allows Shearer and Howard to portray infatuated youth, Zeffirelli's tighter framing highlights Hussey's and Whiting's physical expressivity. At the same time, Zeffirelli does not reduce the actors' work to physiological signs alone. Shakespeare's text remains important with shot changes reflecting transitions in dialogue to create musical phrases that link sound, image, and dramatic significance. The 1968 film balances emotion conveyed by movements, facial expressions, and vocal inflections with impressions created by framing and setting. With significant weight given to all these elements, the 1968 film represents an intermediate point between the 1936 and 1996 presentations of performance.

Baz Luhrman's more "televisual" adaptation of the Romeo and Juliet story coordinates acting choices with other filmic details, even though, as one of the "most media-saturated of all Shakespeare films," the framing and editing do call attention to themselves.[18] The actors' physical signs of heightened emotion become one element in the larger chaotic collage cluttered with bizarre costumes, frenetic camera movement, and dizzying editing patterns. Featuring a design that contrasts with the stately proscenium images of Thalberg's production and Zeffirelli's lush rendering inspired by stained-glass windows and sixteenth-century tapestries, the 1996 film starring twenty-two-year-old Leonardo DiCaprio and seventeen-year-old Claire Danes draws its images from a lexicon that includes news broadcasts, comics, teen magazines, MTV videos, and *Miami Vice* episodes. Luhrman and his collaborators present Romeo and Juliet's ill-fated love as a subject for television news and music videos.

The Luhrman film not only simulates late-twentieth-century film and media conventions, but also comments on those practices from an outsider's point of view. As Peter Donaldson observes, while media "is portrayed with immense energy and even delight," Luhrman also treats it critically "as the cause of the tragic action."[19] Luhrman conveys that critique when Romeo and Juliet first see each other through the distorting water of a tropical fish tank. As Donaldson observes, "This optically mediated courtship dance is in some ways a visual equivalent to the shared sonnet in the text, in the sense that even love at first sight is made possible by a negotiation of formal boundaries, which the lovers alternatively transgress and respect."[20] Even the film's title, *William Shakespeare's Romeo + Juliet,* emphasizes that the film adapts and mediates a prior text.

While produced in the United States with American stars, the film is grounded in Australian cinema. Harold Perrineau, Jr.'s drag portrayal of Mercutio, and the imagery that pervades the Capulet ball allude to the Sydney Gay and Lesbian Mardi Gras Parade (the largest such event in the world) and to Australian films like *The Adventures of Priscilla, Queen of the Desert* (Stephen Elliot, 1994).[21] Luhrman and production design collaborator Catherine Martin came to this project following careers in Australian theater and their success with *Strictly Ballroom* (1992). Cinematographer Donald McAlpine had been responsible for more than forty Australian films that include landmarks in the country's national cinema such as *My Brilliant Career* (Gillian Armstrong, 1979) and *Breaker Morant* (Bruce Beresford, 1980). Editor Jill Babcock came to the project after working on Australian films such as *Muriel's Wedding* (P. J. Hogan, 1994).

As different as they are, the 1936 and 1996 films both presume that audiences are not well acquainted with Shakespeare's play. As if recognizing that canonical literature is foreign ground for film audiences, both identify the principal characters in the opening credit sequences. However, the films differ in how they make the play relevant to their audiences. In the 1996 film, Juliet's angelic purity becomes Danes's angel costume complete with wire and tulle wings. The idea that Romeo and Juliet are ethereal spirits suspended in a state of bliss is translated into literal and ironic terms: Luhrman's Romeo and Juliet kiss while suspended between floors in a moving elevator whose door temporarily shields them from the intrusions of Paris and Juliet's mother.

While the 1936 film establishes its connection with legitimate theater, Luhrman makes his story part of media culture. In contrast to the theatrical model for Thalberg's opening credits, Luhrman's prologue is a televised news event fueled by a barrage of identifiable icons and overt allusions. Cramming ninety-six shots into ninety seconds, Luhrman brings in references ranging from Alfred Hitchcock's 1963 film *The Birds* (the explosion and fire at the gas station) to Federico Fellini's 1960 film *La dolce vita* (the statue on a rope dangling from a helicopter flying over the city). Francisco Menendez sees this approach as a strategy to ease mass-media spectators into Shakespearean verse, noting that "The opening marries the word to the image and the image to the word, an approach that will be the key for the audience to be able to accept the language in this contemporary tale."[22]

The allusions give audiences familiar entry points and ways to access the unfamiliar Shakespearean language. It addresses the audience as television viewers, offers references to Hitchcock and Fellini, and invites viewers to enjoy the innovative way Luhrman incorporates the spectacular and fragmented editing of Hong Kong blood operas, saturated primary colors of Technicolor cartoons, and the *Miami Vice* approach to costume design as the key to character definition. Luhrman explains that they "identified different icons and made veiled associations so you have a way of decoding the story really quickly."[23] While the 1936 film offered a fairy-tale world that contrasted with the economic realities of the 1930s, and the 1968 film took sides in the generational conflicts of the 1960s, Luhrman's film gives voice to young consumer's desire to author their own images in a world of commercial, ready-made images. Here, the star-crossed lovers embody the impossible dream of living an authentic existence in a society that fragments genuine experience to turn a profit.

With that underlying conception, the actors' bodies and voices become the bearers of authentic physiological signs, which accrue significance through integration into the film's montage. Like the characters themselves, the details of the actors' performances belong to a world that includes neither perfectly modulated speech nor evenly measured musical phrases. This media-saturated reality can accommodate only fleeting and off-balance embraces, awkward voices that crack with emotion, and flat, nasal Los Angeles accents that rarely shift in tone. Lovers are continually exposed; the actors appear with little or no makeup, and blocking ensures that there are only a few, frantic moments when they are out of public view. In this world, there are no intimate exchanges in private spaces, only telling pieces of intimate gesture and expression whipped into an audiovisual mixture.

Handheld camera movements and sudden shifts in the actors' energy create an overwhelming sense of instability. The editing does not "follow the conventions of the 'continuity style' [using instead] aggressive camera movement [and] intellectual juxtapositions."[24] In the six minutes of the Capulet ball when Romeo and Juliet first see one another, quick cuts establish a

Claire Danes in 1996: tight framing and short takes offer fleeting glimpses of "natural" expression in a jumble of televisual images

Leonardo DiCaprio in 1996: a crafted moment of authentic, physical gesture

Gesture fragments in the 1996 adaptation: pilgrims' hands in a material world

sense of chaos and imbalance. During the three minutes the lovers are together, wide shots of frenetic crowd movement contrast with extremely tight shots of the lovers locked in their embrace. The combination shows that Romeo and Juliet's passionate affection isolates them further from the cynical world that will always control their lives. With contemporary analogues used to present the play "the way Shakespeare had originally presented his story," Luhrman's film becomes a commentary on the intrusive role of media in contemporary culture.[25]

Sound design completes the chaotic, unstable impression created by coordinated acting and framing choices. In the sixty-shot sequence that begins when the lovers' hands first touch behind the pillar, the handling of sound shifts rapidly: sometimes the actors are close-miked, sometimes their voices are heard from a distance, still other times the musical score completely covers any sound of giggles, gasps, and groans one intuits from the flurry of images that depict the lovers' first tentative touch of hands and subsequent passionate, swirling, and interrupted embraces. Like all aspects of the film, disjointed sound is integrated into the film's design, which creates meaning out of disparate elements boiled down to their simplest components.

All three adaptations of *Romeo and Juliet* give equal weight to framing, editing, production, sound, and performance choices. In the 1936 film, the dreamlike quality of the cinematography and set design resonates with the ethereal feeling created by the actors' controlled and modulated vocal and physical gestures. In Zeffirelli's 1968 film, musical phrases created by framing, editing, miking, and line deliveries come together in moments anchored by the actors' intimate physical and vocal expressions. In Luhrman's 1996 film, acting choices coordinate with the other audiovisual details that are drawn from a dizzying array of social and cinematic allusions. Differences between the three adaptations help to show how acting choices fit into the overall design of the films. Considered together, the films underscore the fact that choices about framing, editing, production, and sound design are also implicitly choices about performance.

ACTING CHOICES AND FRAMING CHOICES IN ADAPTATIONS OF *HAMLET*

However presented on screen, performance begins with actors' physical and vocal gestures. When these gestures resonate with the artistic conception and style of a film, the actor not only makes the editor's work easier, but, more significantly, actively contributes to the final screen product.

Viewing specific gestures and expressions as selections from a range of options helps one see how performance details work in concert with framing and editing to create a film's impact and aesthetic style. Close comparisons of three different cinematic performances from *Hamlet*, act 3, scene 4, in which the Ghost appears to Hamlet in his mother's sleeping chamber (often called the closet scene), show how acting choices contribute to the overall cinematic montage. By examining the same basic scene, we can illuminate the interaction between acting and framing choices. While there are at least forty-eight cinematic versions of this classic play, the three adaptations released in 1948, 1969, and 1990 contain a sufficient range of acting and framing combinations to clarify the different performance options that films offer to actors.

The 1948 adaptation of *Hamlet,* directed by and starring Laurence Olivier, who also performed the voice of the Ghost, won Academy Awards for Best Picture, Best Actor, Best Art Direction/Set Design, and Best Costume. Olivier boldly cut the notoriously long play down to 155 minutes, primarily by eliminating the politicized characters of Fortinbras, Rosencrantz, and Guildenstern, and concentrating on the psychology of the central character. The black-and-white film is distinguished by deep-focus photography and high-angle shots. Olivier prefers to call his abbreviated version "an essay on Hamlet" rather than "a necessarily abridged classic."[26] When Olivier first played Hamlet on stage at the Old Vic in 1937, he was strongly influenced by Ernest Jones's now-famous Freudian analysis of the play. While the sexual nuances between Hamlet and his mother Gertrude, played by Eileen Herlie, were toned down to accommodate a wide commercial audience, critics still found the case study scene "stinging," and they argued that the complex relationship between mother and son was "acted with marvellous intensity."[27]

Tony Richardson's 1969 filmed version of his stage production for the Round House Theatre in London stars Nicol Williamson in the title role and Judy Parfitt as Gertrude. Like Olivier, Richardson concentrates on psychological layers in the play. He also eliminated the character of Fortinbras and substituted a spotlight on Hamlet's face for the tangible and audible presence of the Ghost. Yet Richardson's abridgements alone do not account for the short 112 minutes of the film; Williamson delivers his lines with furious speed. While Laurence Olivier and Mel Gibson take more than three minutes for Hamlet's most famous soliloquy, Williamson delivers Hamlet's "To be or not to be" soliloquy in 150 seconds.[28] Richardson's *Hamlet* is also distinguished by its nearly exclusive use of long takes that frame the actors' faces in continuous close-ups. While Richardson's stage production had been characterized by vast, empty spaces on an enormous stage, his filmic treatment presents a "claustrophobic milieu of enforced intimacy."[29] Neil Taylor observes that the film's orchestration of cinematic elements makes it seem "as if the director [was] a member of the paparazzi pursuing royals in the news."[30]

Garnering Academy Award nominations for Art Direction and Costume Design, Franco Zeffirelli's 1990 adaptation turned Shakespeare's tragedy into an action film. Publicity written for the film's video release announces that Zeffirelli's *Hamlet* is an "immortal tale of high adventure and evil deeds." Zeffirelli cast Mel Gibson after watching him in Richard Donner's 1987 film *Lethal Weapon.* He explains, "There was a scene in which there's a kind of 'to be or not to be' speech. Mel Gibson is sitting there with a gun in his mouth but he can't pull the trigger. When I saw that I said 'This is Hamlet! This boy is Hamlet!' "[31] Glenn Close plays Gertrude, and Paul Scofield portrays the Ghost in this 129-minute-long adaptation. Featuring frequent cuts from one character to another, the film retains only 31 percent of Shakespeare's text, which is reorganized into an action-packed narrative.[32]

Two interlocking questions assist in identifying the actors' choices. What means of expression are available to the actors given the framing in the films? How do acting choices change when framing and other cinematic elements change? The three renditions of the scene with Hamlet, his mother, and his father's ghost reveal ways that actors adjust their performances to suit decisions about other cinematic techniques. Actors and acting teachers confirm that this kind of adjustment is consciously employed by professional actors. Michael Caine teaches screen actors to always ask about the planned shot. "When in doubt," he reiterates, "ask!"[33] Patrick Tucker advises actors to ask the camera operator what kind of shot is planned whenever the director and cinematographer do not offer the information.[34]

In all three *Hamlets,* the actors design their performances to suit the demands of the film. On set, once professional actors know what shot is planned, they select expressive gestures that suit the framing and find the right adjustment for their physical energy and vocal levels. As Caine notes, when a close-up is planned, "the film actor knows how to reduce a performance physically, but not mentally."[35] Vocal choices are keyed to frame composition, not verisimilitude. For example, in *Spartacus* (Stanley Kubrick, 1960), Kirk Douglas matches his voice level to the framing, using low levels for close-ups even in scenes when his character addresses huge crowds.[36]

Contemporary actors' descriptions of such adjustments are remarkably consistent with the approach used by studio-era actors and acting teachers who found that acting for film entails quantitative, not qualitative, changes in technique. In fact, the ability to adjust physical and vocal expression to suit specific framing sets the experienced film actor apart from the beginner. Tucker explains that when you act in film, "part of your brain deals with the acting side, and another part of your brain must function as your own private technical director, keeping tabs on where the camera and microphones are and noting and remembering which marks have to be hit."[37] Editors also bear witness to the distinction between experienced and inexperienced players. For example, Conrad Buff, the editor for *Antwone Fisher* (Denzel Washington, 2002), explains that "the performances were the most challenging thing" for him because Derek Luke, who played the lead, did not have the same experience as Denzel Washington, the film's supporting actor and director.[38] Because Luke's gestures and expressions were not finely attuned to each framing nuance, his performance proved to be "the most difficult to help and balance out" in postproduction.[39]

In the 1948 adaptation of *Hamlet,* Laurence Olivier and Eileen Herlie are often framed in long shots that show the entire bodies of both actors. The wide framing serves to minimize the fact that Olivier is in his forties while Herlie, playing his mother, is in her thirties. In the scene between Hamlet, his mother, and his father's ghost, high angles reveal their whole figures, placing the audience at times in the superior position of the Ghost, who looks down upon the mortals. Long takes preserve the tempo created by the actors' movements and line deliveries. Desmond Dickenson, the film's director of photography, explains that the actors "were able to deliver long speeches and to walk about the set very freely. Often they would walk right up to the camera for a close-up and then walk away again."[40]

Responsive to the framing and editing choices, Olivier and Herlie use full body gestures to express their characters' feelings and relationships. With Olivier on the floor, fearfully looking toward the Ghost, dutifully reaching for Herlie's hand, Olivier creates a son who gives full authority to his dead father. Writhing on the floor like a crazed child or looking like a small beaten boy when still, Olivier gives visual expression to the idea that Hamlet is a child in a man's body. Subtly dropping her head and melting downward with her shoulders, Herlie conveys Gertrude's resignation and sense of helplessness in the face of what she believes to be madness.

The film's deep-focus photography emphasizes the actors' relationship to settings in the same way a well-lit theatrical stage might. Dickenson explains that performances that are designed and choreographed for deep-focus staging place significant demands on actors. He notes that framing and editing in conventional continuity-style cinematography make it possible for an actor to be "built up into a star personality because in the close-up his face loom[s] larger than life upon the screen, whilst everyone and everything behind him [is] shadowy and distorted."[41] He points out that in the early years of cinema the "unreal values of this presentation enabled the star to maintain a position in the film which was often not commensurate with his acting ability."[42] By comparison, with the arrival of deep-focus cinematography in the 1930s that situation became much less likely. Dickenson proposes that "*Hamlet* is a perfect example of a film in which everyone must—and can—act" because deep-focus cinematography allows and requires performers to guide audience attention through physical position (blocking) and vocal styles.[43]

With framing and editing subordinated to acting choices, in the 1948 film Olivier and Herlie convey their characters' relationship through their relative positions in the space. They also direct audience attention by adjusting their gaze to and away from each other and the camera. For example, the actors' close proximity on the oversized bed at the beginning of the scene is indicative of Olivier's Freudian reading of the play. Here, blocking that puts them face to face on the bed gives the characters equal importance and conveys the sexual tension between mother and son. However, after the Ghost enters, Olivier turns his face outward, toward the Ghost and the camera, thus seizing audience attention. Soon after, when Olivier reaches for Herlie's hand without moving his eyes from the Ghost, Herlie helps to keep attention focused on Olivier by remaining in profile as she looks at him. While audiences might hear her voice, their attention is drawn to Olivier, who occupies the center of the frame. Thus, acting choices convey what is important at each moment in the scene.

The orchestration of framing, editing, and acting choices allows Olivier and Herlie to use their physical and vocal expressions in ways comparable to actors working in theatrical productions. No wonder that critics have discussed the film's "stagelike blocking" and have seen the performances reflecting a "theatrical tradition."[44] Olivier and Herlie utilize a full range of facial and bodily expression; their changes of tempo and rhythm are expressed both through carefully executed gestures and through evocative delivery of lines. Herlie clenches her fists as she sits motionless, a combination

Laurence Olivier in 1948: gesture keyed to deep-focus cinematography

that escalates the tension of the moment. Olivier presses the scene forward by making every phrase another step toward the scene's climax. For both actors, each new thought carries a new intonation and a change of tone.

While the 1948 film features gestures, postures, and poses that involve the actors' entire bodies, the 1969 adaptation of *Hamlet* calls upon Nicol Williamson and Judy Parfitt to use physical and vocal expressions suited to the film's nearly exclusive use of close-ups. The actors can communicate information about the characters only through facial and vocal expressions, small gestures of their hands and arms, the subtle angling of their shoulders, the tilt of their heads, and so on. When compared to the options open to Olivier and Herlie, Williamson and Parfitt must draw on a different range of gestures and expressions, most of them so small that they would not be visible in a large theatrical auditorium. Neil Taylor notes that when Williamson addresses the camera directly "the effect is far more winning and controlling [than on stage] because there is no escaping" the actor's gaze.[45] He also explains that Williamson does not "sustain an engagement with the camera's attention for more than a few lines."[46] These shifts, from moments of direct address to times when Williamson's performance is observed, offer evidence about the character through an approach to human expressivity that differs from the 1948 film.

Nicol Williamson in 1969: physical expression confined to tight framing

Bernice Kliman observes that in the 1969 adaptation, even small "changes make for drama in a static frame when one face fills the frame."[47] She explains that this adaptation "concentrates attention on the landscape of the visage."[48] In Richardson's film, the tight framing is designed in coordination with the selection of performance elements that convey especially strong impressions when seen at close distance. In the closet scene with Hamlet, the tight framing draws attention to the evocative power of the wet tears that run down Williamson's and Parfitt's faces. The framing operates in concert with the quality of the gesture when Williamson extends his fingers to cover his eyes completely.

In those moments when Hamlet is transfixed by the ghost of his father, acting and framing choices together convey the impact of Williamson grinding his fist into his cheek, with the close-up amplifying the intense quality of this gesture. Soon after, acting and framing choices work together when Parfitt pitches her shoulders away from Williamson. The diagonal angle of Parfitt's shoulders conveys the mother's emotional distance from her mad son, in part because the gesture-as-presented plays on Western audiences' propensity to read from left to right. As Tucker notes, angling the right shoulder forward creates a strong visual impression because it leads viewers to scan the image the way they would scan a line of print.[49]

While Olivier's use of deep focus allows actors to direct attention, in Richardson's film, compositional choices that dramatize Hamlet's desire for his mother and fear of his father focus attention on Williamson. For the entire closet scene, Williamson is in sharper focus than Parfitt, and the eerie spotlight, which stands for the ghost of Hamlet's father, shines directly on Williamson. Indeed, we never see Parfitt's full face and so the scene belongs to Williamson more fully than Parfitt, whatever her expressive choices are. In contrast to the 1948 adaptation, Richardson directs attention primarily by filmic choices. Even so, Williamson and Parfitt use the expressive means available to them to contribute to the meaning created by the film. For example, placed behind and a little higher than Williamson, Parfitt consistently angles her shoulders away from him and lets her hair obscure her face in a way that works in concert with the filmic choices that focus attention on the son's inner struggle.

The actors also use their voices, one of the primary expressive means available to them, with special creativity. Williamson speaks at almost unintelligible speed; both actors whine and plead. During the run of the stage production, Williamson was often criticized for his nasality and for his limited and inaudible voice. What had been a problem on stage becomes a useful factor in the film because the quality of his voice helps to create a uniquely unsympathetic Hamlet. Moreover, Richardson uses the actors' vocal work primarily for emotional rather than semantic impact. As we watch the film, we lose the rational intelligibility of Hamlet's words even as we respond to the emotional roller-coaster ride conveyed by Williamson's rising and falling cadences.

In contrast to Olivier's and Herlie's intelligent but irrational characters, Williamson and Parfitt create characters caught up in the waves of their nonverbal feelings. While in the 1948 film, physical and vocal expressions suit scenic spaces that are comparable to a theatrical stage, in Richardson's film, actors adapt to the framing and editing choices by using minuscule gestures and vocal sound rather than intelligible words to suggest inner turmoil. While Olivier and Herlie temper their reactions with carefully composed gestures, Williamson and Parfitt ride ebbing and flowing waves of emotion, no longer separating the various thoughts into discrete lines and poetically precise images.

For the 1990 adaptation of *Hamlet,* Franco Zeffirelli uses the more familiar conventions of continuity editing that depend on eye-line match shots and reaction shots. In the scene when the Ghost comes between Hamlet and his mother, Zeffirelli employs long shots working in coordination with

Mel Gibson in 1990: gesture suited for action adventure conventions

the actors' blocking and full body gestures in a way that recalls Olivier's 1948 film. Zeffirelli also brings out the Freudian implications by having Mel Gibson and Glenn Close sit together on the bed in Gertrude's sleeping chamber. Zeffirelli actually pushes their sexually charged relationship to such an extreme that the film has been described as "a fluid, excitingly paced movie about two middle-aged, star-crossed lovers."[50]

The closet scene employs close-ups that focus attention on the actors' facial and vocal expressions, as in Richardson's version. Zeffirelli uses tight framing and shallow depth of field to convey the idea that Hamlet is mesmerized by the Ghost of his father, to the point that he leaves his mother literally and figuratively out of focus in the background. Throughout the scene with the Ghost, Gibson and Close adjust their expressive means to suit the film's conventional combination of wide shots to show action and tight shots to suggest characters' point of view. The acting choices even help to convert the dramatic action into the familiar images of the action genre. To convey a moment of decision, Close pounces on the bed like Catwoman; to suggest Hamlet's inner turmoil, Gibson stands with his hand on his sword staring outward with his eyes full of alarm.

Translating Shakespeare's play into terms familiar to mainstream film audiences, Zeffirelli also frequently cuts from one character to another. As a consequence, framing and editing play a key role in directing audience attention. It also leaves the audience to infer what characters are doing off screen. For example, after focusing attention on the Ghost, when the film cuts to Glenn Close raising her head she appears to have seen the Ghost despite her words to the contrary. The juxtaposition of images creates a complexity in the scene that does not emerge only from the acting choices. Zeffirelli's reliance on familiar editing formulas also makes framing and editing central to the rhythmic pacing of the film. By comparison, in the 1948 film actors' movements and line readings largely determine the rhythmic structure of its long takes; in the 1969 film rhythmic structure emerges from the combination of acting, framing, and editing.

Zeffirelli's framing and editing presume that the film's audience will become more emotionally engaged in the story if the film adheres to familiar cinematic conventions. Those choices, however, present film actors with unique problems. They no longer necessarily depend on interaction with a partner to prompt and stimulate reactions but instead must become self-initiating and self-sufficient.[51] They also cannot expect to direct audience attention through physical position and line delivery. At the same time, their performances must still be designed to suit the framing and editing. Mel Gibson, Glenn Close, and Paul Scofield as the Ghost all adjust their approach to this reality of filmmaking. Often working on isolated pieces of a scene, film actors use the expressive means available to them within the shot and rely on their training and experience to maintain focus and concentration. They draw on their individual preparation, which makes it possible for them to know exactly what their characters are doing at any moment because they have planned every step of their characters' dramatic journey.

CONCLUSIONS

While the complex technological manipulation of cinematic images has made actors' contributions to films harder to identify, the fact remains that mediated performance relies on acting choices working in concert with framing, editing, and other choices. As the case studies indicate, performance choices belong to the host of details that comprise cinematic montage. While studies of stars and directors can occlude what actors do within the frame, close analysis of acting and framing reveals avenues of inquiry that reposition acting as one of narrative film's integral components.

In the same way that performance elements belong to the overall design of the *Romeo and Juliet* adaptations, the three adaptations of *Hamlet* show that acting choices change to suit framing and editing selections. These adjustments reveal that performance details are one of several cinematic elements that combine to create narrative significance. To come to terms with the contributions of actors, it is useful to ask new questions about the interaction between performance and nonperformance elements. What opportunities for expression does a particular film offer an actor? How does an actor adjust his or her means of expression to coordinate with other filmic choices? Answers to these interlocking questions establish a pragmatic foundation for inquiries into whether or not acting choices work effectively with other choices in the film.

Speculations about how actors work, whether they make adjustments consciously, use a specific acting technique, or respond intuitively, do not render the kind of information made available by careful analysis of observable vocal and physical gestures. The Shakespearean case studies show that the selection and combination of actors' movements, gestures, and facial and vocal expressions have a direct relationship to the selection and combination of shots, editing patterns, and audio-visual design elements. Stylistic differences between the films themselves demonstrate that acting choices are consistent with aesthetic decisions about other elements in the film's montage.

Like other members of a production team, the work of performers is designed to contribute to the style of a film as a whole. The perceptible details in the *Romeo and Juliet* and *Hamlet* films reveal that gestures and expressions are not lifeless substance given meaning by directors, cinematographers, and editors. Rather, as Eisenstein proposed and as case studies throughout the book show, images carry distinct tonal qualities that can be shaped by players' gestures and expressions. With connotations embedded in performance details, acting choices interact with other aspects of montage.

CHAPTER SIX

ACTING STYLES AND CULTURAL-AESTHETIC TRADITIONS

Examples in previous chapters show that the myriad details of performance are crafted results of aesthetic choices, and that actors' means of expression (their delivery of text, facial expressions, gestures, and movements) differ from film to film.[1] A look at performances in light of different cultural traditions also illuminates mutual interactions between performance and nonperformance elements. As components of filmic discourse, acting choices reflect the cultural-aesthetic traditions that underlie other aspects of a production. Influenced by conventions indicative of different directors, genres, and time periods, film acting manifests the norms of many different cultural-aesthetic traditions. Emerging from combinations of "ostensive signs" infused with interlocking connotations, screen performances take on narrative meaning and dramatic significance in part because cultural-aesthetic traditions serve as touchstones.

Reckoning with the cultural-aesthetic traditions that inform screen performances makes it easier to pinpoint the observable details that carry connotations. It allows one to see the influence of aesthetic conventions that extend far beyond a star's "personal style." Attending to individual expressions *and* cultural-aesthetic conventions is valuable, for as Prague semiotics suggests, signifiers and systems of signification form an indissoluble bond. Analyzing individual performances in light of cultural-aesthetic conventions proves useful, for as Chaplin's performance in *City Lights* reveals, in composite art forms such as film and theater, meaning and dramatic significance often arise from interactions between individual expressions and culturally defined social gestures.

Earlier chapters have implicitly explored the cultural-aesthetic dimension of performance through examples that show how actors' gestures and expressions interact with other filmic elements in a variety of ways. The contrast between Bresson's *Pickpocket* and Renoir's *The Rules of the Game* illustrates the point that performances are suited to a director's visual style and thematic concerns. *Singin' in the Rain* provides evidence that acting can dominate framing and editing choices; *Weekend* reveals that camera movement can be the dominant factor; *Philadelphia* presents a balance between acting and cinematic choices. In *City Lights,* Chaplin's performance, the most dominant aspect of the film, illuminates the complex interplay between conventional, culturally defined "gesture-signs" and individual "gesture-expressions" that reveal a character's thoughts and feelings. The studies of *Romeo and Juliet* and *Hamlet* examine performance and nonperformance elements working in concert; they show that acting choices belong to cultural-aesthetic conventions that change over time.

Performances belong to cultural-aesthetic traditions that also differ from place to place. This chapter highlights differences that arise from changes in cultural production context. While acting styles are sometimes associated with particular techniques or stars' personal styles, cross-cultural analysis demonstrates that they are perhaps best understood as expressions of cultural-aesthetic traditions. Reflecting their unique production contexts, films from around the world confirm that screen performances are strongly influenced by the aesthetic conventions of theatrical traditions. For example, the rapid shifts in the tone and energy of performances in a Hong Kong film such as *The Killer* (John Woo, 1989) can be traced to performance traditions in Peking Opera; the modulations of mood and feeling in *Monsoon Wedding* (2001) by Indian director Mira Nair show the influence of Sanskrit drama on even internationally produced Bollywood films.

This chapter examines performances in Akira Kurosawa's *Seven Samurai* (1954) and *The Magnificent Seven* (1960), the Hollywood adaptation directed by John Sturges, in light of their respective cultural-aesthetic traditions. Comparative study of *Seven Samurai* and *The Magnificent Seven* is instructive because acting styles in the two films are so distinct. As we will show, while performances in *Seven Samurai* are distinguished by strong, horizontal movements grounded in the actors' pelvic areas, performances in *The Magnificent Seven* play against the vertical axis and feature isolated gestures of the arms. Similarly, while choreography of performance in *Seven Samurai* creates the impression that characters are defined by their communal identity, blocking patterns in *The Magnificent Seven* convey the point that its characters belong to a society that places a premium on individual identity. The sometimes comic, sometimes tragic story is essentially the same in both films. Farmers in an isolated village seek assistance from expert fighters to defend their crops against marauding bandits. After they find a dedicated warrior willing to defend their village, the main samurai/gunfighter assembles a small company of seasoned fighters. Once the handful of brave men arrive in the village, the stories focus on their courageous and finally successful attempt to defeat the determined and much larger band of well-armed thieves. By the end, order has been restored but the mood is far from celebratory because several of the valiant fighters have died in battle, and those who survive return to their uncertain social status as men whose skill is valuable only in time of war.

JAPANESE FILM AND THEATER: *SEVEN SAMURAI*'S CULTURAL-AESTHETIC CONTEXT

In the earliest years of cinema, "the Japanese did not . . . view motion pictures as a new, different, modern, mass produced, machine-driven, autonomous entertainment."[2] One reason is that "in the formative stages of Japanese cinema—from 1904 to 1920—the theater, especially Kabuki, had an immediate impact on film grammar."[3] In addition, filmmakers' reliance on narration, dialogue, and commentary provided by *benshi* (lecturer-performers who stood to the side of the screen) led Japanese audiences to see cinema as an extension of existing performing arts.[4] Joanne Bernardi notes that references to *benshi* practice as lecturers and commentators appear as early as 1909; "by the early 1920s the *benshi* were not only reciting narration and acting out dialogue—they had assumed responsibility for interpreting and analyzing the film as well."[5] In fact, *benshi* satisfied "theatrical expectations" so that even "foreign films were shown in a manner that conformed to Japanese audiences' habits of viewing, as well as to traditional structural premises and methods of narration."[6]

Silent cinema in Japan was also influenced by the fusion of Japanese and Western traditions in the *shingeki* or "new theater" styles developed by the Bungei Kyokai and Geijutsu-za companies in the first decades of the twentieth century. These companies employed conventions of modern Western drama in their productions of *Hamlet*, Ibsen's *A Doll's House,* Maeterlinck's *Monna Vanna,* and Tolstoy's *Resurrection.*[7] The first film to show the influence of *shingeki* conventions was a 1914 adaptation of *Resurrection* directed by Hosoyama Kiyomatsu.[8] The critical and commercial success of

Geijutsu-za's production of *Resurrection* probably led to the film being produced.[9] However, while based on the *shingeki* stage production, the film reveals Kabuki's salient influence on silent cinema in Japan: although the role was first made famous by Geijutsu-za actress Matsui Sumako, the film adaptation featured female impersonator Tachibana Teijiro.[10] Still, *shingeki* had a significant impact on Japanese cinema: *Souls on the Road* (1921), a *shingeki*-influenced film, is sometimes considered "the true beginning of the Japanese cinema"; the film was directed by Murata Minoru and Osanai Kaoru, whose production of Ibsen's *John Gabriel Borkman* in 1909 is sometimes considered "the first real *shingeki* performance."[11]

The connections between Japanese theater and film continued into the sound era. Following World War II, the American occupation required stage and screen practitioners to negotiate the same external pressures. Between 1945 and 1952, traditional theatrical forms such as Noh and Kabuki were "censored and subjected to special control," while occupation authorities supported *shingeki* theater productions because they showed the influence of Western theatrical traditions.[12] In the cinema, *jidai-geki* films (historical films usually set in the Tokugawa period) were eliminated because they were suspected of glorifying feudalism, imperialism, and militarism; by comparison, certain *gendai-geki* films (films about contemporary life) and *Meiji-mono* films (historical dramas set in the enlightened Meiji Restoration 1868–1912) were encouraged.[13] From the occupation period forward, Japanese stage and screen productions have explored "the importance of *no* and *kabuki* as a source of inspiration" and sought to make "the experience of classical Japanese acting techniques meaningful" during a time when there is "a blurring of borders" in Japanese theater and film.[14]

Seven Samurai is one of several Kurosawa films strongly influenced by traditional Japanese theater. He uses Noh theater conventions in *The Men Who Tread on the Tiger's Tail* (1945), *Throne of Blood* (1957), and *Ran* (1985).[15] Emphasizing the importance of Japanese traditions, Kurosawa explains, "If you devote yourself fully to Noh and gain something good from this, it will emerge naturally in your films."[16] However, he does draw on eclectic principles. In Kurosawa's view, screenplays can or should be modeled on Western symphonic structure "with its three or four movements and differing tempos" and on "the Noh play with its three-part structure: jo (introduction), ha (destruction), and kyu (haste)."[17] Moreover, acting choices in Kurosawa's films reflect his view that it is a mistake to "think that the Noh is static and is a performance with little motion."[18] For Kurosawa, Noh performances include "terribly violent motions that resemble those of an acrobat."[19] He believes that the actor "who is capable of such an action performs it quietly" so that the performance is marked by "both quietness and vehemence."[20] His observation prompts one to think of the movements integral to Seiji Miyaguchi's portrayal of Kyuzo, the skilled swordsman in *Seven Samurai.* Like the other experienced samurai, the strong, direct, and sudden quality of Miyaguchi's movements and vocal expressions distinguish him from the bandits, the two novice warriors, and the ordinary men and women in the farming village.

Kurosawa has explained that as a young man, he was deeply impressed by the ability of his mentor, Yanamoto Kajiro, to direct actors.[21] When he became a director, working with actors became extremely important to his production process. Kurosawa begins with a staged reading of the script even before casting is complete.[22] As Takashi Shimura notes, the next steps involve "a walk-through rehearsal; after that a make-up rehearsal; then a number of rehearsals with lights and camera positions; then lots of dress rehearsals, just like on stage."[23] Shimura points out that Kurosawa would use whole weeks of dress rehearsals and sometimes "light a cyclorama at the studio and have the entire film performed as a play, in full costume, over and over again while he, the sole audience, watches."[24] For Kurosawa, rehearsing a scene or piece of action over and over allows "something new to jump forward."[25] He has compared rehearsing to "making a sculpture of papier-maché; each repetition lays on a new sheet of paper, so that in the end the performance has a shape completely different from when we started."[26]

Released in 1954, *Seven Samurai* can be interpreted as a commentary on Japan's lost military power following its defeat in World War II. It pays homage to the forty-seven masterless samurai whose rebellion in the Tokugawa period (1603–1867) provides the subject of "the most famous play in the puppet and *kabuki* repertoire, the *Chushingura,*" and the basis for more than eighty films produced in Japan since 1911.[27] *Seven Samurai* reveals the influence of Kabuki, Noh, and *shingeki* theater traditions.

The film's narrative design suggests the influence of Kabuki drama. Featuring dramatic strength in individual scenes, its "loosely connected episodes" make the story unfold slowly through "a series of climaxes."[28] The film's visual design seems akin to Kabuki theater insofar as it "lies somewhere between the conventionalism of the Noh stage and the illusionism of the Western theatre."[29] Its celebrated battle scenes suggest the influence of Kabuki theater because performances are integrated into the pictorially driven spectacle of the fast-paced sequences. Some of the film's characterizations are thematically and stylistically linked to conventions in Kabuki theater. The battle scenes feature hordes of bandits whose performances suggest the *aragoto* acting style that involves "aggressive confrontational gestures."[30] To represent the youth and inexperience of Katushiro, the apprentice samurai, Isao Kimura draws on the *wagoto* acting style that Kabuki performers use to portray "pale, indecisive, weak young men" who fall in love with fallen women.[31] In addition, *Seven Samurai* does not use female impersonators, although it does play on Kabuki theater's use of *onnagata,* the male actor who specializes in female roles: just before the samurai arrive in the village, the peasant girl who falls in love with Katushiro is forced by her father to cut her hair and dress in men's clothes, thus inverting the *onnagata* convention.[32]

As noted earlier, Noh influences permeate *Seven Samurai.* Linked to Noh plays about warriors *(shuramono),* the film's overarching mood and message harken back to Noh theater's concern with "the mysterious beauty of impermanence" and the exploration of "subdued beauty tinged with sadness."[33] Scenes at the beginning and end of the film that feature Takashi Shimura as Kambei, the first samurai, are marked by the stately quality associated with Noh theater. Early on, Kambei dons the cloak of a monk in a rescue scene that is marked by patient waiting rather than spectacular action; the film's closing images feature Kambei and his fellow samurai, Shichiroji, standing quietly near the graves of the four samurai killed in battle, the powerful force of their spirits suggested by the flags rippling in the wind atop their graves.

Scenes designed around Toshiro Mifune as Kikuchiyo, the renegade farmer who becomes the seventh samurai, highlight another aspect of Noh tradition, this time the *kyogen* character's blend of humor and pathos. Distinguished by his humorous dialogue and pantomime, Kikuchiyo is reminiscent of such *kyogen* characters as the boatman in *Funa Benkei.*[34] Like traditional *kyogen* characters, Kikuchiyo is a peasant. His misadventures are reminiscent of the subjects central to *kyogen* farces (sometimes presented between Noh plays), which include "the unexpected dilemmas [in which] the drunkard, the cowardly *samurai,* ignorant lord, sly servant, greedy monk, shrewish woman, and others find themselves."[35] *Kyogen* theater's emphasis on social situation filters into Kurosawa's film, for Kikuchiyo's impossible situation, suspended between the world of the farmer and the samurai, drives the narrative forward and colors the mournful tone of the film's conclusion.

Noh traditions are especially visible in the acting style that distinguishes the five experienced samurai from the characters around them. Noh acting features "strong vocal technique in which the voice is pushed out from the lower abdomen."[36] Throughout the film, as the leader in the group of warriors, Takashi Shimura uses that vocal technique in moments of action and in the occasional scenes of repose. Yoshiro Inaba, Daisuke Kato, Minoru Chiaki, and Seiji Miyaguchi also push their voices out from the center of their bodies to convey the solid grounding of the other four veteran warriors.

In addition, the acting style used by these players features an "underlying and very controlled sense of energy, a kind of constant yet quiet tension [that] is basic to *no.*"[37] The actors convey that quiet tension of energy even in moments of stasis, for their postures consistently resemble the *kamae* position, basic to the Noh actor, who is "made very much alive by the fact that strength is focused in the lower abdomen."[38] Like traditional Noh actors, they do not lift "the rib cage high, which in the case of Western classical ballet creates its floating quality," but instead push out their lower abdomens, an approach that gives their postures "a downward earth-centeredness."[39] Assuming a position of readiness, the actors' weight is often on the balls of their feet. The torso is straight, the chest is out, and arms "are slightly curved with the elbows turned out."[40]

Drawing on Noh conventions, the actors portraying the experienced samurai convey the warriors' "relaxed strength" and "sense of expectancy."[41] Like performers in traditional Noh theater, they sustain a quiet tension of energy as they move from and return to the basic *kamae* position. Despite the fact the film's many battle scenes and its use of *shingeki* or Western-style realism generally preclude use of *suri ashi,* the Noh technique of "sliding feet," Takashi Shimura and the others often keep their knees "slightly bent to absorb the leg action in a way that the torso remains at a level height"; they also tend to hold their hips in a way that "prevents the upper body from swaying from side to side with each step."[42] These choices are possible because they infuse all their gestures, expressions, and movements with "the same sense of energy and quiet tension found in the *kamae.*"[43] In addition, while the actors do not use specific Noh gestures, some of them, particularly those involving swordsmanship, are akin to *kata.* These performance details do not carry "specific symbolic meaning," but they do convey "the feelings and emotions" of a character or dramatic moment.[44] For example, when the initial members of Kambei's small group first encounter the skilled swordsman, Kyuzo (Seiji Miyaguchi), his fearsome but ethical nature is expressively conveyed by the single cut of his sword that kills his brazen opponent in an instant.

The false alarm sequence in *Seven Samurai* shows the influence of

Kokuten Kodo, the Old Man in *Seven Samurai:* visage as theatrical mask

Kabuki, Noh, and *shingeki* (or Western) theatrical traditions. Working in concert with framing, editing, sound, and production design choices, the performances are marked by varied rhythms. At the beginning of the alarm sequence, the slow tempo establishes the tension that will not be resolved until Kikuchiyo (Toshiro Mifune) and the Old Man (Kokuten Kodo) come face-to-face in the center of the village. When Kambei and his small company of experienced samurai first meet with the village patriarch to learn why they received no welcome, the Old Man sadly explains that the farmers have gone into hiding because they worry about everything, including the consequences of having samurai in their village. Noh-influenced acting choices convey the tension caused by the villagers' inhospitable welcome: actors portraying the seasoned warriors remain almost motionless as they ponder the situation; speaking slowly and quietly, the wrinkled Old Man concludes his sad explanation with a long, heavy sigh. This moment of stasis is abruptly interrupted by rapid, high-pitched taps of the village alarm and the rush of movement that follows. Then, the quick tempo of the alarm, music, and running figures is interrupted when Kikuchiyo/Mifune announces that he is the person who sounded the alarm. This temporal organization reflects patterns in Noh and Kabuki theater and Japanese language itself:

the abrupt changes and shifting rhythms withhold the sequence's meaning and significance until the episode's final moment of resolution when Kikuchiyo and the Old Man make connection and the village patriarch gives his approval.[45]

The forceful masklike visages in the alarm sequence represent another way Noh influences contribute to the film. Echoing Noh's use of highly expressive, nonrealistic masks, some of the actors employ exaggerated facial expressions that transform their faces into mobile masks. For example, when the Old Man reacts to the alarm that signals the approach of bandits, Kokuten Kodo opens his eyes wide and turns down the corners of his mouth; his closed-lipped frown becomes like one of the Noh masks for an old man. Bokusen Hidari, portraying one of the farmers who have brought the samurai to the village, mirrors Kodo's performance choice. In response to the sound of the alarm, he turns his face into a Noh-like mask by popping his eyes and frowning with open lips. The tight framing on their faces underscores the emotional impact of the actors' expressive facial features that take on the appearance of theatrical masks.

Cutting quickly from these powerful images, the film features a series of short takes that show Takashi Shimura and the others racing along the path that leads back to the village. Combinations of wide shots show groups of farmers running wildly into the village. The tension has reached a peak when they close into a tight circular formation that expresses their fear. This blocking conveys the idea that the villagers belong to a community of shared values and concerns. Theirs is a collective identity that finds expression through parallel expressions, gestures, and movements.

Just as the farmers coalesce in the village center, Toshiro Mifune strides into the scene, forcefully tapping out the alarm that had caused the villagers to abandon their hiding places. Putting a sudden halt to their wild anxiety, Mifune's bravura entrance forces the farmers into stunned silence. The samurai relax as they come to see it was a false alarm; these actors return to their postures of sustained, grounded calm. Becoming giddy with relief and embarrassment, the villagers overcome their fear of the men whose help they enlisted. Drawing on Western-influenced *shingeki* conventions, performers use alternating combinations of glazed expressions and small jerking gestures to convey the villagers' transition from frantic hysteria to guilty sheepishness.

By comparison, when Kikuchiyo interacts with the villagers in view of the samurai, Mifune's performance suggests the influence of Noh theater. He portrays Kikuchiyo as a *kyogen* figure who belongs to a realm of "hu-

Villagers respond to the alarm in *Seven Samurai:* blocking conveys their communal identity

morous, stylized, theatrical representation" that illuminates "truth under the veil of the joke."[46] Emblematic of *kyogen* material, the alarm sequence demonstrates the "practical and unpretentious" truth that a peasant, like Kikuchiyo, can know something the samurai do not, namely, that all villages have ways to alert the community of outside danger.[47] Mifune's *kyogen*-based acting style conveys the idea that Kikuchiyo can be forceful like the samurai and in touch with the off-balance, perennially frightened villagers. Mifune uses acrobatic, thrusting gestures that entertain the samurai and initially give the villagers discomfort. He struts in front of the samurai as he flicks insults at the villagers who have become Kikuchiyo's rapt audience. As he addresses the crowd, Mifune's animated and expressive face takes on the appearance of demon masks used in Noh theater. Parading about with his eyes wide open, his nostrils flared, Mifune sticks his tongue out at the farmers in mockery. He clucks at them using animal-like sounds that further transform his visage into a comical and flamboyant mask.

The scene comes to a solid and clear resolution when tall, muscular Toshiro Mifune finally comes face-to-face with spry but hunched-over old Kokuten Kodo. Framing, editing, and blocking emphasize the contrast between the powerful fluidity of Mifune's movements and the frailty of Kodo's bent body. While Mifune's irregular movements control the focus of various

Toshiro Mifune and Kokuten Kodo: Kikuchiyo becomes the seventh samurai by establishing a connection with the patriarch of the village

wide shots in which he moves about the frame, one steady horizontal pan follows Kodo as he slowly hobbles through the crowd. When Kodo reaches an opening in the crowd, Mifune strides forward to meet him. Coming face to face, the actors' equally expressive gestures make clear that the sequence has reached its point of dramatic closure. Beaming joyously at one another, Kodo and Mifune seal the bond between villager and outsider, and the emotion that fills their faces transforms the conventional signs for old men and demons into individual expressions of relief and good-natured amusement.

Mifune's and Kodo's acting choices here exist against a backdrop created by the reserved style that Takashi Shimura, Yoshiro Inaba, Daisuke Kato, Minoru Chiaki, and Seiji Miyaguchi use to portray the experienced, self-disciplined warriors. Grounded in the conventions of Noh theater, these actors keep their torsos in one piece. Sitting, standing, or walking, they often bend forward slightly so that their backs form a straight line. The actors keep their heads erect and their chins pulled back. Often, their arms are curved downward, slightly in front of their bodies, their elbows lifted and hands at their sides.

The numerous wide shots of the experienced samurai traveling to and preparing for battle feature their bodies in strong postures, their knees slightly bent and their feet parallel. Framing, editing, camera movement, and blocking highlight the actors' centered, gliding movements that seem to draw on a constant flow of sustained energy: framing and editing often allow audiences to see the actors in full figure; the men portraying the experienced samurai often move in unison or rest in configurations that suggest their strength, balance, and unity. While Mifune's performance and representations of the bandits and villagers call attention to the energy lost in erratic up-and-down, side-to-side movements, performance details that portray the men of experience are marked by a sustained quietness that gives their sudden moments an effortless strength not found in the movements of the other players. In sum, the influence of Noh theater makes the dominant acting choices in *Seven Samurai* quite different from those in the Hollywood remake.

COMPARATIVE STUDY OF *SEVEN SAMURAI* AND *THE MAGNIFICENT SEVEN*

There are points of contact between *Seven Samurai* and *The Magnificent Seven.* In both films, the first samurai/gunfighter is a man of honor. Yul Brynner's portrayal of Chris Adams resembles Takashi Shimura's representation of Kambei in that they feature an economy of gesture and clear evidence of balance, centeredness, and calm. For the most part, however, portrayals of the main characters illustrate the contrast between the films' respective cultural contexts. As discussed above, Shimura's Noh-influenced performance is marked by sustained gliding and pressing movements. Framing, blocking, and acting present Kambei as an effective leader who establishes connections between people to create community. By comparison, Brynner's performance recalls the use of tableaux in Western theater, for he often presents sculpted poses that illustrate the significance of dramatic moments. Here, frame compositions, blocking patterns, and Brynner's physical and vocal choices create the impression that Adams is a leader because he stands out from the crowd to assume a decision-making role no one else could fulfill. In place of expanding horizontal connections, Brynner is a leader who remains isolated and above the people he defends.

The second character to join the group of seven further highlights cultural and aesthetic differences between the two films. In *Seven Samurai,* Gorobei (Yoshiro Inaba) decides to help because he is impressed and fascinated by Kambei's character; in *The Magnificent Seven,* Harry Luck (Brad Dexter) agrees to join because he suspects the adventure involves hidden treasure. The narrative contrast between the characters' motivations is reflected in choices that distinguish Inaba's and Dexter's performances. Inaba's gliding movements and grounded stance convey Gorobei's attentive concern, while Dexter's jerky and sudden gestures point to Harry Luck's guilty selfishness.

The design and portrayal of the third samurai/gunfighter shows the same contrast. In *Seven Samurai,* Shichiroji (Daisuke Kato) is an old friend of Kambei; both samurai live to watch the villagers plant their fields in the spring after the battles with the bandits. By comparison, in *The Magnificent Seven,* Vin (Steve McQueen) is a recent acquaintance of Chris Adams; the film ends with the two gunfighters riding out of the village looking for new adventures. The characters' differing relationships carries through into the actors' performances. Kato's grounded and measured movements support and mirror Shimura's gestures and expressions, while McQueen's relaxed, limber poses establish an individual whose physicality counterpoints Brynner's upright posture and direct movements.

Although these first three samurai/gunfighters are quite distinct, the fourth pair shows similarities. In both films, he is a wood cutter, a man whose strength allows him to disclose the gentle, nurturing aspects of his nature. Thus, even though Minoru Chiaki's portrayal of Heihachi reflects the influence of Noh theater and Charles Bronson's performance as Bernardo O'Reilly features conventions of Hollywood realism, both players use gestures that are surprisingly soft and light. Chiaki's gestures are especially calm and gentle when he handles the banner he has made for the village; Bronson's voice and gestures are quiet and soothing when O'Reilly is with various children in the village.

The remaining samurai/gunfighters highlight differences in the cultural-aesthetic traditions that inform the two films. In *Seven Samurai,* Kyuzo, the fifth experienced warrior, is a highly skilled swordsman and Seiji Miyaguchi's portrayal is one of the most quiet and violent in the film. Strongly influenced by Noh, his performance provides a baseline against which to measure the quiet tension that infuses performances by the other actors who portray experienced samurai. By comparison, in *The Magnificent Seven,* the fifth gunfighter, Britt (James Coburn), might be an expert with a knife and a gun but Coburn's flexible slouch makes Britt seem barely part of the group. With his body limp much of the time, Coburn will tighten his body in moments of gunfighting action but quickly dissipate this energy once the narrative danger has passed.

The American adaptation includes an additional expert, this time a fading gun-for-hire, Lee, played by Robert Vaughn. In clear contrast to Seiji

Miyaguchi's sustained, energy-filled gliding movements, Vaughn's performance is colored by sudden, slashing gestures and vocal expressions that disperse into lifeless jerks and gasps. Once again, Vaughn's performance establishes the impression that each of the gunfighters is a unique individual, who has little in common with the others and even less connection with the villagers who furnish a reason to kill. Tight shots on Vaughn's face and hands as they twitch with nervous anxiety reinforce the contrast that emerges between this gunfighter and Kyzuo, the skilled samurai swordsman.

In Kurosawa's film, the sixth samurai is Katsushiro (Isao Kimura), a well-born young man whom Kambei takes on as an apprentice. He is the only samurai to fall in love with a woman in the village. This aristocratic apprentice also contrasts sharply with the other novice samurai, the peasant Kikuchiyo (Toshiro Mifune). Kimura portrays Katsushiro as a reserved, sensitive young man, as against Mifune's performance of Kikuchiyo as an animated and highly emotional character whose parents were killed by bandits when he was a boy. *The Magnificent Seven* combines these two very different novice characters into one. Thus, Chico (Horst Buchholz), a farmer by birth, not only manages to become the seventh gunfighter, but also lives to stay behind as the lover of a young woman in the village. The tight, rigid qualities in Buchholz's performance are entirely different from the light, floating style in Kimura's portrayal of the apprentice. Buchholz's bound, nervous energy also contrasts with the loose, free-flowing energy that infuses Mifune's performance as Kikuchiyo. In addition, while Mifune seems to be in constant motion, Buchholz is more static, often holding poses that he strikes. Mifune's *kyogen*-like performance makes Kikuchiyo someone who exists as a mediator *between* the samurai and the villagers, never a samurai but never a farmer. By comparison, Chico becomes accepted as a gunfighter *and*, as their hero, a villager. Buchholz conveys Chico's connection with the story's "natural" leader, Chris Adams, by employing the same direct movement and almost rigidly upright posture Brynner does. When Chico remains behind, it is as someone who has stepped into the elevated role of hero-protector.

The apprentices disclose the cultural traditions underlying the two films. In *Seven Samurai,* class is a social reality that cannot be overturned; in *The Magnificent Seven,* however, questions of class are elided. Kikuchiyo dies in the end: accepted by the seasoned warriors and valued by the villagers, the peasant could never become a samurai in the eyes of his society. Katsushiro must maintain his distance from the villagers and the woman he loves in order to retain connection with the samurai who are of his class. By comparison, Chico has a choice: he can stay behind as the young woman's lover, or join the veteran gunfighters in their search for the next battle. Having attained the status of gunfighter, his elevated position is not in jeopardy; in Western cultural mythology, after a man has proved himself in battle, his decision to be with the woman he desires is an expression of potency.[48]

The following summarizes contrasts between the two films:

Seven Samurai (1954) Director: Akira Kurosawa	*The Magnificent Seven* (1960) Director: John Sturges Dialogue director: Thom Conroy
1st Kambei Shimada (Takashi Shimura)	1st Chris Adams (Yul Brynner)
2nd Gorobei (Yoshiro Inaba) Fascinated by Kambei's character Killed midway	2nd Harry Luck (Brad Dexter) Drawn in by presumed treasure Killed first
3rd Shichiroji (Daisuke Kato) Kambei's old friend Lives to watch planting with Kambei	3rd Vin (Steve McQueen) Chris's new buddy Lives to ride into sunset with Chris
4th Heihachi (Minoru Chiaki) Wood cutter; creates banner Dies first, in early raid on bandits	4th Bernardo O'Reilly (Charles Bronson) Wood cutter; makes flute for child Dies last, protecting boys in the village
5th Kyuzo (Seiji Miyaguchi) Skilled swordsman Third to die, by gunshot in final battle	5th Britt (James Coburn) Expert with knife and gun Third to die in final battle
Kyuzo—disciplined swordsman	6th Lee (Robert Vaughn) Gun-for-hire, losing skill and courage Second to die in final battle
6th Katsushiro (Isao Kimura) Apprentice samurai, young lover Lives, uncertain about his place	Chico—apprentice gunfighter, lover
7th Kikuchiyo (Toshiro Mifune) Farmer's son Killed last in final battle	7th Chico (Horst Buchholz) Farmer's son Lives, assumes paternal role
Old Man (Kokuten Kodo)	Old Man (Vladimir Sokoloff)
Unidentified bandits in a brigade	Calvera, lead bandit (Eli Wallach)

The cultural context of *The Magnificent Seven* includes the eclectic training, experience, and background of the actors, dialogue director Thom Conroy, and director John Sturges, who became known for directing action films such as *The Great Escape* (1963) and *The Eagle Has Landed* (1976). Yul Brynner spent time as a trapeze artist and circus performer and studied with Michael Chekhov, a Russian émigré who developed his own spiritually based approach to acting. Brad Dexter trained at the Pasadena Playhouse, one of the primary training grounds for film actors in the 1930s and 1940s. Steve McQueen studied with Uta Hagen, Herbert Berghof, and Lee Strasberg, all proponents of the American Method, a psychologically inflected version of Stanislavsky's System (see chapter 1). Charles Bronson trained at the Pasadena Playhouse. James Coburn took acting classes at Los Angeles Community College before working with Stella Adler, who devised her own approach to the Method. Robert Vaughn studied acting at Los Angeles Community College. Horst Buchholz, a German matinee idol who won a Golden Globe for portraying a charming rascal in *The Confessions of Felix Krull* (Kurt Hoffman, 1957), combined his experience in German film productions with the studio-era approaches Thom Conroy outlined as the film's dialogue director. Russian émigré Vladimir Sokoloff, the wise Old Man in *The Magnificent Seven,* studied with Stanislavsky and Max Reinhardt; he had also been a member of the Kamerny, an avant-garde theater known for its antirealistic productions.[49] Eli Wallach, who plays the Mexican bandit Calvera, was a founding member of the Actors Studio after studying at the Neighborhood Playhouse, which taught another innovative approach to the Method developed by Sanford Meisner. Thus, as a cast, they represent the kind of diverse cultural and aesthetic backgrounds that often inform Western theatrical traditions.

One can observe, however, that all of the actors in *The Magnificent Seven* learned their craft after "the proliferation of naturalistic literature" and widespread interest in "various psychological determinants" had led Western acting methods to emphasize "*being* instead of mimicking."[50] Despite that, their performances depend on "basic, culturally transmitted gestures to 'write' characters."[51] Acting choices in *The Magnificent Seven* do not parody conventional social gestures as Chaplin's often do in *City Lights.* Rather, they reveal a process of selecting and heightening recognizable social gestures to "render simple, crisp expressions for the camera."[52] In fact, performances in *The Magnificent Seven* bring to light the lasting influence of "the mimetic or 'pantomime' tradition—a performance technique that relies on conventionalized poses to help the actor indicate 'fear,' 'sorrow,' 'hope,' 'confusion,' and so forth."[53] James Naremore notes that the pantomime tradition in Western theater became codified through manuals such as "Henry Siddon's *Practical Illustrations of Rhetorical Gesture and Action* and Gustave Garcia's *Actor's Art,* both published in 1882 and filled with pictures of typical poses and gestures."[54] Acting choices in the pantomime tradition were also outlined in Charles Aubert's *The Art of Pantomime,* translated from French to English in 1927, and *Lessons in the Art of Acting* (1889) by Edmund Shaftesbury, "one of Delsarte's many American imitators."[55] In the United States from the 1870s through the 1920s, Delsarte's "disciples enjoyed a tremendous vogue."[56] Seen as a method for acquiring social grace, variations of Delsarte's work became "so deeply embedded in the culture that a good many actors [in the West] could be described as Delsartean whether or not they even studied him."[57]

Yul Brynner and Horst Buchholz use poses that resemble pantomime depictions of triumph in their portrayals of the "natural" and the aspiring leader.[58] For example, when one or the other makes an emphatic point, he will step back or rock back on one heel, sometimes with a hand raised vertically. Similarly, early in the film when Chico is drunk and fails in his effort to impress Chris Adams, some of Buchholz's gestures recall a pantomime depiction of agony. In a similar fashion, Robert Vaughn uses this pose to convey the anguish experienced by the hired gunman who has lost his nerve. In such instances, the actor juts his chin out and tilts his head back with his face in a grimace.[59]

Some of the acting choices in *The Magnificent Seven* do not reflect conventions once associated with social grace. For example, Steve McQueen's and James Coburn's rounded shoulders likely represent a reaction to early-twentieth-century notions of proper deportment. Similarly, Charles Bronson's casual vocal delivery and Robert Vaughn's breathless line readings indicate responses to traditional elocutionary practice. However, these choices still belong to a tradition deeply influenced by pantomime conventions. First, they involve a selection and heightening of everyday gestures and expressions. Second, they often depend on isolated use of the face and arms or poses that play against the vertical axis. Third, even these "naturalistic" acting choices stand at the intersection of everyday life and aesthetic convention: recall how often the round-shouldered slouch and the intense trembling voice have been used in formulaic productions.

While informed by convention, the portrayals of the seven gunfighters do not generally feature the quiet tension that sustains *Seven Samurai's* Noh-influenced performances. For example, even though Brynner and Buchholz tend to maintain a bound energy that suggests a state of readiness, the actors portraying the other gunfighters consistently leave their bodies at rest, often using small gestures and facial expressions to catch audience attention. Moreover, in contrast to the samurai, none of the gunfighters move from or return to a grounded and centered posture. Brynner and the others often shift their weight back or to the side, tilting their torsos and stretching their limbs. When they lean forward, they hunch over, rather than holding their backs straight. They gather their energy into a series of endpoints or "natural" poses that they assume and then hold. In place of continuous quiet tension, their acting style is distinguished by intermittent, sometimes emphatic "pictures" that convey dramatic significance. In sum, their training in disparate but related Western theatrical traditions comes through in their performances, which make use of full-length poses accented by illustrative gestures and facial expressions.

In the false alarm sequence that begins with the gunfighters arriving in the deserted village, framing and blocking draw attention to the isolated components of the individual actors' performances. In the exchange between Chris Adams and the wise Old Man of the village, Vladimir Sokoloff holds his body very still but uses his face expressively as he delivers his lines in an evenly modulated, singsong rhythm. Brynner confines his response to small shifts in the impassive expression on his face. The church bell that signals bandits are coming abruptly interrupts the exchange between Sokoloff and Brynner. However, the Old Man's reaction is not highly expressive. In fact, framing and editing do not focus our attention on his face; instead, we see Sokoloff and Brynner in a wide shot from the side. The scene cuts to a wide, low-angle shot of the church tower with its ringing bell. Chico/Buchholz steps into view at the top of the tower, the bell swinging behind him. He commands attention by shouting out to the deserted village square below. Announcing his arrival from the top of the church tower, Chico seems to suggest that he is empowered by religious authority.

While the alarm prompts the men of the village to come to the square, their movements do not suggest abject fear but instead hesitant concern. The women have been left behind, and rather than bunching together in a swirling crowd, the men stand apart from one another, considering the situation from separate vantage points. Each man waits to see who has sounded the alarm. With his audience assembled, Buchholz comes down into the square to address the villagers. The wide shots used throughout the scene emphasize the thin, vertical line of his erect posture. With his hips slung forward as he walks, wide framing and low angles show Buchholz pausing to strike a series of poses against the empty background of the blue sky. The men of the village dot the square as if they were individual living sculptures posing for our contemplation.

Horst Buchholz in *The Magnificent Seven:* Chico displays the gunfighters' power as he announces their arrival from the church tower

Blocking that suggests a hierarchical society of isolated individuals in *The Magnificent Seven*

Framing, blocking, and performance style make Chico's address a performance for the gunfighters and the villagers. In place of Mifune's free-flowing movements and comical insults, Buchholz's rigid performance transforms the young gunfighter's speech into an angry lecture. Chico's pretentious display of power over the villagers is designed to impress the seasoned gunfighters and intimidate the farmers. While Kikuchiyo convinces the samurai he is valuable because he can get the villagers to come out of hiding by interacting with them, and mediating between the two groups, Chico demonstrates his worth as a gunfighter by staging and performing his superiority to and separation from the peasants in the village. With a fixed, unsmiling, tight-lipped facial expression, Buchholz punches out his words of scorn and disdain. Punctuating his speech with a collection of conventional

"Prove you're worth fighting for": Chico becomes the seventh gunfighter by asserting his control over the peasants

gestures, Buchholz momentarily lowers himself into a squatting position as if the dumbstruck villagers were small children. Hands on his hips, he sometimes turns his back on his listeners. Finally demanding that the villagers prove their worth, Buchholz raises his voice to a crescendo as he aims his index finger at a villager in a threat. In this scene, resolution does not arise from the joyous connection between the seventh warrior and the village patriarch. Instead, the gunfighters simply give Chico their belated acceptance that he has become one of them.

These changes make *The Magnificent Seven*'s mood and message quite different from the original Japanese film. In *Seven Samurai,* Kikuchiyo is the last samurai to die before the bandits are defeated. As in Noh samurai plays, Kikuchiyo's death leads to a conclusion that allows audiences to savor feelings of disappointment and contentment. The film provides a glimpse of human fragility and impermanence. The sadness and comfort that accompany the characters' return to traditional social divisions is suggested by blocking at the end that keeps the samurai and villagers in separate areas, even though they remain close by and aware of one another. By comparison, the cultural traditions that inform the narrative logic in *The Magnificent Seven* ensure that Chico will live to fight another day. Acting style conveys the point that battle has made Chico a winner, for in the closing scene Buchholz retains the swagger that marked his speech to the villagers.

Acting choices throughout *Seven Samurai* and its Hollywood adaptation contribute to the overall meaning of the films. In *Seven Samurai,* Noh-influenced acting styles and blocking that highlights unison convey the point that tension between community and individual is resolved in favor of communal duty. By comparison, *The Magnificent Seven* suggests that the safety of the community depends on the action of a few isolated individuals. An acting style marked by dramatic but isolated gestures gives physical expression to the idea that society is composed of individuals who sometimes come together for specific missions. Framing, blocking, and acting choices give us isolated characters rather than community members who function as coordinated components of an ensemble.

RETHINKING ACTING STYLES IN THE WEST

Seven Samurai and *The Magnificent Seven* indicate that films are influenced by theatrical traditions in their respective cultures. That connection points to the fact that bonds between theater and film can be as strong as links between films. Theater's influence on cinema is apparent in productions of Tennessee Williams's work, for example. While Hollywood bowdlerized his plays, acting choices in films such as *A Streetcar Named Desire* (Elia Kazan, 1952) and *Cat on a Hot Tin Roof* (Richard Brooks, 1958) bear striking resemblance to performances in the various theatrical productions of these works. Connections between stage and screen can indeed be stronger than those between individual films. Consider, for example, the robotic style of performances in *Un Chien Andalou* (1928), by Spanish surrealist Luis Buñuel, alongside the conventionally modulated performances in *E.T.—the Extraterrestrial* (1982), directed by Hollywood mogul Steven Spielberg.

In the West, theater's influence on the cinema has caused conventional, social "gesture-signs" to be used in screen performance. Put another way, the same cultural-aesthetic traditions that have made recognizable gesture-signs part of Western theater have caused conventional gesture-signs to be used in screen performances. Thus, in the West, daily life experiences play a key role in audience interpretations of and responses to film and theater performances. To a large extent, stage and screen productions influenced by Western traditions prompt audiences to interpret actors' performances through and in terms of expressions, intonations, inflections, gestures, poses, and actions found in everyday life. Exemplifying contemporary naturalistic styles, Meryl Streep's Academy Award–winning performance in *Sophie's Choice* (1983), features quotidian gestures and expressions. In moments of extreme emotion, for example, when she recalls the experience of giving up her daughter to Nazi officers, Streep uses "natural" physical signs to convey the character's tortured inner experience. She creates the image of a woman in anguish through her tears and runny nose, the rising color in her cheeks, the tightness of her voice, her shortness of breath, and her glances that avoid eye contact. Of course, acting choices in Anglo-European cinema do not always feature "natural" behaviors. For example, Orson Welles's portrayal of the title character in *Citizen Kane* (1941) sometimes features expressionistic gestures and expressions. In a moment of extreme emotion, as when Kane smashes the furniture in his wife's bedroom just after she has left him, Welles uses highly stylized expressions, gestures, and movements to represent the character's anguish. His gestures are larger and more extreme than those found in daily life and his facial expressions are far more opaque than facial expressions in everyday interactions.

Differences in Western acting styles are sometimes understood as differences between Stanislavskian and Brechtian performance. Narratives with recognizable characters that have coherent personalities and familiar desires are identified as Stanislavskian and the "Stanislavskian" actor is often thought to create his or her character by merging self with role.[60] Modernist or postmodern narratives that emphasize ambiguity of character and question the nature of identity are linked to "Brechtian" estrangement strategies. In these cases, actors are thought to use "Brechtian" techniques to stand outside their characters and maintain an objective opinion of the role's behavior.[61]

Yet most actors do not work within this binary, nor do they usually experience the one-to-one correspondence between acting technique and performance style that some critics perceive. For example, Split Britches, a feminist theater group, produces performances that are applauded by critics as "Brechtian."[62] However, when discussing their acting methods, Deb Margolin stresses personal identification with the characters as key; she explains, "I think we were just Method actors who didn't bother to clean up."[63] As Ellen Gainor points out, critics who call the group's performances Brechtian, in contradiction to what the company says about itself, are responding to a "hermetic construct of technique, text, and production" that was formed at the Actors Studio in the 1950s when Strasberg moved beyond actor training to work with young directors and playwrights.[64] With acting technique mistakenly linked to dramatic style, the rejection of naturalistic writing and directing led to the rejection of Stanislavsky, whose name had been adopted to legitimize Strasberg's Method, a fundamentally transformed version of the System. In the cinema, modernist filmmakers like Jean-Luc Godard turned to Brecht as an alternative to conventional Hollywood "realism." In the theater, feminists saw a link between women's liberation and "the bold, non-realist style of playwriting and acting which Brecht helped originate."[65]

As the Split Britches example suggests, there can often be a disjuncture between approach used and impression created. Moreover, questions about methods of preparation and execution of performance are separate from questions about the style of performances in individual films. *Un Chien Andalou* features a style of performance entirely distinct from the one found in *E.T.; Sophie's Choice* presents us with acting choices quite different from those in *Citizen Kane*. While the performance details in these films reveal little about the acting techniques used in the productions, the physical and vocal choices that appear on screen offer insight into the cultural-aesthetic traditions that influenced each of the films: surrealism, melodrama, naturalism, and expressionism. Acting styles in these films illuminate their unique traditions and the way specific gestures and vocal expressions convey meaning. Setting aside the attempt to locate one-to-one correlations between acting technique and performance style facilitates analysis of relationships between acting choices, filmic choices, and cultural-aesthetic traditions.

CONCLUSIONS

As the analysis of *Seven Samurai* and *The Magnificent Seven* should suggest, cross-cultural studies can temper sweeping generalizations about film acting per se. Films from different parts of the world reveal that cultural-aesthetic traditions can shape even the way scenes are blocked. Cross-cultural analysis allows one to see that acting styles are not a reflection of an actor's personality but instead the result of choices that are grounded in culturally specific aesthetic traditions. Kurosawa's *Seven Samurai* and its Hollywood adaptation represent one of many possible comparative analyses. One might also consider contrasts between *Throne of Blood* (Akira Kurosawa, 1957) and *Macbeth* (Roman Polanski, 1971), *Do the Right Thing* (Spike Lee, 1989) and *Quartier Mozart* (Jean-Pierre Bekolo, 1992), or *Le samourai* (Jean-Pierre Melville, 1967) and *The Killer* (John Woo, 1989).

The comparative study of *Seven Samurai* and *The Magnificent Seven* reveals that use of social gestures and "natural" signs in Western stage and screen productions is an aesthetic choice. *The Magnificent Seven*'s use of conventional social gestures to convey characters' thoughts and feelings is indicative of theatrical and cinematic conventions in the West. Considered alongside the other case studies in part 2—Chaplin's portrayal in *City*

Lights, performances in the various adaptations of *Romeo and Juliet* and *Hamlet*—the contrasting acting choices in *Seven Samurai* and *The Magnificent Seven* illuminate the fact that cultural-aesthetic traditions in the West have made "natural" signs and interactions between conventional gesture-signs and individual gesture-expressions a profound source of meaning in Western film and theater. Because films influenced by Western aesthetic traditions often feature physical signs seemingly drawn from daily life, viewers' interpretations can productively draw on personal experiences. However, an increased awareness of traditions in the performing arts can make screen acting choices seem less like "natural" behavior captured on film and more like decisions influenced by the West's pervasive use of culturally defined gestures in stage and screen productions. Part 3 explores ways that terminology from the craft of acting can enhance understanding of the "natural" physical signs used in screen performances.

PART THREE

TERMS AND CONCEPTS FROM THE CRAFT OF ACTING

CHAPTER SEVEN

DELSARTE AND THE DYNAMICS OF HUMAN EXPRESSION

One hears that some actors work "from the outside in," while others develop characterizations "from the inside out." Outlining the approach that starts with characters' physicality, Laurence Olivier explains: "with one or two extraneous externals, I begin to build up a character, a characterisation."[1] To create his portrayal of Richard III, for example, Olivier used the histrionic voice of his predecessor, Henry Irving, and the "physiognomy of Disney's Big Bad Wolf."[2] By comparison, players identified with the Actors Studio and hence the American Method will often draw on personal experiences to create performances. For instance, describing her work in the stage production of *Summer and Smoke,* Geraldine Page recalls, "I consciously worked on revealing my own self on stage."[3]

While useful in some ways, this binary of working methods also obscures salient insights into the craft of acting. For instance, although different techniques tend to feature different aspects of performance, actors from dissimilar eras and schools share the sense that external and internal aspects of their work are at base inseparable. As the next section explains, practitioners who create varied aesthetic styles and use diverse creative approaches all recognize the fundamental duality of the acting craft. All seek to make physical, hence visible, something of the invisible aspects of human experience, whether it be psychological or spiritual.

At the same time, whether performers tend to work from the outside in or inside out, their contributions are necessarily conveyed through physical gestures and expressions. As studio-era screen-acting teacher Josephine Dillon reminded her students, "the lenses of the cameras, or the lenses of the human eyes, see only the body, not the thought, nor the wish, nor the emotion, nor the soul—just the body."[4] This verity makes the otherwise elusive and apparently subjective art of acting legible and accessible to analysis.

Of course, the evocative material details of acting are colored by the cultural and aesthetic conventions of which they also partake. Thus, in the West stage and film players' "natural" behavior often serves as a conduit through which characters' interior, subjective experiences are made legible to the audience, while in Japan stylized conventions of Noh allow a more obviously histrionic physical vocabulary (see chapter 6). Moreover, the material tools of acting enrich both film and theater alike. Audiences of both forms attend to the "outside" in order to intuit something about the "inside." Whatever approach actors employ, their gestures and expressions, not their working methods, combine with other aspects of a production to affect audience impressions. Attending to that fact can enhance analysis of both stage and screen acting.

Through training and experience, actors learn that connotations can be conveyed by particular gestures and expressions. They use this sometimes conscious, sometimes intuitive knowledge "to determine exactly what part of the body may most effectively be manipulated to convey a given type of emotion."[5] Actors' vocal tones and bodily movements as well as their verbal and physical rhythms condition audience responses to performances as much as their anatomies and physical types do. As avant-garde theater artist Jerzy Grotowski explains, performance is a process in which "the actor transforms from type to type, character to character . . . in a poor manner, using only his own body and craft."[6] Performance details can serve as visual or auditory signs of characters' inner experience because, as Grotowski points out, actors "compose a role as a system of signs."[7]

This chapter examines the recognition scene in *Smoke* (Wayne Wang, 1995) to show how characters' thoughts and feelings are conveyed by actors' gestures and expressions. Looking at the carefully composed details in the performances of Forest Whitaker and Harold Perrineau, Jr., the analysis draws on the work of French elocutionist François Delsarte to describe acting choices in the scene. While ostensibly out-of-step with current acting trends, Delsarte's system offers useful avenues for analyzing screen performances that rely on "natural" physical signs to communicate meaning. In fact, his taxonomy proves especially useful for performances that seem so "natural" that, as philosopher Suzanne K. Langer suggests, audiences generally see right through the crafted details of the performance into the fictional world they create. To clarify the operation of "natural" performance signs, the chapter closes with a look at Langer's insights into the seamless "transparency" of performances found in so many Western film and theater productions.

MULTIPLE AVENUES TO CREATING "NATURAL" PERFORMANCE SIGNS

In the West, practitioners associated with contrasting moments in theater history have prized performances for their physical expression of emotion. Compare, for example, the opinions of three diverse figures: the leading force in gestural acting, François Delsarte (1811–71), the surrealist Antonin Artaud (1896–1948), and the creator of the American Method, Lee Strasberg (1901–82). Delsarte wrote: "Gesture is the direct agent of the heart. It is the fit manifestation of feeling": as such "it is the spirit, of which speech is merely the letter."[8] Similarly, Artaud called the actor "an athlete of the heart," marking the physicalization of emotion as the actor's special expertise. Artaud proposed, "One must grant the actor a kind of affective musculature which corresponds to the physical localizations of feelings."[9] Strasberg valued the expression of emotion and by the 1930s had made the emotional memory exercise his central technique. As he explained, helping the actor find "the beads of emotional memory . . . was the task I was to devote myself to in establishing the Method."[10] However, by the 1950s, Strasberg realized that the corporeal and vocal manifestations of emotion could become "a central problem in acting" because "the actor could 'struggle with his own blood' and find 'the cue for passion,' and yet somehow be unable to express it."[11]

Centuries earlier, the Greeks and Romans saw the recognizably physical signs of emotion as arising from "inspiration," moments when the gods literally breathed creativity into the orator and actor. To harness inspiration, the Roman orator Quintilian mentally visualized the images in his speeches to endow his performances with greater passion. Others tapped personal experiences to create legible physical signs to convey their characters' inner experiences. One story tells of the Greek actor Polus, who, "clad in the mourning garb of Electra, took from the tomb the ashes and urn of his son, embraced them as if they were those of [Electra's dead brother] Orestes, and filled the whole place, not with the appearance and imitation of sorrow, but with genuine grief and unfeigned lamentation."[12] Both imaginative visualizations and the use of emotional memories register as familiar to actors today.

While Strasberg's emphasis on actors' genuine emotion and Stanislavsky's initial experiments with "emotional memories" and his later insistence on visualizations are reminiscent of these ancient acting techniques, Stanislavsky passionately refused to call either approach "inspiration." In *An Actor Prepares,* the fictionalized teacher, Tortsov, upbraids his student for labeling a successful performance in this way, because for Stanislavsky, inspiration could not reliably organize the "poetry" of acting through the "grammar" of technique.[13] Waiting to be "inspired" stands in opposition to his sense that acting is a craft that can be learned. Moreover, to establish more dependable working methods, Stanislavsky made the actor's powers of observation, contemplation, and imagination a central focus. Developing a series of physical "lures" to make creative processes more conscious, he established ways for actors to harness imagination and emotional expression through script analysis, *raja* yoga, techniques grounded in behaviorist psychology, physical and vocal training of the actor, and so on. In other words, looking to the material side of acting's duality can help actors control and shape even their most emotional and seamlessly "natural" performances.

Echoing Stanislavsky's skeptical view of inspiration, Delsarte, Artaud, and Strasberg similarly recognized that imagination and emotion are not sufficient in themselves to produce a physically legible performance, but that the actor needs to activate both the internal and the external equally. Moreover, they all recognized to some extent that working "from the outside in" could sometimes lead more reliably to expressive "natural" performances. Even Strasberg, so identified with the inner techniques of Method acting, on occasion used physical methods to access emotion. For example, he created the "Song and Dance" exercise to complement his "Emotional Memory" technique in an effort to activate actors' bodies and voices. Strasberg would have an actor dance and sing a familiar tune and then demand changes in movement and vocal rhythms, tempos, keys, and so on, until the directions became so onerous the performer would collapse in tears or freeze in confusion. This controversial exercise uses physical movement to induce emotional experience and observable physical expression.[14]

Just as the emotional layer in performance had been identified centuries earlier, training in the physical dimension of public performance emerged when actors and politicians in ancient Greece were required to master oratorical skills. Aristotle points directly to "the management of the voice to express the various emotions," especially "the volume of sound, modulation of pitch, and rhythm," as the basis for successful performances.[15] During the Enlightenment, the era's propensity to discover "natural laws" through scientific observation encouraged players to codify expressive gestures of the hands, face, and body. Similarly, in the nineteenth century, acting and elocution manuals outlined ways that actors and public speakers could master "laws" of expressive communication (see chapter 6).

In the twentieth century, some practitioners integrated physical approaches to characterization into comprehensive working methods. Recall that in Stanislavsky's earliest experiments at the First Studio founded by the Moscow Art Theatre in 1911, he discovered that harnessing emotional memories agitated actors more than it helped them (see chapter 1). Thus, already working to enhance actors' concentration, imagination, and communication, beginning in the 1920s and 1930s Stanislavsky also provided ways for actors to explore physical actions as a way to develop characterizations. His earliest delineation of a "method of physical actions" represents a rehearsal technique through which "emotional life may sometimes be more easily aroused and fixed for performance through work on the physical life of the role."[16] Here, "the actor discovers and then performs the logical sequence of physical actions necessary to carry out the inner, purposeful actions" that an actor has previously identified through careful script analysis (see chapter 9).[17]

Coming to international attention in the 1960s, Polish director Jerzy Grotowski saw his contributions to training and rehearsal as a continuation of Stanislavsky's work on "the domain of physical actions."[18] Concurring with Stanislavsky's emphasis on "daily training and ongoing professional education," Grotowski required "actors under his direction to engage in regular physical and vocal training . . . to strengthen the actor's physical and receptive capacities."[19] Like Stanislavsky, he also understood that physical exercises alone could not prepare actors for performance. Instead, according to Grotowski, training should develop "the actor's imaginative and associative capacities," and directors should guide "the actor to develop the most subtle nuances of inner life within the framework of the role."[20] Drawing on this psychophysical training, an actor in Grotowski's theater sought to become "a holy figure, a type of 'secular saint' whose extraordinary discipline and ability allowed him or her to cast aside daily life masks" that could hinder the process of creating expressive performances.[21]

While Grotowski might describe the actor in unique terms, his intense interest in exploring the process of creating gestures that make feeling manifest can be traced back to figures like Delsarte.[22] Articulating a perspective shared by Stanislavsky and movement specialist Rudolf Laban (see chapter 8), Grotowski argues that whether working from the outside in or the inside out, training and preparation should "enhance the actor's receptivity to impulse," which "in Grotowski's terminology, refers to a seed of a living action born inside the actor's body which extends itself outward to the periphery, making itself visible as physical action."[23]

Indeed, attention to physical training and an awareness of performance's visible, physical dimension have often characterized work by theater companies like Grotowski's that are associated with the avant-garde. For example, in the 1920s, Russian theater director Vsevolod Meyerhold, a founding member of the Moscow Art Theatre, built on the idea that "every stage action must be justified or motivated" to develop a biomechanical system of training and performance, combining his aesthetic views with a desire to cut all superfluous motion from acting.[24] Meyerhold stressed that actors must "be able to move and to think" for their characters but with the maximum efficiency and efficacy.[25] Focusing "on the physical formulation of the movement" to be used in performance, Meyerhold's actors excelled in physical control, spatial and temporal rhythmic awareness, and "responsiveness to the partner, to the audience, to other external stimuli, especially the ability to observe, to listen and to react."[26]

The fact that many contemporary actors and twenty-first-century actor-training programs across the globe are turning once again to the physical dimension as the central entry point into the duality of acting can be seen in both Eastern and Western interest in the methods developed by Japanese theater director Tadashi Suzuki. Using Suzuki's methods, actors prepare by stamping rhythmically on the floor, literally grounding themselves in the physical world. As Suzuki explains, "The actor composes himself on the basis of his sense of contact with the ground, by the way in which his body makes contact with the floor. With his feet, the performer proves he is an actor."[27]

As these notes suggest, there is no simple recipe for approaching performance, and yet actors are charged with the task of translating invisible thoughts and feelings into visible signs that audiences can understand. In the West, that often means crafting "natural" signs seemingly drawn from daily life.

DELSARTE, EKMAN, AND PHYSICAL SIGNS

Writing about celebrated English actor David Garrick (1717–79), Denis Diderot, the French philosopher, essayist, novelist, playwright, and critic, called attention to Garrick's exemplary control of his physical and vocal expression. In his volume on acting, *Le Paradoxe sur le comédien* (*The Paradox of Acting*, 1830), Diderot explained:

> Garrick will put his head between two folding-doors, and in the course of five or six seconds his expression will change successively from wild delight to temperate pleasure, from this to tranquility, from tranquility to surprise, from surprise to blank astonishment, from that to sorrow, from sorrow to the air of one overwhelmed, from that to fright, from fright to horror, from horror to despair, and then he will go up again to the point from which he started.[28]

François Delsarte was also interested in actors' physical and vocal expression. Building on the eighteenth-century interest in natural laws, the French elocutionist further refined ideas on gestural acting, focusing on the relationship between external signs and inner states. As he wrote, "Semeiotics [*sic*] studies organic forms in view of the sentiment which produces them."[29] On the basis of his studies, Delsarte crafted "aesthetics" that described "gesture [as] the direct agent of the heart."[30] He began his study of human expression by examining corpses in the Paris morgue. Noticing that the thumb turns inward at death, he postulated that the thumb is an indicator of vital energy.[31] Delsarte moved on to study living subjects, classifying postures, stances, physical positions of the body, facial expressions in the brows, mouth, and eyes. He studied the joints of the body, the expressive musculature, and the dynamic qualities of motion.

Today, Delsartean drawings of postures, hand gestures, and facial expressions look old-fashioned and needlessly mechanistic. They seem tied to histrionic acting. As acting teacher John Delman, Jr., wrote in 1949, "No doubt the nineteenth century, in its eagerness to perfect the traditional language of pantomime, reduced it to absurdity."[32] Dancer Ted Shawn, who incorporated Delsarte's observations into modern dance techniques, explains that in his own childhood he "saw only the distorted and already outmoded falsifications" of amateur entertainers who "took 'poses' supposedly expressive of grief, joy, shyness, anger, defiance, etc. etc. etc. ad infinitum, ad nauseam."[33] He points out that the amateurs' "statue-posing" was actually "a complete reversal and falsification of the science which Delsarte taught."[34]

In contrast to eighteenth-century studies of static poses, however, Delsarte examined the dynamics of gesture. He found that forward movement often suggested openness and confidence, while movement away often conveyed defensiveness and repulsion. He looked to the sequences in which motion occurs, noting that physical gesture consistently precedes speech. Delsarte found that parallelism in the body (for example, when the right arm moves together with the right leg) indicates intentionality and that oppositions (right arm, left leg) could be expressive of strength. Delsarte observed how unfolding the arm from the shoulder to the wrist differed from folding the arm inward from the wrist to the shoulder. Over time, his advocates charted 59,049 signs that could be linked to specific emotional states. Delsarte himself "contemplated an almost infinite number of variations."[35]

Even if one acknowledges that Delsarte's taxonomy is more nuanced than histrionic performances might suggest, some observers find it difficult to accept Delsarte's position that gesture is a global language, "comprehensible to people of every tongue; whereas their different forms of speech must be laboriously learned before they can be employed or understood."[36] Delsarte's taxonomy of gestures and expressions recognizes that different cultural groups employ different gestural accents, but it is grounded in the view that human physical and vocal expression originate from a basic, universal human physiology. Growing awareness of cultural differences has made Delsarte's interest in expression that arises from physiology seem misguided.

However, increasingly more sophisticated studies in contemporary neuroscience have shown that human expression, cognition, and emotion are indeed connected to physiology. Assessing the implications of research in body language studies, Patsy Ann Hecht observes that "one might be tempted to scoff at the scientific pretension of the [Delsarte] system" but that "psychologists have been delving more and more extensively into the meaning of human movement and expression."[37] Discussing computational theories of the mind and the work of neuroscientist Antonio Damasio, Rhonda Blair writes, "For theories of theatre and performance to be complete, they must engage in science that can illuminate [physiological] phenomena, since it is sentient beings with material bodies and brains who are the performers and its percipients."[38]

The work of psychologist Paul Ekman demonstrates the legitimacy of Delsarte's conclusion that certain aspects of human expression are linked to physiology. Ekman's studies of facial expression reveal transculturally legible expressions of emotion. He explains that human physiology "has shaped the affect program, determining which facial movements are likely to occur with one or another of the emotions, and perhaps also the timing of those movements."[39] His research reveals that "changes in visual appearance are not arbitrarily associated with emotion" but instead that for some emotions—disgust, happiness, sadness—the changes in visual appearance is "the same for all people."[40]

Ekman accounts for cultural differences in behavior, making a distinction between the social and the biological aspects of human expression. He distinguishes between gestures that are tied to specific messages, such as nodding the head yes or no—these are what he calls "emblems"—and gestures that are linked to human physiology, for example, turning the mouth downward and crying or wrinkling the nose in disgust. Echoing the Prague school's observations about gesture-signs, Ekman notes that emblems often have a "specific verbal meaning, known to most members of a subculture or culture and typically employed with the intention of sending a message."[41] In *Smoke,* gestures and expressions of greeting that the actors use in the scenes set in Auggie's cigar store might thus be called emblems of friendship, recognized as such by the group. By comparison, the gestures and expressions of grief featured in the exchange between Perrineau and Whitaker in the recognition scene belong to the category of human expression grounded in transnational human physiology.

In sympathy with Delsarte's work, Ekman's research shows that what prompts universal expressions of emotion is not fixed or universal but instead specific to a culture or individual. While situations that provoke disgust might be distinct for different cultures, its expression (nose wrinkled, upper lip raised, etc.) will be universally identifiable.[42] For example, in a cultural setting other than the one suggested by *Smoke,* the initial moments of shared recognition between an estranged father and son might provoke the expression of joy rather than the expression of shame and rage. In another cultural setting, rage and shame might be the characters' response to a situation in which the son never identifies himself to his father. Ekman's research shows, however, that in these cases, the specific display of human emotion would be globally identifiable.

More refined than the work of Delsarte, Ekman's research on the difference between gestures and expressions in private (recorded through hidden cameras) and in public shows how socially constructed "display rules" affect people's repression of expression. Studies reveal, for example, that Japanese expression of emotion in private is universally recognizable but that culturally specific display rules lead to discernable processes of hiding the expression of those emotions in public. In *Smoke,* the recognition scene approximates a private situation in which the expression of basic emotion flows quite freely.

While Ekman, like Delsarte, has drawn criticism for concentrating on static images of facial expression, his research demonstrates that close attention to the dynamics of human expression produces insight into the externalization of inner experience. Like Delsarte's early taxonomy of gesture and expression, the work of Ekman and other neuroscientists shows that physical and vocal expression can convey meaning even to audiences whose cultural background is distinct from the performers. As Delman notes, even though Delsarte's taxonomy is outdated, it is still true that "bodily action, simplified by selection, moderately exaggerated, provides a language of expression more universally intelligible than words."[43]

Although generally overlooked by actors and scholars today who are more cognizant of Stanislavsky's reforms, Delsarte deserves attention if only because his system was of great importance to actors throughout the era of silent cinema. While Delsarte experimented with oratory and singing, Steele MacKaye (Delsarte's only American student and one of his most sophisticated interpreters) turned the master's semiotics into concrete methods and techniques for acting. MacKaye founded the first professional training program for actors in the United States in 1871, the St. James School.[44] Through his offices, American Delsartism (as MacKaye's adaptation became known) provided one of the key acting methods in the United States until Stanislavsky's ideas took hold in the late 1920s and 1930s.[45]

Even after Stanislavsky's tours to the United States in the 1920s brought greater attention to the inward aspects of acting, external training remained of central importance in actor training. Just as Stanislavsky had insisted on the actor's physical and vocal development, drama schools in the United States throughout the 1930s and 1940s considered work on the actor's instrument as important as instruction in imagination and script analysis. Moreover, stage actors who began working in film discovered that they were in fact required to pay special attention to the physical and vocal dimensions of performance. The degree to which this type of attention is necessary is reflected, for example, in the series of exercises developed by studio-era drama coach Josephine Dillon for strengthening physical control over the eyes to prepare actors for close-ups.[46]

Thus, as noted earlier, despite the seemingly profound distance between nineteenth-century elocutionist François Delsarte and twentieth-century Method acting guru Lee Strasberg, practitioners from both schools see physical and vocal expressions as "signs" that convey meaning. Paul McDonald's point that acting is "the form of performance specifically involved with the construction of character" echoes the views of practitioners from Delsarte to Grotowski, namely, that audiences gain access to characters through the physical signs performers make available.[47] A look at the recognition scene in *Smoke* shows that Delsarte's taxonomy illuminates actors' use of "natural" physical signs to convey characters' emotions.

DELSARTE TERMS APPLIED TO *SMOKE*

A collection of films by Hong Kong–born director Wayne Wang, Jim Jarmusch, John Sayles, and others ushered in a new era of independent filmmaking in the 1980s. Geoff Andrew notes that Wang, who "virtually invented the Chinese-American movie single-handedly," was exploring "issues of ethnic and cultural identity several years before Spike Lee came to the fore."[48] With crises of identity at the heart of his stories, Wang's hybridized films also reveal his "ability to juxtapose apparently incompatible cinematic styles."[49] Developing "a postmodern and post-national film language all his own," Wang has explored "the notion of identity in flux . . . on both formal and thematic levels."[50] Directing films for art house and mainstream audiences, Wang's first commercial success, *The Joy Luck Club* (1993), was followed by the collaboration with screenwriter Paul Auster that led to *Smoke* (1995) and *Blue in the Face* (1995). Even though the two films do not address Chinese-American concerns, they reflect Wang's interest in cultural hybridity.[51]

Following its release, *Smoke* gained notice at the 1995 Berlin Film Festival, with the Special Jury Prize going to Wayne Wang and Harry Keitel for his performance. At the 1996 Independent Spirit Awards, Paul Auster received the award for Best First Screenplay and Harold Perrineau, Jr., garnered a nomination for Best Supporting Male. Considered today, *Smoke* reflects the kind of attention to evocative "natural" acting that is also illustrated in William Hurt's Oscar-winning performance in *The Kiss of the Spider Woman* (Hector Babenco, 1985) and Forest Whitaker's Oscar-winning performance in *The Last King of Scotland* (Kevin McDonald, 2006).

Smoke allows audiences to engage emotionally with various characters. Paul Benjamin (William Hurt), the novelist mourning the death of his pregnant wife, is one who brings audiences into the story. Auggie Wren (Harvey Keitel), the cigar store owner who takes a photograph of his street corner every day at exactly the same time, is another. These two characters function as the figurative voice in the film, for their conversations carry the film's overt philosophical perspective, and much of the action is seen through their eyes. Thomas Jefferson Cole (Harold Perrineau, Jr.), the street-smart African-American youth who saves Paul from being killed in traffic, is one of the characters who shape the underlying mood of the film. His estranged father, Cyrus Cole (Forest Whitaker), is another. The central crisis of their story is whether and how Thomas and his father can reconcile after years of separation.

Years before the narrative begins, Cyrus abandoned his son in the aftermath of a drunk-driving accident that killed Thomas's mother and caused Cyrus to lose his left arm. The prosthetic Cyrus wears is a constant reminder that he is responsible for his wife's death. For Thomas, the long absence of his mother and father has caused an extreme adolescent identity crisis: the character not only adopts a series of different names over the course of the story, but also resists identifying himself even to people who care for him. After staying at Paul's apartment for a short time, Thomas disappears and goes in search of his father, who now lives outside the city with a new wife and young child. Thomas finds Cyrus's auto shop and, borrowing the novelist's name, starts working for his father as "Paul Benjamin."

Both father and son have delayed their painful reckoning for as long as possible. Cyrus chose to disappear after the drunk-driving accident, while Thomas, after locating his father, puts off the confrontation by hiding behind his assumed identity. Their delay has only increased the inevitable explosion of emotion endemic to moments of recognition and reconciliation. The sequence begins by suturing us into Thomas's point of view. We see him painting a workroom at his father's garage. He hears a car drive up and comes out to see Cyrus/Whitaker drive up with his young son and new wife, Doreen (Erica Gimpel). Doreen invites him to join in eating the picnic lunch they have brought. Thomas/Perrineau turns to wipe off his hands but immediately hears another car's horn honk; we cut to see Auggie/Keitel and Paul/Hurt arriving. In the next shot, the tightened muscles in Perrineau's face and body display Thomas's sudden concern; the camera follows Perrineau as he races down the steps to meet the car.

The next take, which lasts roughly two minutes, begins with introductions and handshakes. Initially, Perrineau stands to the side of the frame, but as the scene develops, blocking leaves Perrineau boxed in between Hurt and Keitel on one side and Whitaker and Gimpel on the other. Conveying the point that Thomas needs to get some breathing room, Perrineau steps out from between them, into the foreground of shot with his back to the audience.

However, Whitaker too steps forward, conveying Cyrus's determination to retake control of his surroundings. With the pressure building on Thomas, the scene cuts to a medium close-up of Perrineau. As Thomas prepares to tell Cyrus his real name, Perrineau's mouth hangs open and his eyes are wide in a look of trepidation. His face suggests Delsartean images of terror. He shifts his weight from side to side, ambivalently approaching and retreating from his father and the truth. Perrineau pulls his head backward

In *Smoke,* Harold Perrineau, Jr., reveals Thomas's need for breathing room by coming toward the camera as he backs away from the adults closing him in on both sides

Harold Perrineau, Jr.: his head drawn back and his wide-eyed, open-mouthed expression conveying fear and distrust as he admits to being "Thomas Jefferson Cole"

Forest Whitaker in *Smoke:* his eyes, nostrils, and mouth conveying the anger and astonishment Cyrus Cole feels when he hears his son's name

slightly in retreat from the confrontation. The performance details concur with observations made by Delsarte, who noted that "the complex feelings of scrutiny and distrust will produce an attitude of suspicion, jealousy, hate, or envy, which first lowers the head and then draws it backward."[52]

In a reverse shot, Whitaker's facial expressions register the rage and pain welling up in Cyrus. Thrusting his head forward, Whitaker responds angrily to his son, who has tricked him by not identifying himself. He moves aggressively in toward Perrineau, his mouth open, lips distended. In contrast to Perrineau, Whitaker's eyes grow small and focus downward. His nostrils quiver as he seems to repress his urge to weep. Here again, the performance details concur with observations made by Delsarte, who found that the "nostrils dilate in anger, passionate resentment, and the like."[53] Both actors use open mouths for most of the scene; even that acting choice is consistent with evidence collected by Delsarte, who discovered that the lips are often "parted in astonishment, suspense and awe."[54]

In a wide shot, Auggie and Paul pressure Thomas to say who his mother is. Now Cyrus tries to buy time and save face; he asks his wife to leave them alone. When Thomas/Perrineau says his mother's name, Cyrus/Whitaker responds by slugging him. Keitel and Hurt move forward to help the young man but Doreen/Gimpel intervenes and kicks Keitel in the leg. Keitel and Hurt bumble away into the background and off screen. We see Perrineau get up off and race across the space to tackle Whitaker. The two wrestle on the ground while Gimpel tries to break up the fight, all the while yelling, "He's your son, he's your son." Finally, Gimpel pulls Whitaker away from Perrineau.

When Thomas is forced to say his mother's name, father and son give vent to their pent-up anger. The father's attack is sharp and sudden, quickly expressed and quickly discharged. But when the son responds by tackling his father around the waist and abdomen, the movements carry an entirely different tone. In Delsarte's view, the torso represents procreation and passion; for Thomas, it seems the right place to connect with his lost father. The wrestling, in the fullness of its bodily contact and its similarity to hugging, conveys the complexity of a relationship that encompasses violence and affection. While the single punch that Cyrus delivers expresses his position of authority, Thomas's tackle prolongs connection between father and son. As they wrestle on the ground, their embattled embrace expresses their respective anguish; the fight ends only because Cyrus's wife forcibly interrupts it.

Tight shots frame the culminating confrontation between father and son. Using his good right arm to point at Perrineau, Whitaker accuses the boy of lying; in the background we hear Gimpel's continuing screams to stop the fighting. Whitaker's mouth is open and his lips are turned down and distended but also pulled back. His eyes are lowered. His hand reaches forward but his head leans back, thus creating equilibrium across his body. The gesture recalls Delsarte's law of opposition in which full-body gestures tend to create equilibrium. In this case, the equilibrium depends on a "gesture with the arm [while] the head moves [back] in opposition."[55] Finally, the balance of the gesture, in contrast to his disequilibrium at the top of the scene, conveys Cyrus's painful acceptance of his son, and by implication, the events of his past.

The next shot features Perrineau's face twisted in fear and, from off screen the sound of Whitaker's anguished cries join those of Gimpel's. Perrineau's gestures and expression suggest that Thomas holds on to his ambivalence and anger. He shifts his weight and pulls his head backward, creating disequilibrium and a physical expression of avoidance. His eyes narrow more than in the opening shots of the confrontation but his mouth remains open with lips turned downward. This physicality in comparison to Whitaker's more balanced stance suggests that Thomas has traveled a shorter emotional distance toward reconciliation than has his father.

The next shot shows Whitaker, crying and gasping for air, his prosthetic left arm crossing his body. Having just pointed *at* his son with his good arm, Whitaker reveals that Cyrus is truly reckoning with his past as he points *to* Thomas with the arm lost in the accident. His weapon-like hook further suggests the violent ambivalence of this reconciliation and thus further intensifies the emotionality of the moment. The character's lost arm metonymically tells the whole story of abandonment.

In this final image of Cyrus, Whitaker's face is more pained than angry, a copy of the many Delsartean drawings that depict weeping sorrow: eyes squinched up, mouth open and turned downward, head moving downward. Whitaker's gesture might be balanced but his stance simultaneously indicates a loss of equilibrium. In the last moments of the scene, he appears about to fall forward, suggesting not only the character's vulnerability, but also the fragility of Cyrus's emotional acceptance. We cut from Whitaker's anguished expression to the final image of Perrineau's face, which conveys the boy's deep concern that his father will not accept him, particularly after this confrontation. The event has left all members of this family spent, for in this final image, the cries from off screen have also finally stopped.

Framing, editing, and blocking serve to support and enhance the emo-

Forest Whitaker in *Smoke:* his eyes, head, mouth, and stance illustrating Cyrus's sorrow for the grave mistakes that included the abandonment of his son

tional intensity conveyed by the actors' gestures and facial expressions. Prior to the final confrontation between Cyrus and Thomas, frame selections do not call attention to Whitaker's or Perrineau's facial expressions. That delay gives the later shots of their emotion-filled faces greater impact, for in the closing moments of the scene, frame choices allow us to carefully study their intense facial expressions. As the sequence progresses, framing and editing also allow one to explore the expressive qualities in the actors' arms and shoulders, which feature physical signs that Delsarte discovered in his studies of human expression. He had described the joints of the arm as "great articular centres" that are able to reveal the degree of intensity felt by the person who gestures; the most pertinent joints of the arm in the recognition scene in *Smoke* are "the shoulder for pathetic actions" that serves as a "thermometer of passion," and the hand that serves as a "volitional" indicator.[56] As the scene's dramatic conflict develops, Whitaker and Perinneau forcefully lift and retract their shoulders. Their hands quickly reach out in attack and accusation or pull back in retreat and pain. These physical signs convey the inner turmoil that Cyrus and Thomas experience.

The rhythm of the scene traces an arc from nervous stasis through furious action and a return to relative balance. The rhythmic structure that underlines the intensity of the scene is another dramatic component that Delsarte identified. He explains, for example, that any dramatic "state of being is outwardly shown by great physical exertion, and is immediately followed by intense calm."[57] Wang emphasizes the ensuing calm by cutting abruptly from Perrineau's frightened face to the next scene, a quiet picture of acceptance, with the newly constituted family and their friends resting as they sit around a picnic table.

It is unlikely that Perrineau and Whitaker worked from an acquaintance with Delsarte. Yet their performances result in gestures and expressions that can be analyzed according to Delsartean concepts of expression. This case study reveals that Delsarte's taxonomy can describe the apparently "natural" physical signs actors use to convey character emotion. Using Delsarte's terms to analyze such "natural" details of their performances makes it possible to identify the type of gestures and expressions that seem to emerge not from craft but from the fictional characters themselves. Cultural-aesthetic traditions in the West have made it a challenge to see the craft from which naturalistic performances emerge. Exploring distinctions between the transparent and opaque dimensions of performance sheds light on the process of representation exemplified by Perrineau's and Whitaker's use of "natural" physical signs.

MAKING "TRANSPARENT" ACTING CHOICES "OPAQUE"

Aesthetics philosopher Suzanne K. Langer has described the imagined realm of drama as "virtual," formed from the "actual" material reality of embodied performance. Echoing the Prague school's observations about "ostensive signs" (in performing art, things that stand for themselves), she explains that by using actual hands, faces, arms, legs, torsos, and vocal chords that obey biological and physical laws, actors create virtual, imagined realities (see chapter 4). Langer observes that performers establish this virtual realm by distinguishing actual reality from illusion and manipulating the actual to produce the desired illusion. When this manipulation is hidden from the viewer by the use of familiar, quotidian gestures, the otherwise opaque actor's craft now seems "transparent," even as it provides "insight into the [virtual] reality to be expressed."[58]

When audiences encounter naturalistic performances designed to create dramatic characters, various factors prompt them to lose awareness of the actual performance elements and to focus instead on the illusion those gestures and expressions establish. As was examined in the opening chapter, film audiences are often prompted to see naturalistic performance details as natural behavior captured on screen. Even a bravura performance like Chaplin's in *City Lights* can become invisible, hence transparent, because it mobilizes familiar, socially defined gesture-signs to create meaning. Similarly, the scene from *Smoke* illustrates the way films can use "natural" signs to convey emotion. With recognizable physical signs in place, audiences tend to overlook the crafted dimension of acting. The performance elements that have been crafted and carefully selected for inclusion in the film seem somehow inevitable and thus become a transparent window through which fictional characters are viewed. The conventions of naturalism require acting choices that emphasize the illusion of characters. Such performance elements are meant to disappear by calling attention neither to themselves nor to the skill of the actor. Thus, the opaque body and voice of the actor becomes the vehicle for the virtual realm of the story.

Audiences "see right through" the details of performance to varying degrees, often depending on how trained their eyes are to the nuances of observable performance elements. A particular acting choice might draw one person's attention to the opaque dimension of the performance even though that same moment is transparent for another. For example, at the conclusion of *City Lights*, the image of the Tramp gently holding the flower might prompt one person to reflect on Chaplin's use of the conventional gesture of giving flowers, but lead another to ponder the Tramp's tender feelings. Similarly, as the discussion of *The Magnificent Seven* suggests, increased awareness of cultural-aesthetic traditions can affect perceptions about the transparent and opaque dimensions of performance. Acting choices that seem natural can, upon reflection, reveal the influence of aesthetic conventions. Considered in relation to early-twentieth-century postures of "good deportment," the gunfighters' limber slouches and hunched shoulders are not simply "natural" poses but also responses to earlier aesthetic conventions.

Sometimes moments of performance will emphasize an actor's physical or vocal skill. Recall, for example, Chaplin's flamboyant display in the scenes with the monument to "Peace and Prosperity" and the sculpture of the nude female in *City Lights*. In other moments of performance, an actor's skill is only implied by the successfully created illusion of character. The scene between Perrineau and Whitaker exemplifies the latter circumstance. As James Naremore observes, the physical details of a performance become more noticeable when they include strange, overt, or what Naremore refers to as ostensive gestures and expressions.[59] By comparison, the concrete details of a performance can be easily taken for granted and thus overlooked when they include gestures and expressions so familiar to audiences that they seem to be drawn from everyday life.

Yet acting choices that feature seemingly natural behavior warrant analysis of their opaque dimension, for as Naremore points out, even naturalistic performances by actors such as Spencer Tracy and Robert Duvall involve "a degree of ostensiveness that marks it off from quotidian behavior."[60] Similarly, when actors use naturalistic styles, moments of "expressive incoherence" violate realism's demand for consistency of character and expose actors' use of physical and vocal signs to portray characters.[61] In these instances, conflicting "natural" signs allow audiences to see that a character is concealing his or her true feelings from the other characters. *Far From Heaven* contains many of these moments. For example, early in the film when Cathy leaves the house to get her husband Frank at the police station, she "acts" as if she were calm in front of Sybil, but viewers are allowed to see that she is in fact emotionally shaken; Julianne Moore keeps her voice soft, even, and perfectly modulated as she asks Viola Davis to mind the children but one can see the tension in her hands and face.

Like Langer's insight into opaque and transparent dimensions, Naremore's contrast between ostensive and quotidian acting choices can be applied to any sort of stage or screen performance. In fact, distinctions between acting styles can be charted by assessing the varying place of ostensive performance choices and the degree to which gestures and expressions create virtual characters and worlds of imagination. As Naremore observes,

> At one extreme, the actor develops the body as an instrument, learning a kinesics, or movement vocabulary; at the other he or she is encouraged to behave more or less normally, letting gesture or facial expression rise "naturally" out of deeply felt emotion. Professional players have always spoken about the value of both skills, but . . . modern dramatic literature strongly favors the second.[62]

Naremore's identification of modern dramatic literature with gestures that rise "naturally" underscores the fact that contemporary forms of realism and naturalism give priority to creating transparent performances that draw attention away from the concrete, opaque aspect of performance elements. As suggested by the discussion of films by Renoir, Sayles, and Cassavetes, conventions in poetic realism and neonaturalism invite audiences to focus on the characters, with performance elements serving primarily as a means to access the virtual realm of fictional representation (see chapter 2).

In Western cultural-aesthetic traditions over the centuries, productions have offered various means of accessing fictional characters. Eighteenth-century audiences lingered over representative images of the virtual during "moments of stupefaction" when all action stopped; these "freeze frames" at moments of high emotion allowed for the specific contemplation of the virtual in the midst of predominantly histrionic, opaque performances.[63] By the end of the nineteenth century, conventions had changed. The use of an invisible fourth wall now turned staged worlds into seemingly self-contained and complete illusions.

The naturalistic convention of the invisible fourth wall influenced stage and screen productions throughout the twentieth century. *A Streetcar Named Desire,* on stage (1947) and screen (1951), drew audience attention to Stanley Kowalski, not Marlon Brando. For contemporary audiences, the actor's work in developing Stanley's famous "mumble" is hidden by its quotidian familiarity. Yet research reveals the craft Brando employed in creating the physical dimension of his performance. Considering himself "an ear man," Brando found his way into the part by experimenting with vocal placement and diction. As David Richard Jones explains, Brando found his vision of Stanley's character in "that hard, flat, unSouthern voice, big enough to have grandeur in screaming 'STELL-LAHHHHH!' and nasal enough to bite when Stanley confronts Blanche."[64] With that sound established, Brando could manipulate it to show how Stanley "loses control of language" in the trunk scene, in his comments on bowling, and elsewhere. He could use it to make audiences imagine that "Stanley didn't give a damn how he said a thing."[65] As the work of Brando suggests, performances created by the careful selection and combination of seemingly quotidian elements can lead audiences to "see through" the actor's craft to the fictional character.

Critical attention needs to be paid to the opaque dimension of film performance. The influence of late-nineteenth-century naturalism led film audiences to expect screen actors to use the gestural language of the everyday (handshakes, grunts, and nods). Voices might be allowed to soar and range in film musicals but conventions of realism prompt audiences to expect dramas to feature the narrower modulations of daily life, including, for example, the flat sound of "Stanley Kowalski's" voice. Films that depend upon such familiar vocal and gestural expressions make the agency and control that actors exert in their performances difficult to detect.

The opaque dimension of screen acting is submerged, for example, in a film such as *The Birdcage* (Mike Nichols, 1996), which includes performances constructed out of seemingly quotidian gestures and expressions. In the opening scene, Robin Williams crosses through the nightclub, arranging a free coffee here, upbraiding a clumsy waiter there. In his first seconds on screen, Williams creates his character by manipulating small everyday gestures. His mannered gait and expressive hand and eye movements tell us that he is not only the proprietor but also gay. Williams's work, however, registers without being noticed. Only extratextual information about the actor's life as a husband and father allows audiences to intuit that he "acts" this role. Williams's subtle performance is all the more remarkable in its juxtaposition to his nightclub's transvestite act. In contrast to Williams's transparent work, the flamboyant female impersonators on the stage behind him suggest the potential opacity of performance.

Because audiences draw information from the small details of gestures and vocal expression, performance demands a body and voice trained in what is sometimes called "craft" and sometimes "virtuosity."[66] Performances that lay bare an actor's physical control can illuminate the discipline that is the foundation of acting. Characterizations that require actors to play more than one role especially highlight the skill behind the selection and combination of performance choices within a single production. They can also illustrate shifting emphases in acting traditions because dual roles such as Jekyll and Hyde are often taken up by actors from different generations. For example, following his critically acclaimed stage performances as Richard III, John Barrymore continued to demonstrate he was more than a matinee idol by portraying the dual role in *Dr. Jekyll and Mr. Hyde* (John S. Robertson, 1921), a silent film based on Richard Mansfield's theatrical production of Robert Louis Stevenson's novella. In his performance as the giddy, idealistic young doctor and the gnarled, spider-like sadist, Barrymore rises to the challenge posed by Mansfield's legendary portrayal. On more than one occasion in the film, he performs the transformation in full view, using his face and body with only a minimum of assistance from makeup and cinematography. Moving from Jekyll into Hyde, Barrymore's expression goes from a gentle frown of concern into a grimace; his posture retreats from an elegant carriage into a hunched lumbering walk; his elegant fingers tense and gnarl, their fake fingertips exaggerating the arch of his hand.

Performances that feature an actor's physical control remain an integral part of cinema. Far from belonging to a histrionic past, screen performances continue to feature virtuoso performances. Consider, for example, Edward Norton's transformation from a shy, modest choir boy into the assertive, wise-cracking murderer in *Primal Fear* (Gregory Hoblit, 1996). Despite aesthetic and technological differences between the 1921 and the 1996 films, both actors rely primarily on virtuosity to morph from one personality into the other. Barrymore and Norton both develop distinct vocal and physical repertoires or "physics of movement and gesture" for their two characters.[67] Because their performances remain relatively free of cinematic intervention, and the actors themselves effect radical transformations in voice, stance, and gesture, the opaque dimension of their performance comes into view more easily.

Transformations, which present two distinct characters within the body of the same actor, make performance eminently visible. Actors' contrasting portrayals in different films can also illuminate the opaque dimension of performance. For instance, Jack Nicholson's extreme physicality in Stanley Kubrick's 1980 horror film *The Shining* is marked by Nicholson's "long sweeping gestures" and the dynamic walk that carries him through the hotel halls as if he were a "demented derelict."[68] However, in *Five Easy Pieces*, Bob Rafelson's 1970 low-key story about a drifter, Nicholson's performance is "understated" and his "mostly naturalistic" gestures and expressions reflect the subdued tone of the film.[69] The contrast between these two performances suggests the range of "natural" physical choices available in acting.

CONCLUSIONS

An actor's physical and vocal instrument is essentially the same as that used by other performers. An actor extends a hand, looks up or down, lets a breath escape as a sigh, and chooses specific postures and gaits. These types of physical and vocal gestures comprise the material of acting, as handstands and flips do for an acrobat. While circus gestures are always extraordinary and musical performances call attention to the opaque skill involved, actors' performances can range from the extraordinary to the usual, from big, impressive choices to a simple handshake or nod. The analysis of acting choices that feature "natural" signs follows a line of inquiry that inverts the path audiences generally travel. Normally, actors' physical signs become more and more transparent as audiences enter into the fictional world of the characters. By contrast, the opaque dimension of actors' performances becomes more and more evident as one pinpoints connections between impressions and the specific "natural" signs crafted into performances. Delsarte's taxonomy facilitates such analysis. The case study of *Smoke* reveals that even a seemingly outdated taxonomy can illuminate the integral connection between the opacity of performance elements and audience impressions about the virtual world of filmic characters.

Framing and editing choices in *Smoke* do not highlight the virtuosity of the actors. Working in concert, performance and nonperformance elements do not draw attention to the actor *qua* actor but instead allow performance details to pull audiences into the experiences of the characters. Delsarte's taxonomy supplies a way to identify acting choices in this seemingly "natural" sequence. It provides terms and concepts for describing the way Perrineau and Whitaker as actors create emotional illusion through their physical gestures and movements. Using Delsarte's terms to examine their work makes the actors' otherwise transparent contributions visible and clarifies that actual performance details provide a window into the virtual realm of their fictional characters.

A film such as *Smoke* is perhaps ideally suited to an analysis that considers "natural" signs in performance because the film itself explores "the subtle uniqueness of the everyday," a concern made explicit in the photographs Auggie takes of his street corner every day.[70] Auggie shows Paul that some of the images seem identical at first but that a closer look reveals that the minute details of the content are "infinitely varied."[71] In a similar fashion, performances with recognizable social and "natural" gestures might initially not seem to require analysis. However, upon careful consideration, they disclose "the subtle uniqueness of the everyday" and the potentially profound interaction between sign systems and individual expressions.

Analysis shows that even performances composed of "natural" physical signs depend vitally on actors' bodily skills and imaginative abilities to create a virtual world peopled by fictional characters. While some cultural-aesthetic conventions lead audiences to "see through" quotidian performance elements, Delsarte's terminology provides one way to isolate and describe the physical and vocal features that create impressions of fictional characters and their interactions. His work offers terms and concepts for describing the dynamics of human expression integral to screen performance. The next chapter shows that Laban Movement Analysis complements the Delsartean system. Like Delsarte's work, Laban Movement Analysis can facilitate description and analysis of gestures, expressions, poses, movements through space, and modulations in voice as physical actualities that convey imagined characters' thoughts and feelings.

CHAPTER EIGHT

LABAN: TEMPORAL AND SPATIAL DIMENSIONS OF MOVEMENT

In the first decades of the twentieth century, cultural, aesthetic, and technological developments placed human movement in a new light. As Hillel Schwartz notes, "Motion pictures, like modern dance, corporeal mime and, soon, the schools of naturalistic . . . acting, demanded much more than a simple reading of one discrete attitude after another."[1] Instead, audience encounters with these new forms "demanded a reading of the body in motion and an appreciation of the full impulse of that motion."[2] In the case of cinema, audiences were required to "watch for those subtler motions of face, shoulder, rib cage and pelvis that reflected inner states but had been scarcely visible from the distant galleries and boxes of 'legitimate' theater, vaudeville or burlesque."[3]

Modern dance practitioners greatly contributed to the new way of thinking about human movement. Schwartz explains that between "1840 and 1930 the dance world in Europe and the United States [experienced] a shift in attitudes toward physical movement."[4] 1840 is significant because "by that year François Delsarte had begun his lectures in Paris."[5] 1930 is the year of the Third Dancers' Congress, an event that brought international attention to the work of Rudolf Laban, Mary Wigman, and Kurt Jooss, all leaders of European modern dance.[6] In 1929, Essen, Germany, became the center of all the Laban schools; Rudolf Laban had been named the director of movement and dance for the State Opera in Berlin; and Laban's work was recognized by his colleagues as "the common basis for modern dance."[7] In 1930, Mary Wigman's tour in the United States "raised public awareness of

Modern Dance."[8] In 1933, Ballets Jooss's unprecedented combination of theater, dance, and modern media captivated American audiences.[9]

Differences between perspectives associated with Delsarte and Laban represent a shift in emphasis. In America, dancers like Isadora Duncan set aside Delsarte's "rigid equations of specific gestures with specific meanings [but] took from Delsarte his concern for the absolute integrity of gesture, his attention to the expressive power of the torso and his desire for movements liberated from highly mannered codes of motion."[10] Similarly, Laban and his colleagues created notation systems that emerged as "an outgrowth of, and reaction to, ballet."[11] They worked from ballet notation's "static, documenting positions and floor patterns" to develop a transcription system that could effectively characterize the changing, goal-directed qualities of human movement.[12] Laban Movement Analysis was designed to describe temporal-spatial phrases of human movement rather than isolated moments of codified postures or "natural" behavior. Its terms and concepts address movements arising from and ending in any part of human bodies. Grounded in the view that human movement is an expression of feelings and desires, Laban Movement Analysis sees gestures as "expressive *releases* rather than practiced achievements."[13]

A "subtle but remarkable" contrast exists between nineteenth-century theories of gesture and the view shared by Laban and other leaders in modern dance.[14] Their twentieth-century perspectives reflect the arrival of motion pictures and naturalistic theater, which required audiences to "read not merely the attitude but the entire stretch of the outlooming motion of which the last position struck was just the finishing touch."[15] Of course, staging practices that recall nineteenth-century forms of expression can still be found. In *The Magnificent Seven,* Horst Buchholz employs a series of codified gestures to perform Chico's speech to the villagers and experienced gunfighters (see chapter 6). However, many screen performances are not usefully described through reference to theories of expression exemplified by orators like Edmund Burke, William Pitt, or Daniel Webster.[16] Instead, as this chapter suggests, the density and fluidity of performances like those of Denzel Washington and Ethan Hawke in *Training Day* (Antoine Fuqua, 2001) can be better understood by turning to taxonomies like those developed by Rudolf Laban. This chapter shows how Laban's terms can be used in studies of screen performance; the next extends the application of that vocabulary by examining the temporal and spatial dimensions of actors' movements, gestures, and expressions in light of principles central to script analysis.

BACKGROUND NOTES ON LABAN MOVEMENT ANALYSIS

Laban built on the gesture theories of François Delsarte and the music theories of Emil Jacques Dalcroze to develop a conceptual framework that facilitates observation and analysis of human movement. Born in 1879 in what is now Bratislava, Slovakia, Laban participated in the aesthetic developments of his time. Working in Germany during the Bauhaus and expressionist periods, he established "theatrical and recreational dance programs," founded schools, and produced books, journals, and other publications.[17] He worked closely with many European dancers, choreographers, directors, and teachers; between 1913 and Laban's death in 1958, Mary Wigman, Dussia Bereska, Kurt Jooss, Albrecht Knust, and Lisa Ullmann made key contributions to the terms, concepts, and notation systems that comprise Laban Movement Analysis.

Prior to World War II, Laban's dance theory and practice had "established his reputation as the . . . founder of the Central European School of Modern Dance."[18] However, in 1936, at the height of his career, the German government put Laban under house arrest, his work was banned, and "Laban's name was forbidden to be used anywhere in the Third Reich."[19] Laban fled Nazi Germany and in 1938 began a career in England as a movement consultant to educators and factory owners. After World War II, collaborations between Laban's Art of Movement Studio and Joan Littlewood and Ewan McColl's Theatre Workshop in England led to rehearsal methods that employed Laban's taxonomies "to structure the expressive techniques of performance."[20] Actors in the Theatre Workshop Company explored different uses of time, weight, direction, and flow in theater games and improvisations that established in part "the rhythmic patterns" of performances produced by the company.[21] Laban's *The Mastery of Movement on the Stage* (1950), the first comprehensive guide to movement analysis and physical characterization for actors in the West, emerged from his collaboration with the Theatre Workshop.

Since the 1970s, Laban's work has been integrated into many training programs. Some practitioners see it as "a perfect complement" to central principles in Stanislavsky's System (see chapter 1).[22] Laban methods are especially compatible with work grounded in Stanislavsky's insight that "emotional life may sometimes be more easily aroused and fixed for performance through work on the physical life of the role, rather than through inner work."[23] Laban principles have also been used in courses that draw on methods outlined by Strasberg, Adler, and Meisner, as well as acting approaches developed by Jerzy Grotowski in the 1960s at the Laboratory Theatre in Poland. While courses in mime, stage combat, tai chi, and so on teach specialized skills, work that draws on Laban Movement Analysis gives actors "the means for finding and developing whatever is needed in movement for *any* production, *any* style or character."[24] For studies of completed performances, the Laban system provides a comprehensive network of terms and concepts for describing the "impelling inner action" that colors the movements an actor performs to convey a character's disposition, goals, and tactics.[25]

CONTRASTING QUALITIES OF MOVEMENT IN *TRAINING DAY*

Training Day uses familiar genre formulas to mount a critique of power in contemporary American society. Drawing on the conventions of the gangster film and the crime thriller, *Training Day* takes audiences into the literal and figurative underworld of Los Angeles in ways not usually seen in Hollywood studio films. Shot on location in neighborhoods closed to outsiders, the film is distinguished by its gritty realism. Working within its genre conventions, the film features spectacular moments of violence and physical action. Yet *Training Day* is also distinguished by the film noir elegance of its framing, editing, and lighting design, which focus attention on the emotional and ethical conflicts disclosed by performances in the film. From the moment we are introduced to Alonzo Harris (Denzel Washington) and Jake Hoyt (Ethan Hawke), the film creates tension by keeping the characters constantly on the move in a story that takes place in one day. The film increases that tension by keeping Alonzo and Jake penned in by their surroundings. Some of the film's most searing dramatic conflicts are played out, not in the open or when the characters are on the move, but when Washington and Hawke are confined by the interior of Alonzo's black Monte Carlo automobile, or the small, dark living room of Alonzo's Vietnam War buddy, or the heavily fortressed apartment complex where Alonzo keeps his mistress, young child, and reserves of weapons and cash.[26]

Training Day is one of many films in which Denzel Washington reconfigures "the concept of classic movie stardom."[27] Washington had already collected an Academy Award for Best Supporting Actor for his performance in *Glory* (Edward Zwick, 1989); for his depiction of rogue narcotics officer Alonzo Harris, Washington received the Academy Award for Best Actor, with Ethan Hawke getting a Best Supporting Actor nomination. Washington's performance also earned him the Golden Globe Award for Best Actor in a Motion Picture Drama, the American Film Institute Actor of the Year Award (Male, Film Category), and best-actor awards from film societies across the United States. Writing about his portrayal, critics noted that "Washington plays Alonzo like a con man with a one-two punch" who has a "confident stream of palaver but always a hidden agenda."[28] Touching on performance elements that we will examine in detail, reviewer Bob Graham observed that Alonzo/Washington "disarms the neophyte with a joke and then punches home his real point."[29]

While there is no evidence Washington and Hawke used Laban principles to develop their characterizations, the Laban system provides a coherent set of terms for analyzing (1) the spatial aspects of the actors' movements, (2) the temporal dimensions of their movements, (3) the weight or strength that infuses their movements, and (4) the contrast between the energy flow in Washington's and Hawke's portrayals. Laban terms help one pinpoint the *direction* and *speed* of their movements, as well as the *degree of resistance* and *degree of control.* Laban's taxonomy prompts one to identify *direct* and *flexible* movements, *sudden* and *sustained* gestures, *strong* and *light* expressions, and *bound* versus *free* movements. Laban terms enhance performance analysis because they highlight the expressive qualities of actors' choices that are revealed by the relationship of expressions, gestures, and movements to space, time, weight, and flow.

Spatial aspects
Place, direction, shape of movement
Direct versus flexible or indirect movement

Temporal aspects
Speed and rhythm of movement
Sudden versus sustained movement

Weight/strength
Degree of resistance to gravity
Strong versus light movement

Energy flow
Degree of control of movement
Bound versus free-flowing movement

Early in the film, streetwise cop Alonzo Harris and novice narcotics officer Jake Hoyt meet in a greasy diner. Although the film opens with brief scenes of Jake starting his day at home with his wife and infant child, the scene in the diner is the first time audiences see Alonzo and Jake interact. The two actors' gestures and expressions establish a clear contrast between their characters. Washington's movements are direct, whereas Hawke's are flexible. The irregular rhythm of Washington's movements has a sudden quality, while Hawke's regular rhythm often makes his movements seem more sustained. Washington's performance is marked by strong movements, but Hawke's are lighter. Washington's portrayal features tightly bound movement, whereas Hawke uses free-flowing physicality to represent Jake. These contrasts appear in the opening seconds of the scene. As Hawke blithely enters the diner, he uses a light and free-flowing gait. Washington is already in a secure position for the confrontation, his posture strong and bound.

Consider the spatial dimension of their performances. The contrast between Alonzo and Jake emerges from the actors' movement placement (high or low space), direction (forward, backward, side-to-side, or diagonal movement), and shape (curved, linear, spiral, or circular movement). Once the two men sit opposite one another, Washington maintains a lower, more guarded plane than Hawke, whose body flutters and squirms throughout the scene. In addition, Washington moves forward several times during the scene, darting, almost lunging at Hawke, who is confined to awkward side-to-side movements during the encounter. He sometimes even glances away as if looking for a way to escape.

Washington also uses linear movements, pointing at Hawke, placing his hands on the table in straight, even lines, whilst the more circular movements of Hawke's hands and head convey the young cop's repeated attempts to catch his balance and find a safe space to land.

Washington's physical and vocal movements are much more direct than Hawke's. Each glance and hand gesture is like an arrow zinging toward a target. Washington delivers his lines *at* Hawke. When he says "Hoyt," the word comes out like a poke or a punch aimed at Hawke's belly. Washington's physical gestures and vocal expressions are focused on their point of arrival and designed to move directly toward their point of impact. When he commands Hawke to tell him a story, he turns his reading glasses into a fencing foil as he directly challenges the young man to find something entertaining to say.

Washington's use of space is economical, even restricted. His sits motionless before and after making gestures and vocal jabs that pierce the space between the two men. The directness of his gestures and line deliver-

In *Training Day,* the novice, Ethan Hawke, uses a light, free-flowing gait that contrasts with the strong, bound position of the veteran cop, Denzel Washington

ies establish that Alonzo pays close attention to potential threats. In this initial meeting with his new partner, the veteran officer carefully observes how the young man deals with his attacks.

By comparison, Hawke uses indirect physical and vocal gestures to convey the rookie's ignorance. Where Washington transforms the diner booth into a bunker from which he fires direct shots, Hawke blunders about, squeezed into his side of the booth. Early on, Hawke glances about, his attention scattered around the room, as if he has discovered he is exposed and on display. As Washington continues to challenge him, Hawke turns to a series of light, indirect gestures: he twiddles his thumbs, glances down, licks his lips, and taps his thigh. His eyelids flutter, his words come out in a breathy rush, he breaks into smiles, gasps in moments in surprise, and drops into stunned, hollow-cheeked stares. Throughout the scene, Hawke moves his shoulders in a flexible, wavelike fashion and continually shifts his weight, never really coming to rest.

Hawke's unbalanced gestures show that Hoyt does not see Alonzo as a threat, but instead as someone whose attention he must get. In contrast to Washington, who uses his hands, arms, and shoulders as a forceful coordinated unit, Hawke often uses his right hand in flimsy, isolated gestures to embellish his statements. While these feathery moves might catch Alonzo's eye, they are rookie mistakes because they leave Hoyt unguarded. Still, Hawke's performance conveys the sense that Hoyt is not without resources. In this first confrontation, Hoyt is outmatched; Hawke's elastic and uneven movements suggest that Hoyt is smart enough to know that direct responses would lead to more trouble. His flexible movements show that Hoyt understands he has to get his bearings. Hawke's flexible movements establish character traits that will become more visible as the narrative develops; over the course of the film Hoyt emerges as someone who will take the time to assess situations in ways Alonzo does not.

The temporal dimension of the actors' characterizations creates that same impression. Washington's gestures and expressions are marked by an irregular rhythm. Variable temporal patterns arise from his gestures and vocal expressions that have unexpected shifts in tempo. When Hawke arrives, Washington casually tosses out the order to "get some chow," but within seconds he presses out the command, "Tell me a story," then he drops his voice as he adds, "Hoyt." His smooth chuckle over Hoyt's female training officer shifts suddenly to the single shout "Boom" that causes Hawke to flinch and throw up his hands in defense. Delighted that he caught the young man so off guard, Washington breaks into a grin and points at Hawke, who keeps his hands up as if under arrest.

Changes in the temporal rhythm of Washington's performance might be the most salient feature of the scene that marks the beginning of the daylong test that Jake endures and that proves to be too much for Alonzo. In their initial meeting, the irregular tempo in Washington's gestures and expressions show that Alonzo is determined to keep any and all challengers off balance. In contrast, Hawke portrays Jake as a character who depends on regular, almost metric movements. As the rookie cop who begins his training day playing very much by the rules, Jake attempts to engage in social interaction structured by the regular temporal patterns of conventional gesture-sign behavior. As Hawke squirms in his seat while Washington reads his newspaper, he injects his remarks, "It's nice here," and "Won't mind not roasting in a hot black and white all summer," at such regular intervals it sounds as if he is following a script of conventional social interaction. Jake's predictable rhythm makes him completely vulnerable to Alonzo, who uses irregular temporal movements that keep Jake reeling.

The contrasting rhythm in Washington's and Hawke's performances becomes even more pronounced when considered in relation to other temporal aspects of their portrayals. Throughout the scene, Washington's gestures and line deliveries are marked by accelerating movements that are executed in short durations. That combination is visible when he snaps his newspaper taut, taps the pistols in his shoulder holster together, and abruptly replaces a smooth flow of dialogue with sharp, minced words punched out at Hawke. Without warning, he will suddenly raise an eyebrow, drop into a whisper, or fix Hawke in a cold stare. The unexpected quality of his movements estab-

Ethan Hawke's high, side-to-side, and circular gestures convey Jake's off-balance attempts to escape and then gain a foothold in the confrontation with Washington

Denzel Washington's direct, linear gestures pierce the space between the two men

Washington literally pokes fun at Hawke, who still registers his shock that Washington suddenly shouted "boom" just as Hawke began his "most entertaining" story

lishes that Alonzo thinks quickly and reacts instantly. As the story progresses, one can see that Alonzo is also a man who sometimes acts too hastily.

Working in temporal counterpoint, Hawke uses gestures and line deliveries marked by decelerating movements completed over longer durations that suggest a sustained quality.[30] The sustained feature of Hawke's performance becomes more dominant over the course of the scene. With a glazed look coming into his eyes, Hawke puts longer and longer pauses between his words and phrases. He replaces his nervous glances with open-eyed stares at Washington. His increasingly decelerating movements of longer duration convey the idea that, while Jake begins as a hopeful, even cocky, young officer, by the end of the scene he has been reduced to a stunned novice.

The difference between the weight and degree of resistance in the actors' movements deepens the impression that the characters have very different temperaments. The contrast also clarifies the trajectory of the scene, which ends with a decisive win for the seasoned combatant in round one of the characters' training day matchup. Washington's strong movements, which emerge from an inner reserve of energy and determination, establish Alonzo as someone who has learned to anticipate resistance to his objectives. His voice deep and full, Washington shows that Alonzo enjoys his role of authority. Strong movements, which fight against the downward pull of gravity, reveal that the veteran has a clearly defined objective in his initial meeting with the novice. As Washington's movements become stronger over the course of the scene, Alonzo's immediate and long-term intention to dominate the bright young rookie is made visible.

Even at the beginning of the scene, Washington's strong, forceful movements contrast with Hawke's light, untethered gestures and expressions. Hawke's weightless movements lack energy and determination. They establish that Jake's comparatively protected life has led him to expect that other people will indulge or yield to him. The light, unfocused kinetic force in Hawke's movement creates the impression that the rookie does not have a clear objective in his first meeting with his superior officer. Weightless, without a center, Hawke loses affect as the scene goes on. After Washington dismisses his story about arresting the drug dealer on his way to kill someone, the energy drains out of Hawke's eyes, face, and body. He becomes like a limp flag barely waving in the breeze, more and more lifeless as Alonzo takes the wind out of Jake's sails.

The contrast disclosed by the different weight that informs Washington's and Hawke's movements is equally visible in the flow or control of movement in their respective performances. The movement flow in Washington's performance falls into the category that Laban describes as bound. Starting the confrontation from a compressed position of readiness, Washington keeps his chin down and his eyes steadily focused on Hawke. He presses his lips together when he speaks and, with the expression in his eyes constantly changing, he retains an impassive facial expression. Throughout the scene, the controlled quality of Washington's performance creates the impression that his "action can be stopped at any given moment."[31] Like actors whose performances are influenced by traditions in Japanese Noh theater, the controlled flow of movement in Washington's performance conveys a sense of fluency even in moments of rest. These periods, for example, when Alonzo ignores Jake by silently studying his morning newspaper, signal occasions when the veteran is controlling his movement to the utmost.[32]

Jean Newlove explains that pauses in bound movement "can occur for a variety of reasons": a character might sense an error, discover a need to adjust an approach, or find a reason to put a particular action on hold.[33] In the initial encounter between Alonzo and Jake, there are several instances when the streetwise officer suspends movement as he shifts strategies to overpower the untrained rookie. For example, Washington pauses for a moment when reading the newspaper fails to keep Hawke quiet and Alonzo has to find another way to dominate the young man. Similarly, when Hawke finishes his entertaining story, Washington holds very still again, this time figuring out how to deflate Jake's pride for having served justice.

In contrast, Hawke's free-flowing movements reveal the rookie's vulnerability and convey the sense that young Jake approaches life without expecting errors or the need to adjust.[34] When he first arrives, Hawke swoops into the booth opposite Washington. He moves without hesitation into his story about his arrest that prevented a murder. He keeps smiling and extending himself throughout the confrontation, hesitating only after Washington has beaten him down. Unprepared for and outmatched by someone who stays on guard, in this first round Jake loses more energy and more ground each time Alonzo disrupts the young man's free flow of movement.

CONTRASTING "EFFORTS" IN *TRAINING DAY*

Specific combinations of spatial, temporal, and weight qualities in the players' movements also reveal the logic of their respective acting choices. Laban referred to these combinations as *efforts*. While in everyday usage the term suggests actions that require a substantial commitment or use of energy, in Laban Movement Analysis *effort* designates the inner impulse revealed by an expression, gesture, or movement.[35] Through study, Laban and his collaborators located eight basic efforts: pressing, thrusting, wringing, slashing, gliding, dabbing, floating, and flicking.

	Sustained	*Sudden*
Strong and direct	Press (crush, cut, squeeze)	Thrust (shove, punch, poke)
Strong and indirect	Wring (pull, pluck, stretch)	Slash (beat, throw, whip)
Light and direct	Glide (smooth, smear, smudge)	Dab (pat, tap, shake)
Light and indirect	Float (strew, stir, stroke)	Flick (flip, flap, jerk)

This rubric facilitates nuanced descriptions of acting choices, for even in its simplest formulation the system identifies variations of the eight basic efforts.[36] For instance, if the *weight* or strength of a pressing movement is more visible than its direct and sustained aspects, it becomes a crushing movement. If pressing's *direct* quality is emphasized more than the strong or sustained qualities, it becomes a cutting movement. If its *sustained* quality is more pronounced than the strength and directness of the move, then pressing becomes a squeezing movement. Similarly, a shove is more weighted than a thrust; a punch is more direct than a thrust; a poke is more sudden than a thrust. At the opposite extreme, a flipping gesture is lighter than a flick; a flapping movement is more flexible than a flick; a jerking movement is more sudden than a flick. In the diner scene, Washington's series of strong, direct, and sudden physical and vocal expressions can be described as variations of thrusting, shoving, punching, and poking movements. By comparison, Hawke's light and indirect movements seem to alternate between forms of floating and flicking.

The qualities of physical and vocal expression in the first confrontation between Alonzo and Jake make the scene a clash between distinct and opposing characters, and distinguish the actors' performances throughout the film. Subsequent scenes maintain and amplify the structural opposition between the strong, direct, and sudden qualities in Washington's performance and the light, indirect qualities that infuse Hawke's. Throughout the film,

Washington's acting choices suggest that Alonzo will never be satisfied with anything less than all-out victory over every challenger. He is always fighting against space, time, and gravity. In scene after scene, he uses advancing movements, gestures that expand into the space around him, and line readings marked by increasing speed, pressure, and directness.

By comparison, Hawke's acting choices reveal Jake as someone who would be satisfied with a draw. Throughout the film, his flexible, light, and often sustained movements indulge the forces of space, time, and gravity. Even in moments of tension, his line readings often feature diminishing speed, pressure, and directness. In scene after scene, when responding to Washington's advancing and widening movements, Hawke will usually move so that he takes up less and less space. The contrasting qualities in their acting choices can be described in terms of the efforts made visible by Washington's and Hawke's movements, gestures, and vocal and physical expressions.

The contrasting efforts that infuse their performances come to light even in passing moments. For example, when Alonzo and Jake are about to leave the apartment where Alonzo's son and mistress (Eva Mendez) live, Alonzo takes a moment to check in with the boy. Alonzo, who is seated next to the child with his shoulder holster on, shows almost no affection. The only display is the sudden, direct, light dabbing or tapping gesture that Washington uses to transfer a kiss from his hand to the boy's head. By comparison, moments before we saw Hawke and the boy asleep next to one another on the couch. There is a floating quality to the image of the youths napping on the sofa. That impression is carried over into the sustained, flexible, and light qualities of Hawke's sleepy movements when Washington prods him with his gun to wake up.

The qualities of the actors' efforts also disclose the developing stages of the opposition between Alonzo and Jake in the important pair of scenes that involve the well-connected drug dealer Roger (Scott Glenn). In the first scene with the three characters, the gentle calm suggested by the morning light belies the sinister nature of Alonzo's plan to make the rookie cop an accessory to crimes that will eliminate the threat that Roger, Alonzo's longtime drug contact, might pose to the veteran who operates on both sides of the law. The calm also establishes a contrast with the chilling afternoon raid on Roger's bungalow that will cause Jake to become an enemy Alonzo cannot afford to leave alive.

The scene begins with Alonzo and Roger exchanging a boisterous greeting. The thrusting, punching, and poking movements that Washington and Glenn use convey the characters' need to demonstrate their strength and their ability to keep opponents off balance. In the first part of the scene, Glenn pokes his words at Washington as Roger hints that his own access to high-level city officials gives him an advantage over Alonzo. Washington reveals that Alonzo is antagonized by the taunt but that he elects to remain guarded; he responds by pressing himself deeper into the huge leather chair that serves as his latest bunker.

When Roger turns his attention to Jake, who sits opposite the two veterans and remains dazed from the PCP Alonzo had forced him at gunpoint to smoke, the young man's floating vulnerability prompts the cagey drug dealer to become less guarded. As he talks to Hawke, Glenn removes the bathrobe he has been wearing over his undershirt and trousers. His line readings become colored by dabbing, patting, and tapping qualities as he questions Jake and discovers that he had been a star defensive player on a local high-school football team. His voice light and direct, Glenn explains, "I follow all the good players." In another situation, he might pat the young man on the shoulder.

The gentle quality of Glenn's gestures changes suddenly when he is interrupted by a phone call. Tightening his voice and body, he punches out instructions to a drug contact in trouble. He quickly hangs up the phone, returning immediately to the softer, more relaxed movements he used when focused on Jake. Then, as if responding to Washington's long silence during the various interactions, Glenn quickly shifts his attention to include Washington. Roger knows that Alonzo's botched drug deal in Las Vegas has put both of them at risk; he now suspects that Alonzo has gotten in over his head. Getting down to the business of telling Alonzo to change his ways, Glenn's voice becomes colored once again by strong, direct, and sudden poking qualities as he tells an allegorical story about a determined snail who does not know when to quit.

When Glenn finishes the story, Washington dismisses it but Hawke bursts out laughing and then suddenly stops himself. With his voice squeezing into a whimper, Hawke says, "It's not funny." He then rubs his head and stares blankly in front of him. The sudden revelation of Jake's complete confusion prompts Glenn to give him a wink. The quick dabbing movement brings the young cop over to his side and encourages Jake to share what he has learned about life, namely, that people need to protect their smiles and cries. The simple, genuine quality of Jake's insight touches Roger and causes him to drop his guard, even though he should have seen that the story prompted Alonzo to raise his defenses.

Moments later, Alonzo seizes that opportunity. With Washington controlling his movements so that they approximate the dabbing quality that now infuses Glenn's interactions with both cops, Alonzo gets Roger to reveal what he plans to do now that Alonzo has put their futures in jeopardy. With Roger still thinking about Jake's childlike insight, he casually volunteers the information that he plans to retire soon, forgetting that Alonzo knows retiring kingpins often secure their immunity by exposing others' crimes. In this seemingly unimportant moment, Roger becomes vulnerable to Alonzo. Reflecting that new dynamic, as the scene closes, Glenn's gestures become lighter and more flexible while Washington's become stronger and more direct.

Alonzo and Jake return to Roger's house later that afternoon, with an arrest warrant and Alonzo's hand-picked, fully armed team of narcotics officers. The story's pivotal confrontation between the streetwise cop and the novice begins the moment Jake turns down Alonzo's offer to share in the financial spoils of the raid. Hawke's light, offhand declining to participate in what is presented as standard undercover procedure sets off Washington's sustained gliding gestures that quickly increase the tension as Alonzo raises the stakes and tells Jake he has to kill Roger. To convey Alonzo's increasing pressure on Jake, Washington uses stronger pressing movements. In response, Hawke shifts to strong, sustained, but flexible wringing movements. He then conveys Jake's need to defuse the horrible tension of the moment: using a strong slashing movement, Jake/Hawke suddenly pretends to fire a gun at Roger/Glenn.

Jake's sudden gesture prompts Alonzo to shift plans again. Without warning, he grabs the shotgun, kills Roger, and then frames Jake for the killing. When Jake quietly but firmly resists this new plan, Alonzo ups the stakes again by threatening to kill Jake. In these moments, Washington communicates Alonzo's unwavering determination by using increasingly stronger crushing gestures and vocal expressions. Hawke conveys Jake's newfound resolve through the quality of his movements—sustained wringing suddenly gives way to slashing movements that allow him to take the shotgun from Washington. When Hawke turns the shotgun on Washington, Washington's repertoire of pressing, cutting, and crushing vocal expressions equals and then overcomes Hawke's strong, sustained, but flexible wringing movements. Jake backs off, and Alonzo lives to fight Jake later that evening.

Laban terms and concepts allow one to see the strong, direct pressing and thrusting movements that mark Washington's performance. When Alonzo works to keep an opponent off balance, Washington uses sudden and off-speed gestures and expressions. Sometimes, he will diminish the pressure of his movements so that they become lighter and more disarming. However, in confrontations that prompt Alonzo to take complete control of the people around him, Washington uses increasingly stronger gestures and expressions that have a pressing and then a crushing quality. By the end of the film, the constant fighting against space, time, and gravity leaves Alonzo depleted of energy, and finally vulnerable to attack.

Giving physical expression to the opposite scenario, Hawke's performance features light and flexible floating movements that shift into light but direct dabbing or gliding movements when Jake engages in philosophical conversation with the men of experience. In moments when Jake finds it absolutely necessary to resist Alonzo's control, Hawke shifts from light floating movements to strong wringing and slashing movements. The film uses the contrast between Washington and Hawke to show that Jake, whose movements are not constantly fighting against space, time, and gravity, can call on a reserve of energy when he eventually decides to rise up against Alonzo. That energy not only allows him to remain morally upright in the face of Alonzo's threatening and alluring advances, but also makes it possible for Jake to return home at the end of the day, ultimately outlasting Alonzo in the daylong battle of wills.

TEMPORAL-SPATIAL PERFORMANCES IN FILM

In addition to illuminating the qualities that infuse actors' performance choices, Laban taxonomies clarify key principles of movement. One concerns the difference between human movement and the motion of inanimate objects that have no "inner aspect."[37] In cinema, both provide information about characters but in entirely different ways. Film audiences indeed make inferences about characters based on the motion of objects. For example, watching the famous car chase in *The French Connection* (William Friedkin, 1971) one deduces that Popeye Doyle (Gene Hackman) will do whatever it takes to succeed, but that does not involve attributing intention, thought, or feeling to the car, of course. By comparison, in film and everyday life, human movement is a window into individuals' thoughts, feelings, attitudes, and temperaments. Laban explains that movement reveals inner experience because "even the most minute [human movement or] exertion demands some kind of effort."[38] In addition, even when effort is unconscious and involuntary, it is "always present in any bodily movement."[39] By comparison, "no inanimate object can make an effort."[40] Thus, audiences learn about characters indirectly by considering the motion of inanimate objects, but directly by examining the efforts that infuse human movement and vocal expression.

With its rubrics for analyzing the *process* of human movement, the Laban system facilitates insight into the things audiences watch when they watch screen performance: movements, gestures, and expressions with specific spatial, temporal, and energetic qualities that are combined to create meaningful sequences. It illuminates the qualitative features of the endlessly changing gestures, expressions, and intonations viewers find in films. Laban taxonomies enhance analysis of the connotations carried by the qualities of actors' physical and vocal expressions. Such qualities cannot be accurately represented by "a series of snapshots," even though publicity stills might suggest that impressions about film characters are based on single images of frozen motion, and even though confusion between inanimate motion and human movement might lead people to imagine that interpretations arise from perception of motion rather than apperception of human movements that have specific spatial and temporal qualities.[41]

As the case study indicates, Laban Movement Analysis directs attention to "actual movement, rather than its completed result."[42] That focus is crucial to studies of screen performance because the meaning of a gesture is not disclosed by a still image but instead is best understood by analyzing the movement as it exists in space and time. Cinema studies already recognize that films convey meaning through the positioning of figures in cinematic space; Laban Movement Analysis can clarify the way films convey meaning through the spatial and temporal dimensions of performance.

The profound meaningfulness of film actors' gestures and expressions might have escaped notice because of certain Western ideas about movement itself. Vera Maletic points out that in the seventeenth century, René Descartes saw movement as "a purely mechanical act which belongs to the realm of bodies, completely separate from the world of intelligent minds."[43] However, publications in the twentieth century by Edmund Husserl, Maurice Merleau-Ponty, Laban, and others challenged that view, proposing instead that movement should be seen as a way to discern "the intent of human action."[44] Merleau-Ponty sees human movement as a process that involves aiming at things through one's body.[45] The notion that film acting is produced by mechanical reproduction conforms to seventeenth-century Cartesian views of movement. By comparison, reckoning with the meaningfulness of actors' movement on screen is consistent with the vision of human movement articulated by phenomenologists such as Husserl, Merleau-Ponty, and Laban. A post-Cartesian conception of movement also leads one to see cinema not simply as a recording medium or visual art or mass media form, but also as a dramatic art form in which performances have spatial and temporal dimensions.

Structural studies in cinema have already explored the temporal dimension of film narratives. Gérard Genette's structural approach to literature has provided a model for work that examines the temporal flow of narrative information, especially how the order, duration, and frequency of elements help to establish the primary voice in a film as well as its more subliminal mood.[46] The temporal dimension of acting can be analyzed by drawing on Laban's work. His structural approach to movement demonstrates that order, duration, frequency, accent, and counterpoint are basic features of movement as well.

Genette's approach to narrative considers five factors. These include (1) order, that is, the order of scenes; (2) duration, the time given to individual characters and story elements; (3) frequency, the number of times an element of the story is presented; (4) voice, the character who takes readers or audiences through the story and provides the clearest voice or literal point of view; and (5) mood, the characters, circumstances, and landscapes that disclose the story's unresolved ethical dilemma, figurative point of view, and underlying mood.

Laban's work shows that these five aspects can also be found in movement. It is possible to examine (1) order, or "the regulation of tempo and duration of movements into ordered sets"; (2) duration, to determine "how long it takes to complete a movement, or set of movements"; (3) the frequency of movement elements that determines how quickly a "movement phrase is complete"; (4) the voice or accent that conveys the "strongest and most significant movements in a movement phrase"; and (5) the mood or counterpoint movements that reveal "two or more contrasting sets of time elements existing simultaneously, either within one person's movement, or between two or more people."[47]

Genette's structural approach to literature and Laban's structural approach to movement are both grounded in musical terms and concepts. While it seems that the musical dimension of Genette's approach has not drawn a lot of attention, students of Laban have explored the connection between musical theory and movement analysis. In the 1950s, training in the Laban system at the Art of Movement Studio in Manchester, England led Warren Lamb to see the eight efforts as akin to "eight notes of music" one could combine "in an unlimited number of ways."[48] More recently, movement experts such as Carol-Lynne Moore and Kaoru Yamamoto have proposed that movement is like music because it too "combines a sequential melodic line of single notes sounded over time with a simultaneous harmonic structure of many tones being sounded together."[49]

Following Laban's example, contemporary movement experts see a crucial difference between human movement and language, which consists of basic elements that must be arranged in certain ways to build up sequences that finally have meaning.[50] Movement is less like language than like visual art, which can create an "instantaneous, global, and complex" nonverbal impression.[51] Closely related to musical compositions, human movement features successive development and simultaneous effects.[52] Like a musical composition, a sequence of movement "can only be appreciated as the piece sequentially progresses through time to its ending."[53]

Movement experts believe that music provides "many useful concepts, such as harmony, rhythm, dynamics, scales, and chords" that contribute to movement analysis, but that human gestures and expressions require analysis grounded in the recognition that "only movement *is* movement."[54] Echoing insights into human gesture articulated by Delsarte and Ekman, Laban and others have found that human movements can convey "multiple meanings, some that are pan-human, others that are culture-specific, and still others that are singularly individualistic."[55] Like the Prague school's work on interactions between conventional gesture-signs and individual gesture-expressions, research by Laban and others demonstrates that human movement is meaningful because it "is at once natural *and* contrived, visceral *and* symbolic, personal *and* social, ever present *and* constantly disappearing."[56] Screen acting, which features movements that become meaningful in cinematic time and space, becomes legible when considered through these semiotic and structural approaches that reckon with the complexity of human expression, gesture, and movement.

CONCLUSIONS

Laban Movement Analysis facilitates study that seeks to understand the connotations conveyed by actors' physical and vocal expressions. As earlier discussions suggest, those connotations are not accurately represented by even a series of snapshots. Kuleshov's initial experiment showed that the connotations of a single image are often different from connotations suggested by images in motion pictures. Our discussion of "iconic" and "ostensive" signs in *City Lights* also shows that the picture or single image of Chaplin resting on his cane might suggest nonchalance but that when seen in the context of the Tramp's encounter with the sculpture of the female nude, the moment is actually one of intense focus and tightly bound erotic energy (see chapters 2 and 4).

Addressing aspects of performance touched on in the discussion of tableaux in *City Lights* and the limp-then energized gunfighters in *The Magnificent Seven,* the analysis of *Training Day* highlights the fact that acting often features sequences of movement marked by what Laban termed alternating rhythms of stability/mobility and exertion/recuperation. Employing rubrics developed by Laban, the case study of *Training Day* shows that characterizations are crafted through the specific spatial design of movements and gestures, their place of origination in the body, and the energy quality in actors' movements, gestures, and expressions. Laban taxonomies of goal-directed human movement illuminate the expressive qualities of movement that become visible in relation to space, time, weight, and flow. Rather than starting performance analysis each time from scratch, one can begin by asking if an actor's movement through space is primarily direct or flexible, whether a certain gesture or line delivery is sudden or sustained, whether a movement is light or strong, whether the flow of movement in an actor's portrayal is bound or free.

Laban rubrics make it possible to locate the underlying efforts that color the movements, gestures, and physical and vocal expressions in film performances. As the study of *Training Day* reveals, Laban terms allow one to see that even on screen, "human movement involves not merely a change of position, but also a change in the activation and involvement of the body and in the quantity and quality of energy necessary to effect the motion."[57] Laban Movement Analysis can illuminate the inner impulse in actors' movements and clarify their spatial and temporal dimensions, their strength and flow. It provides a system of terms for describing the interactions between performance elements that lead to distinct and contrasting characterizations. Building on this chapter's analysis of goal-directed movement facilitated by Laban taxonomies, the next uses principles of script analysis developed by Stanislavsky to show how actors' gestures and expressions communicate the conflicts and evolving interactions between characters in a scene.

CHAPTER NINE

STANISLAVSKY: PLAYERS' ACTIONS AS A WINDOW INTO CHARACTERS' INTERACTIONS

Crafting film performances often begins with script analysis that reckons with four fundamental elements: the characters' "given circumstances"; the "objectives" they seek to achieve; the "actions" they take to attain their goals; and the "beats" or units of action that reveal the string of tactics characters use to reach their objectives.[1] This chapter draws on these principles to discuss acting choices in a completed scene from *The Grifters* (Stephen Frears, 1990). Focusing on the final confrontation between Lilly (Anjelica Huston) and her son Roy (John Cusack), the case study shows how players' actions communicate emotional dynamics in the scene and the changing relations of power between the characters. This study uses terms from script analysis to describe the fictional interaction made visible by the actors' performances. It shows how the actors' gestures and expressions function as "ostensive signs" that affect viewers' sense of the characters' respective situations, their diametrically opposed goals, and their increasingly desperate strategies to get what they need.

Interpreting action is often fundamental to encounters with fictional characters. In his structural analysis of literature, Roland Barthes argues that action is the central principle in narrative; characters' actions are not simply "trifling acts," but in fact make the narrative possible.[2] By defining literary sequences in terms of action, Barthes's structural approach to fictional narrative shares common ground with dramatic theories. Since Aristotle, action has also been placed at the heart of dramatic literature. Moreover, in the embodied art of acting, action becomes a central expressive tool for players whose performances convey interactions between fictional characters. Stanislavsky identifies action as "what the actor does to solve the problem or fulfill the task set before his or her character by the play."[3] At base, actors "take action," a literal translation of the word that Stanislavsky uses for the actor's main function during performance. In film and theater, action is thus a fundamental organizing principle in both the narrative and the physical realization of the narrative.

Following this line of thought, Stanislavsky finds drama's core dynamic in the "event" produced when "contradictory" actions of various characters clash. His last, most innovative approach to performance, called "Active Analysis" in Russia, explores "actions" that collide with "counteractions" to produce "events" that become the focal point of script analysis for actors.

Throughout his career, Stanislavsky connected action with the basic duality of acting as an art form (see chapter 7). For him, dramatic action is always both "inner" (mental, psychological, spiritual) and "outer" (physical and vocal, rhythmic and expressive). He taught players to seek actions that are "apt" in relationship to the character's circumstances (as "given" by both text and production decisions) and that follow each other "logically" and "consecutively" in relationship to how the script and production develop the story. Stanislavsky's work suggests a series of interrelated, analytical questions for actors and directors to explore as they seek to physicalize a written scene. The following list provides an overview of such questions, using the language of Active Analysis.

1. What is the context of the scene (its sequence in the play, its place in the story) and the characters' backgrounds (their historical, social, and personal experiences)? In other words, what are the *given circumstances*?
2. Which aspects of the script are *fixed clues* to its potential performance? In other words, what textual details (visual descriptions, word choices, style, tone, etc.) must the production and performances honor?
3. Which aspects are *open clues* to potential performance, allowing for interpretation?
4. Is the scene *emblematic* (representing action that has occurred before in the characters' fictional lives, as, for example, sibling skirmishes) or *historical* (representing action that has never happened before and thus moves the story further along)?

Questions 1 through 4 establish overall aspects of the scene and condition answers to the questions below.

5. Who impels the scene forward toward its *main event*? What does this character *do* to make the scene happen (an active verb)? This verb describes the scene's *impelling action*.
6. Who resists this action forward? What does this character *do* to resist (an active verb)? This verb describes the *counteraction*. What is the quality of resistance (*direct* or *oblique*)?

Questions 5 and 6 define the scene's primary *conflict* and condition its *main event*.

7. What is the *main action* in the scene (persuading, pleading, attacking, confessing, proposing, or teasing, etc.)? What is its *main event* (a farewell, forgiveness, etc.)?
8. Is the scene primarily *active* (with characters creating new situations) or *reactive* (with characters coming to grips with circumstances)?
9. Is there an *activity* (setting the table, watching television, packing one's bags for a trip, etc.) that forms a physical context for the *main action*?
10. Does the scene reach a *point of resolution*? In other words, does an *event* occur as a consequence of which characters need to change their actions and counteractions?

Questions 7 through 10 seek to uncover the underlying dynamics of interaction in the scene and hence its *subtext*.

For Stanislavsky, discrete units of action serve as the building blocks for story and scenes. Each new "bit" (as he called these units) begins whenever the strategy of taking action or the action itself shifts. In the United States, actors generally call these segments "beats," a term that most likely derives from the Russian pronunciation of "bits" by émigré teachers. While the term "is widely misunderstood to mean changes in mood, or pauses, or something to do with the pace or tempo-rhythm of the scene," it actually only concerns logical units of developing action.[4] For Stanislavsky, when actors identify the bits of a scene, they discover the structural dynamics that undergird their future performance.

Playwrights and screenwriters sometimes use *beat* to indicate a pause in the action or dialogue. However, speaking to screenwriters, Denny Martin Flinn points out, "There is no such thing as (a beat) and using this within dialogue because you want the actor to pause is incorrect."[5] Flinn explains that "a beat is an actor's term, and has nothing to do with timing," even though there are instances when shifts between character/player actions can be suggested by a pause.[6] In *Training Day,* Denzel Washington sometimes pauses when Alonzo shifts tactics (see chapter 8). The study of the scene in *The Grifters* will also reveal that the actors sometimes pause as one character/actor changes tactic and causes one unit of action to change into another.

While Stanislavsky is indeed concerned with pauses and with physical and vocal rhythms, he does not use *bit* as a directive or even as a descriptive term for them, but rather as a structural device to mark the shifts in action and interaction that construct a performance. His actual use of musical metaphor is more global and interesting. He sees dramatic texts as "scores of action" that suggest potential physical performance, in much the same way that written musical scores notate the potential sound for music. Like the orchestral conductor, the director keeps the performers playing in synchronicity.[7]

For Stanislavsky, the words of a text, like the notes in music, lay out an outline for performance to be completed through the interpretive and physical work of the actors. Thus, script analysis is one of the foundational aspects of actor training. Stanislavsky's work with script analysis led to a series of methods for reading and connecting with texts. Early in his career, he focused on an intellectual and imaginative analysis of the play, inviting actors and director to discuss characters and dramatic conflicts before moving into rehearsals. He called this "Cognitive Analysis" and conducted it with the actors seated around a table. In his last years, he developed the technique of Active Analysis, which allows and requires actors to test their understanding of a text by physicalizing its actions and counteractions through improvisational studies of the story from the first day of rehearsal.[8]

As noted in the opening chapter, the approach used by Hollywood actors in the 1930s and 1940s mirrors Stanislavsky's assumed primacy of text, for they too relied on scripts as scores for performance. Concurrently and in the years that followed, Stella Adler taught a script analysis course that became renowned among Method actors.[9] Adopting some of Stanislavsky's language for script analysis, she stressed the need for actors to ground their portrayal of characters in the text's given circumstances and to investigate a play's social and historical mores. Even Lee Strasberg, who emphasized actors' work on themselves as emotional instruments, rather than interpretive analysis of plays, assumed actors would begin with analysis of story and character. At the Actors Studio in New York, he often likened an actor's expert reading of a text to a doctor's reading of an x-ray.[10] Today, most training programs teach actors to read scripts analytically, teasing out the facts from which characters with imagined autobiographies can emerge. In interviews, filmmakers often point out that script analysis is the foundation for performance and all aspects of production.[11] In sum, a script is a source of information about characters and their fictional world, as well as a performance score that lays out the structures and sequences of the characters' actions and interactions.

While actors and directors study scripts to identify the dynamics of character interactions, audiences study the aural and visual details of completed films to understand these dynamics. Even though films create meaning in numerous ways, like other forms of dramatic art they convey information about characters' dispositions, aspirations, desires, and psychological complexes largely through the qualitative details of the movements, gestures, and expressions that constitute the players' observable actions. Audiences also study the actions that players perform, searching them for meaningful clues. That search proves useful precisely because "human movement is intentional . . . actions are guided and purposeful, and the intentions of the mover are made clear by the way in which a person moves."[12] Accusing actions will probably feature strong and direct movement, while flattery will likely be conveyed by gestures and vocal expressions infused with floating or dabbing qualities.

In daily life and dramatic art, when "the impelling inner action is different . . . the coloration of the movement also differs."[13] Viewers study the details of actors' physical and vocal expression to identify the actions they are performing. Based on that evidence, they make inferences about what the characters want and what they will do to satisfy their needs and desires. Audiences "discover" that a character has shifted his or her tactic because there is an observable change in the quality of the actor's gestures and expressions. Terms for the eight basic Laban "efforts" provide a useful starting point for describing the players' actions in a scene (see chapter 8). Later in the chapter, the study of performances in *The Grifters* will employ those terms along with terminology from the craft of acting that illuminates the structure of actions and counteractions.

TERMINOLOGY FROM THE CRAFT OF ACTING

Acting in narrative films is a process that generally involves the representation of fictional stories by means of recognizable human gestures, expressions, and movements. Basic considerations in script analysis can serve as touchstones to study completed scenes. As noted at the outset, the first factor concerns the given circumstances of a scene (or story). Second, each character strives to solve a certain problem in a scene (or story); often this is called the character's objective. The third consideration concerns the series of actions each character takes to achieve his or her objective. Characters change actions or tactics in response to the obstacles and resistances they encounter as they strive to realize their short- and long-range objectives. The details in actors' performances disclose characters' tactics and the moments when shifts take place; they reveal which character initiates the action and which one resists over the course of the scene. Fourth, units of action or beats emerge from the series of actions characters/actors employ. Change in the actors' gestures and expressions signals the end of one unit of action and the beginning of another, thus making the units of action detectable to the viewer. Players' actions also disclose who initiates and who resists in each unit of action. In what follows we list key considerations for studies of performance that draw on the principles of scene analysis. Script analysis considers the following components:

The *given circumstances* of the scene (or story) and for each character in the scene (or story)

Each character's *objectives* in the scene (or story), or, put more precisely, each character's *problem* as posed by the given circumstances

The targeted *actions* or *counteractions* each character undertakes to achieve his or her objective, or, put more precisely, to solve his or her problem

The *units of action* or beats that mark the sequence of actions and counteractions and the moments when characters shift the tactics they employ

Building on script analysis, studies of performance consider the following:

Each unit of action, to see which character/actor initiates the action and which one resists

How units of action are colored by the goal-directed tactics used by the actors in the scene

How a change in the quality of an actor's expressions, gestures, and movements conveys a change in the character's intended action or counteraction or a shift in tactic

Stanislavsky's vision of action and dramatic structure outlined above has become common currency in contemporary acting.[14] Two commonly used handbooks for film practitioners, *Action! Acting for Film and Television,* by Robert Benedetti, and *Directing Actors: Creating Memorable Performances for Film and Television,* by Judith Weston, reflect the widely accepted usage of Stanislavsky's terms and concepts. For example, Benedetti explains that a "purposeful action is formed when *a stimulus arouses an attitude, alternatives are considered, and a strategic choice is made that results in action directed toward an objective.*"[15] He argues that screen performance should disclose "an *inward* flow of reaction leading to a choice [that is] followed by an *outward* flow of action directed toward an objective."[16] Similarly, Weston defines the objective as "what the character wants the other character to do," and action as what characters/actors do to achieve their goals.[17] Outlining an implication of that insight, Benedetti observes, "Like people in real life, a character will usually choose an action that seems to have the best chance for success in the given circumstances, and when possible they will select a *direct* action such as persuading, demanding, cajoling, begging, and so on."[18] He adds that "when there is either an external or internal obstacle in the way of direct action, they will choose an *indirect* approach and hide their real objective beneath some other activity."[19]

In *The Grifters'* final scene, Lilly needs her son Roy to prove that he loves her, and Roy needs his mother to prove she loves him. The way each character wants the other to demonstrate love puts them into direct conflict and requires them to use direct actions of accusing, persuading, and pleading along with indirect actions such as disarming, amusing, and inspiring as they seek to achieve their objectives. As do most scenes, this one features a series of direct and indirect actions because achieving objectives is not a simple process. Benedetti explains: "As we do in life, characters will usually pursue an action until it either succeeds or fails. If it fails, they will shift to a different action."[20] Those moments of change warrant careful consideration by actors and directors; they also have importance in studies of completed scenes because any change in the players' action "can be felt as a change in the rhythm of the scene; each creates what Stanislavsky called a new 'unit of action.'"[21]

As Weston further notes, an actor often finds it helpful to create "a strong sense of need or objective and then not think about when to change action verbs, but rather let the changes come out of his interactions with the other actor."[22] Benedetti also confirms the value of actors' interaction in a scene. He argues that it "is as important for actors to agree to the phraseology of their shared action as it is for members of an orchestra to work together to fulfill the phraseology of a piece of music."[23] To create portrayals, actors search for the rhythm of the scene, "feeling where the beats change, as if they were dancing with one another."[24] That rhythm emerges from the combination of related units of action. As Benedetti explains, "a beat will not have a strong resolution since that would interrupt the momentum of the scene; rather, *the resolution of one beat begins the rising action of the next.*"[25] In sum, "Beats change when one of the characters forms a new action, causing a counteraction in the other character, thus the structure of the scene is inextricably tied to the thoughts and feelings of the characters."[26]

Making thoughts and feelings visible to audiences presents actors with one of their key challenges. Speaking to actors, Benedetti writes: "When you find a way of understanding your character's action in a way that springs naturally from their objective, you have found what actors call a *playable* action."[27] Weston acknowledges the challenge, noting that it is difficult "for producers, directors, writers, and even actors to understand and trust that if an actor commits to a playable choice rather than to a decision about vocal inflection or facial expression, the movie will be better."[28]

Understanding how difficult it is to set aside "intellectual" decisions about how a certain moment should look or sound, Weston argues that one of the film director's principal tasks is to help actors find playable actions. She explains: "Although we can't decide how to feel, we can decide what to do. This makes the verb, something that we are doing, a playable *choice* and a playable direction."[29] As Weston explains, "Using action verbs instead of adjectives is a way of approaching the emotional center of a scene in a way that is experiential and playable rather than descriptive and result-oriented."[30] By playing actions, rather than employing preselected poses, gestures, and expressions to represent moods or feelings, film actors create emotional events.

Performing actions requires players to use transitive, action verbs that have an object. As Weston notes, words like *defensive* and *angry* "are not verbs (they are adjectives). *To accuse* is an example of an action verb. It takes an object; you accuse someone else of something, of lying, of underhanded behavior, whatever."[31] Today, contemporary acting or directing manuals sometimes include lists of such action verbs. Weston's *Directing Actors* includes two different lists of action verbs. The following is Weston's short list of action verbs.

Accuse	Convince	Persuade
Beg/plead	Dazzle	Pry

Belittle	Demand	Punish
Brag	Encourage	Ridicule
Cajole	Flatter	Scrutinize
Challenge	Flirt	Seduce
Charm	Goad	Soothe
Coax	Incite	Stalk
Complain	Knife	Tease/tickle
Compliment	Nail	Warn

Action verbs are players' basic tools. Weston argues that an "excellent way to make transitions [from one unit of action to another] is to make a simple full change of action verb."[32] She points out: "If an actor changes suddenly and completely from begging to accusing, we (the audience) will know that a transition has taken place."[33] In *The Grifters,* there is a beat change when Huston suddenly shifts from seducing to attacking Cusack: one moment she kisses him; the next moment she grabs his crotch hard enough to make him flinch. Directors can communicate simply and straightforwardly with actors by using verbs. For example, a director might describe a beat change by saying: "She pleads with him all the way to here; then she punishes."[34] Action verbs help players create the "central emotional event" that should take place in each scene; they make it possible for players to communicate the sense that something "*happens* between the characters who are interacting."[35]

Actors and directors identify the scene's "event" by studying "the bits, the little sections of a scene."[36] A change in subject or discussion topic usually suggests a new unit of action. In *The Grifters,* Cusack starts a new unit of action by introducing the new and seemingly unrelated topic that he plans to "get off the grift." Generally organized into beginning, middle, and end segments, units of action are often "connected by small events or issues."[37] In addition, as the confrontation between Lilly and Roy reveals, changes are also often "punctuated by some physical movement."[38] Thus, just as actors rehearse one unit of action at a time, studies of completed scenes profit by proceeding beat by beat.

Analyzing actions and counteractions, Robert Cohen identifies a collection of threatening tactics. He notes that one "basic threat tactic is simply to dominate a situation by confidently and assuredly issuing commands"; he explains that the determined action of taking charge often "frightens people and makes them subservient and obedient."[39] Another threat tactic features overpowering actions such as huffing and puffing, setting the jaw, narrowing the eyebrows, flaunting one's size, or raising the volume of one's voice.[40] A third involves observing intently; as Cohen explains, "investigative power is an intimidating and threatening force."[41] Conclusiveness is a fourth threat tactic. Cohen notes: "a forceful person does not willingly prolong discussions; he concludes them to his benefit"; gestures and vocal expressions that indicate there is nothing more to be said often compel "silent attention, respectfulness, and adherence."[42] Huston's portrayal of Lilly features all of these threatening tactics.

Still other threatening tactics, identified by Cohen, can be found in Huston's work. Seizing the right to speak, attacking the beginning of lines, and hitting command words or the name of the person addressed are all examples of attack, a fifth type of threat.[43] Concluding a speech by demanding a response is still another type, precisely because "giving up the floor and observing the person who takes it can be a [very] powerful act."[44] "Implying a hidden arsenal" can also be used to threaten an opponent, because hidden weapons, including information or "awareness of a special talent," strengthen the person's position in relation to the opponent.[45] Cohen points out that even screaming can be a threat tactic because it shows that the character is "beyond rational control" and "beyond the restraints of reason."[46] Huston's performance in the final scene is composed largely of these eight threatening tactics.

Along with threatening tactics, Cohen groups together inducing tactics that involve "projecting onto the other person the same behavior you wish him [or her] to adopt."[47] Characters and actors often use such tactics to color their chosen actions when more direct tactics seem unwise, unnecessary, or unproductive. These strategies are distinguished by the fact that someone takes "an active part in *leading* and *guiding* the attitudes and responses" of others.[48] Cohen points out, for example, that nodding and smiling "work like a magnet" to draw the other person out.[49] These actions confirm the other person's worth because they demonstrate agreement and shared sense of values. Disarming the other person can be another inducing tactic. In daily life or acting, "openness and harmlessness" often induce the other person to adopt the same stance.[50] Lulling can induce gentle behavior in response. As Cohen notes, "soft music, euphonious sounds, and the 'love hum' of people who make soft sounds when they kiss or caress are all lulling activities which, however spontaneous, do have tactical results."[51] Amusing someone can also bring him or her into one's desired frame of mind. Cohen explains that "wit, joking, and engaging in humorous interplay are among the most wonderful induction tactics possible, since they connote a sharing of values . . . and a childlike playfulness in which union is both possible and desirable."[52] In the final confrontation between Lilly and Roy, Cusack tends to use inducing tactics such as these more often than Huston.

Cohen identifies a fifth inducing tactic in the ability of teachers, salespeople, and politicians to give "an inspiring appeal."[53] He points out that "the expression of wonder—at life, love, the theatre, the universe—and the commitment to values, ideals, causes, and people" can genuinely inspire others.[54] Similarly, flattery can be "an entirely benign and gentle act which simply means discovering the best parts of someone else and singling them out for a little praise."[55] As an effective inducing tactic, flattery gives the recipient "an expectation of improvement, and an identity to live up to."[56] Cohen notes that "frankness is a special kind of flattery [because it] is a confirmation of another's adulthood and intelligence."[57] In the final scene in *The Grifters,* Cusack's actions show that Roy needs his mother to confirm his adulthood; seeking to induce that behavior, he flatters her several times by praising her intelligence and ability. Huston's actions also reveal Lilly's need for approval, for she eventually turns to seduction, which involves using "the kind of physical behavior you want the other person to adopt."[58] The following provides a summary of Cohen's observations on threatening and inducing tactics. Threatening tactics feature actions that allow a character to:

1. Take charge: issue commands with confidence
2. Overpower: raise volume of voice, draw self to full height, and so on
3. Observe intently: watch closely, investigate for clues
4. Conclude discussion: there is nothing more to be said
5. Attack the conversation: seize the floor, emphatically call the other character by name
6. Demand a response: explicitly or by giving up the floor and watching the answer
7. Imply a hidden arsenal: weapons that are physical or psychological, e.g., information
8. Scream or throw a tantrum: show that the character is beyond restraint and reason

Inducing tactics involve actions that allow a character to:

1. Confirm the other character/actor: nod, smile, express agreement
2. Disarm: shake hands, bow head, give alluring glance

3. Lull: use gentle sounds or soft motions that soothe
4. Amuse: use jokes to let shared values emerge
5. Inspire: make an earnest appeal to the other's ideals and shared goals
6. Flatter: discover the best parts of the other character/actor and praise them
7. Be frank: confirm the other's maturity, intelligence, and so on
8. Seduce: initiate behavior that you want the other to adopt

Even though Huston's performance in the final confrontation between Lilly and Roy exemplifies threatening tactics, Huston and Cusack both strive to dominate the situation by "intimidating, frightening, or overcoming" the other.[59] They both issue commands and overpower the other with large gestures and raised voices. At different times, they observe each other intently, demand answers, and try to conclude the discussion. Both use verbal attack actions: Huston punches out the name "Roy"; Cusack slashes out the word "listen." As the scene reaches its conclusion, Lilly's use of sexual allure as a weapon conveys her increasingly desperate determination to make Roy give her the thousands of dollars he has carefully saved from his career as a small-time con artist who always works alone.

However, both actors also use inducing tactics at various points in the scene. They begin with strategies that suggest agreement and mutual support. Cusack opens with soothing tones designed to lull Huston into a calm and complacent state. Early in the scene, Huston lowers her eyes and head to suggest vulnerability and thus disarm Cusack. Later, Lilly makes passing attempts to amuse and gently trifle with Roy. Several times during the confrontation, Roy tries to inspire, flatter, and speak frankly with Lilly.

In a completed scene, the spatial, temporal, and energy qualities of the actors' actions provide the evidence for such assessments. Put in the simplest terms, Huston's and Cusack's strong movements (pressing, punching, and slashing) convey the characters' threatening tactics, while their light movements (gliding, dabbing, and flicking) convey the characters' inducing tactics. For example, when Huston's performance is marked by strong, direct, and sudden gestures, one infers that Lilly is demanding something from Roy. When she shoves, thrusts, and punches her words across the room at Cusack, Lilly clearly goes on the attack. When Cusack uses light, direct, and sudden gestures, he creates the impression that Roy tries gently to disarm Lilly. When his vocal expressions have a dabbing or tapping quality, one sees that Roy makes himself seem vulnerable to get Lilly to let down her guard.

PLAYERS' ACTIONS IN *THE GRIFTERS*

The Grifters follows a trio of con artists. As the story develops, each time Roy becomes more involved with the alluring con artist Myra (Annette Bening), he pulls back to spend time with Lilly. When Roy declines Myra's demand that he become a partner in her complicated con schemes, Myra sees Roy's refusal as a sign that he loves Lilly. She decides to get Lilly out of the way, but Myra loses her own life in the attempt. However, because Myra had told Lilly's boss, Bobo, that Lilly had skimmed thousands of dollars off the gambling money she had collected for him, Lilly is forced to go on the run.

Like other films directed by Stephen Frears, *The Grifters* does not have clearly defined heroes and villains. The main characters have flaws and limitations but they are also worthy of compassion. Not surprisingly, that tone of acceptance informs Frears's approach to directing as well. In interviews, he emphasizes the contributions of writers and actors and explains that the director's job is simply to make everything work.[60] Frears always has a clear sense of camera and lighting setups, but he believes that the director's primary job is to create the conditions in which actors can work to illuminate the underlying significance of dramatic conflicts.[61]

In *The Grifters,* a simple, elegant trajectory informs the evolving interaction between Lilly and her son. It begins when she visits Roy after having lost contact with him for several years. Early in the scene, the two garish clown pictures, where Lilly will later find his life savings, catch her attention as she peruses his dim, sparsely decorated apartment. Initially, Roy is guarded, suspicious of his mother's sudden interest, but seeing her awakens his confused longings for her. To collect himself, he offers to make instant coffee, just as Lilly will later regroup by getting glasses of ice water. Their first brief visit brings them closer together when Roy passes out and she rushes him to the hospital for surgery to repair the internal bleeding caused a few days earlier by a blow to his stomach served up by a local bartender who caught Roy trying to ply his trade.

When Roy discovers his mother in his apartment, about to leave with his cash stuffed in a briefcase, the climactic final scene between them unfolds. The characters play out their objectives in clearly etched units of action, as each fights for physical and emotional survival. Desperate to save her life, Lilly knows that keeping Roy's money represents her only chance to survive Bobo's inevitable efforts to kill her. For Lilly, the objective in the scene is simple: to get Roy's money. However, her greater problem in this scene is integral to the overarching problem that has shaped her interactions with Roy from the beginning of the story: she needs Roy to show his love for her. In this confrontation, she must persuade him to demonstrate his love by giving her the money and allowing her to leave as quickly as possible.

Just before this final encounter, Roy has discovered that Lilly has killed Myra and assumed her identity. With Myra gone and his mother officially dead, Roy seems to imagine that Lilly can now become in some way his intimate partner. He knows she is in a vulnerable position, and he believes he can and should protect her. When he finds her trying to escape with his money, he sees her action as a childish and unnecessary move. He tries to straighten her out, unaware of the danger she is in. However, once Lilly hammers home the point that Bobo is after her, Roy becomes increasingly desperate. He knows that if Lilly leaves with his money, he will never see her again. For Roy, the objective in the scene is also simple: to make Lilly stay. However unsafe for Lilly, he cannot let her abandon him again, even if he is not quite sure whether she should be his mother or his lover.

The qualities that infuse many of Huston's movements in the scene reveal that Lilly has one point to make to her son, namely, that she cannot go on without his money. The qualities that color Cusack's gestures and expressions show that Roy too has one point to make, namely, that he cannot go on without being close to her. Lilly wants to go; Roy wants her to stay. Frears presents their doomed confrontation in a twelve-minute scene that uses almost one hundred shots to present Lilly's desperate desire to get to safety and Roy's equally desperate need for her to stay. Their objectives put them into direct conflict, making it impossible for both characters to succeed. The following list provides an overview of the scene, the characters' given circumstances, and their objectives.

Scene: Roy's apartment, night.
Roy returns from Phoenix to find Lilly in his apartment about to leave with his money.

Given Circumstances
Lilly has only a short time to escape before Bobo's men find her and kill her for stealing a percentage of Bobo's gambling money.

Roy has only a short time to convince Lilly she cannot abandon him again—as she did eight years ago and when she failed to make her date in Del Mar, and, most recently, when she appeared to be dead in Phoenix).

Objectives

Lilly needs Roy to show that he loves her (by giving her the money and letting her go).

Roy needs Lilly to show that she loves him (by staying with him and starting a new life).

The scene is divided into beginning, middle, and end segments. In the opening round, Roy/Cusack attempts to take charge of the situation. This segment escalates in intensity until Huston and Cusack suddenly stop yelling at one another and rush to grab the briefcase filled with money. The middle segment, when Lilly leaves the room to get ice water from the kitchen, gives both characters a chance to regroup. In the concluding segment, Lilly's actions drive the scene to its resolution. She makes a series of attempts to bring Roy around to her position; each time Cusack resists, Huston switches to a new and more deadly strategy. The entire scene's sequence of tactics can be seen as eight units of action that convey the escalating stages of the dramatic conflict. In units 1 through 3, Huston and Cusack fight to a draw; in units 4 through 8, Huston regroups and then turns to a series of increasingly threatening tactics.[62]

The scene begins when Cusack glides into the room, pausing to survey the chaos caused by Huston's frantic search. Here, in this initial unit of action, Roy initiates and Lilly resists. Both characters/actors use inducing tactics to coax the other into agreement. With a light, direct dabbing quality in his voice, Cusack quietly takes charge as he tells Huston to take a minute. Huston responds positively to the quiet request and allows the conversation to draw Cusack's attention away from the fact she is stealing his money. Encouraged by Huston's seemingly conciliatory stance, Cusack moves toward Huston and, with quiet assurance, tells her to relax. He then glides forward as he tells her to put the briefcase down. Pausing to search for ways to get back on track, Huston sits down and puts the briefcase on the coffee table. Still impelling the action forward, Cusack disarms Huston; he cajoles her into staying by asking her to tell him what happened in Phoenix. Coming to see inducing tactics as a way to get the money, Huston confides in Cusack as she recounts the scene in the hotel room. Then, with Cusack softened up by being brought into her confidence, Huston glides into telling him that she's sorry that she had to take his money. That move, however, triggers Cusack to press out his command, "You're not taking it." As he says the line, he drops his voice and pulls his chin back and in, which gives him a more pow-

Anjelica Huston and John Cusack in *The Grifters:* Lilly/Huston and Roy/Cusack square off as they get ready for battle in the second unit of action

Roy/Cusack takes command as he tells Lilly about her new life "off the grift"

erful position. Cusack's departure from inducing tactics suddenly kicks the conflict into a higher gear. With his resistance out in the open, Huston now goes on the attack.

That transition marks the change into the second unit of action. Blocking conveys the idea that Cusack and Huston are poised to enter full-fledged confrontation, for at this moment they stand squarely face-to-face, their bodies tensed for battle.

In the second unit of action, Lilly initiates and Roy resists; both characters use threatening tactics. While the opening segment was colored by direct but generally light dabbing and gliding qualities in the actors' physical and vocal expressions, the second is marked by the strong, sudden, and direct thrusting quality that infuses their larger, more emphatic gestures and expressions. Huston throws her arms out in front of her as she paces across the room. Punching her words out, Huston demands that Cusack give her the money. She keeps her cheeks sucked in and makes the tension that runs through her body clearly visible. But Cusack fights back and at moments goes on the offensive. Barking orders at Huston and getting right in her face, Cusack insists that Huston get a legitimate job.

He does not let up. He circles her and jabs his finger at her as he maps out her new life. However, Huston does not back down. Alternating sharp, sudden vocal thrusts with bound and sustained commands, she orders Cusack not to tell her what to do. Hands on her hips, her head thrown back, eyes and nostrils flared, Huston demands that Cusack back off. With his voice cutting across the room, Cusack battles back. His words tumble out in rapid fire, his neck is tense, and his eyes remain fixed on points in front of him. Having fired alternating volleys of attack from across the room, they pause to reload their emotional arsenals. Roy realizes that it will be difficult to overpower Lilly, and he changes to an inducing tactic.

The battle moves into the third unit of action, with Roy initiating the action and Lilly resisting. Roy suddenly changes the subject; he announces that he has decided to change his life, and he attempts to inspire Lilly to change. But Lilly quickly pierces his attempt. As if thrusting out her words, Huston drives to end the discussion. She claims the right to have the money because she is the one in danger. Made desperate by the validity of her claim, Cusack fights back more wildly. He thrusts his words at Huston as he condemns her for failing to recognize that he should keep his life savings because he is willing to share it with her, if she stays. They are both right. They both deserve the money. They both rush to grab the briefcase of money. Cusack physically overpowers Huston as he slams his foot down on it. He presents Huston with an obstacle that she must acknowledge. If she is to succeed, Huston will have to use indirect measures. The battle has reached a stalemate. If it were possible, the characters might call it a draw, but their circumstances and objectives make that impossible. The following list provides an overview of these first three units of action.

1. *From Roy entering to Roy telling Lilly she is not taking the money*
   Roy initiates the action—Lilly resists

Roy uses inducing tactics—Lilly uses inducing tactics
Roy flatters Lilly (says her plan is working very well)
Lilly disarms Roy (shows her gentle side by confiding in Roy)

2. *From Lilly demanding the money to Lilly rejecting Roy's attempts to tell her what to do*
Lilly initiates the action—Roy resists
Lilly uses threatening tactics—Roy uses threatening tactics
Lilly commands Roy to give her the money
Roy commands Lilly to get a regular job

3. *From Roy proposing a new life to Roy blocking Lilly's grab for the money*
Roy initiates the action—Lilly resists
Roy moves from inducing to threatening tactics—Lilly uses threatening tactics
Roy tries to inspire Lilly; then he overpowers her and concludes discussion
Lilly attacks Roy's proposal; then she overpowers him and concludes discussion

The fourth unit of action opens with Lilly's signal that she is prepared to use indirect strategies to bring Roy around to her side. Echoing Cusack's gestures at the beginning of the scene, Huston's voice is hushed as she asks Cusack if he would like a drink. Undeterred when he resists, Huston keeps asking the question in different ways, as if lightly dabbing at him until she gets him to agree. Roy's consent is significant, for it lets Lilly know that Roy might let her win, if she can find the right way to convince him.

Like a seasoned bridge player assessing her opponents' strengths and weakness during opening bids, Huston tests Cusack in the fifth unit of action by trying out various related strategies. Huston glides into the room with the glasses of water and toys with Cusack by seeming harmless and threatening by turn. Cusack remains unmoved. Sitting across from Cusack, Huston tries again to disarm him as she recalls that when she gave birth to him she herself was too much a child to prove a good mother. Letting her words float into the air, Huston feigns weakness. Cusack resists this ploy as well, lightly flicking back his disgust at her threadbare ruse. Shifting to stronger physical and vocal expressions, Huston presses her words out as she pleads with Cusack to give her the money. She now tries to shame him into giving it to her, and then she simply demands it. Cusack conveys his re-

Huston, hand on her hip with a new plan of attack: Lilly/Huston begins the sixth unit of action by using the threatening tactic of observing intently

sistance to Huston's elaborate repertoire of tricks by poking out the word "no."

Cusack's simple and dismissive expression triggers the sixth unit of action. Enraged, Huston gets up and leaves behind her attempts at ladylike tactics. After she looks out the window to collect herself, Huston turns back with her hand on her hip. Focused on Cusack who remains seated, she is ready to deliver another attack.

Gliding with assurance as she paces back and forth in front of the windows, Huston probes to find out why Cusack needs the money. Questioning him, she puts him on edge by observing him intently. When reasoning with him does not prompt him to concede, Huston uses stronger, more direct thrusting movements as she again attempts to shame Cusack into compliance. She then threatens him by demanding that he tell her why she cannot have the money.

Coming to the realization that Lilly needs the cash more than he does, Roy still fights back because something else is becoming very clear: once she gets the money she will probably leave him forever. In peevish, childish desperation, Cusack leaps out of his seat and comes over to Huston, who stands at the window. He grabs Huston's right hand, the one scarred earlier in the film when Bobo punished her for disloyalty. She grabs it away but Cusack still runs through a repertoire of strategies as he tries to get Huston to see things his way. Pressing his words out, Cusack flatters her, tries to inspire her, and works to convince her by speaking frankly to her. Concluding the

Lilly/Huston gets the money she needs through seduction: Roy/Cusack almost gets her to stay by yielding

stream of words that verges on an implied proposal of marriage, Cusack moves to the opposite side of the room as he rests his case.

Although she clearly resists Cusack's offer, Huston's eyes light up because Roy's physical contact has given Lilly an idea for a new plan of attack. In this seventh unit of action, Huston starts in front of the apartment window, a place that has become her corner of the boxing ring. With her voice smooth and low, and her eyes fixed on Cusack, Huston comes toward him in a slow and even glide that increases in strength as she approaches. Using the threatening tactic of implying a hidden arsenal, Lilly suggests that she might not actually be Roy's mother. She invites him to imagine this possibility. Lulling him into the idea, she tells him that she knows he would like that. As she moves across the room toward him, Huston relaxes her body, her soft, floating movement showing none of the tension so visible before. Still filled with energy, Huston's actions initiate the behavior she wants Cusack to follow. Visibly pressed against the wall on the opposite side of the room, Cusack begins to stutter, confused and as if begging Huston to take a less powerful tactic. Weakly resisting the new idea, Cusack makes an effort to end the conversation. However, Huston has won before she even reaches him: Cusack is stunned, trembling with fear and excitement. Their brief but passionate kiss creates a pause in the conflict; Lilly now knows she will get the money and, for a second, Roy can imagine she will stay.

When Roy drops his guard, there is a chance Lilly will also. Huston's action reveals that Lilly is frightened that Roy will persuade her to stay with him; she abruptly changes tactics and drives the scene into its final unit of action. Quickly dropping her alluring strategy, Lilly breaks off their gentle kiss as soon as she proves that she can seduce him. Without warning, Huston turns the kiss into an attack; Cusack suddenly jumps as if Huston has grabbed his crotch. Stunned by this abrupt change in Huston's actions, Cusack pulls back and turns away, raising his water glass to take a drink as if to put some kind of physical obstacle between them. However, his resistance to Huston's assault is feeble, for this gesture at best conveys a weak attempt to end the conversation.

Following through with overtly threatening action, Huston picks up the briefcase full of money and slaps Cusack across the face with it. The water glass breaks, cuts into Cusack's neck, and blood spills out as he drops to the floor. What makes the action all the more horrific is that Huston's simple gesture is so like a parent slapping a child who has said a dirty word. Momentarily overwhelmed by the consequence of her action, Huston gasps and cries out. However, Huston does not change course; sobbing as she leans over Cusack lying on the floor, she soon starts to gather some of the paper money now strewn around the room. The scene ends as Huston stumbles out, carrying the briefcase filled with a disheveled pile of bloodstained bills.

The following list is an overview of the final four units of action.

4. *From Lilly offering Roy a drink to Lilly returning with ice water*
   Lilly initiates the action—Roy resists
   Lilly uses inducing tactics—Roy uses inducing tactics
   Lilly lulls Roy (by offering something to drink)
   Roy confirms Lilly (being frank and agreeing with her suggestion)

5. *From Lilly toying with Roy to Lilly demanding the money*
   Lilly initiates the action—Roy resists
   Lilly uses inducing and threatening tactics—Roy uses threatening tactics
   Lilly tries to disarm Roy; she then pleads with, shames, and demands
   Roy concludes the exchange

6. *From Lilly getting up to observe Roy to Lilly dismissing Roy's proposal for a new life*
   Lilly initiates the action—Roy resists
   Lilly uses threatening tactics—Roy uses inducing tactics
   Lilly observes Roy intently and then demands a response
   Roy tries to inspire Lilly (to start a new life with him)

7. *From Lilly suggesting she is not Roy's mother to Lilly kissing Roy*
   Lilly initiates the action—Roy resists
   Lilly uses threatening tactics—Roy uses inducing tactics
   Lilly pulls out hidden weapons (of new information and allure of sexual contact)
   Roy tries to persuade Lilly (to use less powerful weapons)

8. *From Lilly grabbing Roy's crotch to Lilly leaving with the money*
   Lilly initiates the action—Roy resists
   Lilly uses threatening tactics (beyond reason)—Roy makes final gestures of defense
   Lilly overpowers Roy
   Roy weakly tries to end the conversation

As this case study suggests, audiences infer characters' psychological and mental action from the physical actions of the performers. Stanislavsky labels this duality in acting "psycho-physical" and uses scene analysis to draw actors into the hidden inferences in scripts that he calls "subtexts." Acting choices in Huston's and Cusack's performances shape impressions about the characters' evolving interaction. Variations in the players' vocal pitch, volume, and rhythm and in the spatial, temporal, and energy qualities of their gestures and movements inform interpretations of the characters' dramatic conflict.

The tightness in Huston's face, voice, and gestures convey Lilly's conviction that she must have Roy's money. The forcefulness of Huston's line deliveries, gestures, and movements communicate Lilly's utter determination. Even if Lilly's original idea had been to slip secretly away with Roy's life savings, Huston's increasingly persuasive tactics demonstrate that Lilly needs more than money; she needs Roy to express his love by giving it to her freely. Similarly, the rising tension in Cusack's voice, face, and gestures reveal that Roy cannot let his mother leave. He needs Lilly to show she loves him by staying and starting a new life with him. At moments, Roy is poised to attain that goal, circling Huston, blocking her exit, forcing her to stay within reach. Ironically, he comes closest to keeping her with him when he yields to her seduction. The outer actions that concern the money betray the inner subtextual actions that concern their love.

Individual moments in the performances become significant in light of the expressive details throughout the scene. Like all human movements, which gain full significance when related to what precedes and follows, the tactics in each unit of action become meaningful in relation to *(a)* each actor's series of strategies and *(b)* the specific ways in which the two actors' corresponding strategies intersect. Stanislavsky's Active Analysis is especially helpful in establishing the complexities in such interplay, because it distinguishes between impelling actions and conflicting counteractions in the scene, and it invites one to specify the exact ways (directly, obliquely, or otherwise) in which dramatic forces clash.

For example, in the second unit of action, the characters both have a chance to achieve their goals because Huston and Cusack alternate between listening and demanding to be heard. Action and counteractions hold parity in this interaction. However, in the third unit of action, when both characters simultaneously shout to make their points, the equally matched action and counteraction reaches stasis and leads to deadlock. Written, staged, and performed like a boxing match, the first three units of action present the characters as striving to secure their mutually exclusive objectives until they reach a draw and take a break to regroup. Later in the scene, when Huston's action gains force and weakens Cusack's counteraction, the stasis is broken and the dynamic conditions for resolution arise from within their continued interaction. When they return, Lilly's well-practiced repertoire leads to victory. The goal-directed impulses that color Huston's and Cusack's actions provide material evidence about the characters' given circumstances, their objectives, and their changing tactics. Principles of script analysis provide vocabulary for describing the "intensities" in the actors' performances (see chapter 2). They offer a way to analyze how their acting choices "deflect reference" from the actors to the fictional characters.[63] They also supply terms and concepts for describing how Huston's and Cusack's actions function as "ostensive signs" that stand in for the characters' actions, and why their performances become "transparent" as audiences "see right through" them into the "virtual" realm of the fictional characters (see chapters 4 and 7).

CONCLUSIONS

Writing about the cinema often uses craft terms to describe shot-to-shot relations, frame selections, lighting design, camera movement, and sound design. References to close-ups, tracking shots, low-key lighting, and shot/reverse shot sequences are part of film scholarship and popular film criticism. By comparison, acting/directing terms such as given circumstances, objectives, and actions are still rarely found in film literature, and many of the analytically useful concepts outlined by Stanislavsky remain unexplored in cinema studies. However, terminology that clarifies the ways that players' actions reveal character will enhance critical practice. As the case study of *The Grifters* demonstrates, Huston's and Cusack's performances serve as the primary basis for interpretations about the characters' desires, thoughts, and feelings, even though their gestures and expressions work in concert with other aspects of the film's representation. This concluding chapter suggests that principles of scene analysis provide a window into completed scenes, just as players' actions create a window into characters' circumstances, objectives, and evolving strategies.

CONCLUSION

Two objectives have guided this book. The first has been to offer alternatives to some deep-seated misconceptions about acting and film. By drawing on Prague semiotics and selected work in film and theater studies, the book clarifies that acting is constituted by interrelated actions that create emotional and intellectual responses in audiences. This perspective counters the intransigent equation of "true" acting with live theater and the related view that film captures "natural" behavior. Similarly, several of the book's case studies show that "cinematic" strategies often focus audience attention on the expressive details crafted by actors. These examples dispel the notion that framing and editing "do" the acting in cinema. While Metz once proposed that viewers respond to films because they identify with the look of the camera or with the characters, this book offers evidence that actors' physical and vocal choices can influence audiences' impressions as well. Thus, by argument and example, the volume creates a hearing for the alternative view that screen acting is best understood as a full-fledged component of film, no more and no less important than framing, editing, lighting, costuming, sound design, and so on; gestures and expressions in the cinema warrant analysis because they are one of many factors that influence audiences' interpretations.

The book's second objective has been to illustrate the various ways one can productively describe and analyze acting in cinema. By using readily available terms, concepts, and taxonomies developed by acting practitioners, Prague semioticians, and others, the volume's collection of brief examples and extended case studies fulfill this promise by modeling strategies for studying and discussing screen performances.

The book's overarching point of view acknowledges and argues that viewers encounter performance in relation to other cinematic elements. This understanding of screen acting enables fresh insights into film practice generally, for the corollary is that audiences also interpret nonperformance elements through and in terms of their conjunction with acting choices. Put another way, performance details are no more or less mediated than other aspects of cinema. Viewers reconcile the impressions conveyed by a certain shot selection with the connotations suggested by other choices in the cinematic representation, including those derived from performance. Similarly, audiences might interpret a sound element, such as the enhanced echo of a character's footsteps (created by Foley artists and sound editors), through and in terms of the many filmic details that accompany it. These might include a slow, ground-level tracking shot that maintains a close-up on the feet (framing); a dissolve leading into a long take (editing); low-key lighting (lighting design); smooth dark pavement (production design); polished steel-toed work boots (costume design); and a slow, measured rhythm in the steps (performance element). As Prague theorists suggest, audiences interpret connotations conveyed by all filmic elements through their relation to concomitant textual details.

This book also acknowledges that impressions about acting and other cinematic choices are mediated by narrative and extratextual information. As the discussions about *A Woman Under the Influence* and *Far From Heaven* indicate, facts provided by previous scenes allow the connotations carried by performance elements to acquire narrative meaning and dramatic significance (chapter 2). Similarly, as noted in the observations about *Touch of Evil,* audiences also often bring dense extratextual knowledge and expectations to their understanding of scenes and sequences (chapter 3). Additionally, as the comparative studies suggest, viewers' knowledge about genre conventions, star images, aesthetic traditions, and directors' bodies of work can affect how they approach and respond to screen performances.

While recognizing extratextual factors, the book primarily focuses on acting choices and their relation to other cinematic elements in narrative films. The contrast between *Pickpocket* and *Blow-Up,* on the one side, and *The Rules of the Game* and *Matewan,* on the other, suggests the many ways that films integrate performance and nonperformance components (chapter 2). The observable differences between *Seven Samurai* and *The Magnificent Seven* reveal that acting styles are best understood, not as personal behavior or effects of acting technique, but as reflections of narrative demands, directorial visions, and cultural-aesthetic traditions (chapter 6). The adaptations of *Hamlet* and *Romeo and Juliet* show how conventions change over time and how acting choices change as well to suit the respective framing, editing, sound, and design schemes. These adaptations thus demonstrate that nonperformance elements do not trump acting, but that conventions specific to cultural-aesthetic moments affect all cinematic choices (chapter 5).

Systematic thinking about screen acting allows one to see that performance details belong to filmic representations. As cinematic elements, they are comparable to lighting and framing choices. Gestures and expressions can be signs of actors' labor, just as details in lighting and framing are signs of work by gaffers and cinematographers. Fans can use performance details to access idealized star images in much the same way film buffs might examine lighting and framing choices for evidence of a filmmaker's genius. However, as Heath explains, cinematic gestures and expressions are not simply signs of someone offscreen, but instead are best understood as "intensities" that exist in filmic representations, independent and "outside a simple constant unity of . . . some *one.*"[1] In other words, filmic gestures are different from actors, aspects of narrative (agents and characters), and films' mobilization of extratextual factors (star images, figures, and *typage*) (chapter 3). Prague theorists also emphasize that performance elements are distinct from both characters and actors. Zich identifies the unique place of performance details when he explains that "the sensorily perceptible substratum" is what provides evidence for impressions about "the dramatic character" (chapter 4).[2] Likewise, Langer directs attention to the expressive potential of crafted performance elements by noting that "transparent" acting choices establish a window into the "virtual" realm of fictional characters (chapter 7). Heath, Zich, and Langer chisel out a conceptual space for the performance elements that are this volume's central concern.[3]

Metz overlooked the remarkable expressivity of gestures and expressions, when he equated framing with fragmentation, rather than selection, and identified editing elements with linguistic units instead of ostensive sign components that direct viewers' attention. Focused on "absent" actors, theorists such as Metz and Benjamin found no "acting" in films. By contrast, Kuleshov (who has been wrongly associated with the view that editing creates screen performance) demonstrated early on that details of performance matter in film (chapter 2). Furthermore, recent research by Crary amplifies Eisenstein's insight that shot selections and combinations do not fragment "reality" as much as they focus attention on the salient details of crafted, often conventional signs of "actuality" (chapter 2). Prague theorists have provided a comprehensive alternative to linguistic-based semiotics by envisioning variable and mutual interactions between all cinematic elements (chapter 4). They highlight the complex interplay between conventional "gesture-signs" and individual "gesture-expressions" and show that vocal elements, facial expressions, gestures, poses, and movements function in relationships of subordination, domination, equilibrium, and parallelism with each other and with other formal elements such as framing and narrative. Kuleshov, Eisenstein, Crary, and Prague theorists thus not only facilitate analysis of film performance, but also provide a more comprehensive vision of cinema.

Having cleared the ground of commonly held misconceptions about acting and film, productive description and analysis can proceed by adopting a number of existing taxonomies. As the *Smoke* case study reveals, Delsarte's comprehensive study of physical gestures can illuminate the crafted, meaningful components in performances that use "natural" physical signs to convey emotion (chapter 7). Laban Movement Analysis also offers useful terms for discussing performance. As the examples from *Training Day* suggest, one can identify direct and indirect movements, sudden and sustained gestures, weighted and light postures, and bound versus free-flowing vocal expressions (chapter 8). Connotations carried by acting choices are also clarified through the analytical terminology developed by Stanislavsky. As the study of *The Grifters* shows, principles of scene analysis can serve as effective tools for observing the ways in which performance details convey fictional characters' thoughts and feelings (chapter 9). Delsarte's techniques may not be widely used today, but his taxonomies of expression remain useful as analytic tools. Likewise, not all practitioners develop characterizations using Laban principles, yet Laban Movement Analysis still offers valuable terms for describing film performances. Similarly, even though Stanislavsky's approach to script analysis is not employed in the same way by all actors and directors, its basic principles can enrich the understanding of existing performances. The field of cinema studies has long depended on craft terms to describe framing choices, editing patterns, lighting schemes, soundtrack elements, and camera movements; this book shows that craft terminology can be used to describe screen performances.

The analytic value of acting and directing terms makes it especially unfortunate that misconceptions about film acting have emerged from lack of information about ways that performers prepare for working out of sequence, without rehearsal, and without scene partners. Sustained by marketing rhetoric, anecdotes have suggested that screen actors do not draw on the kind of training and preparation employed by stage actors. However, while film actors adjust their performances to suit framing, editing, and other directorial choices, their approaches to characterizations are not venue-specific. Whether working on stage or screen, players influenced by developments in Western twentieth-century actor training generally explore their characters' given circumstances, objectives, and actions along with the dramatic structure of any given scene.

In fact, the unique demands of film production do not make training unnecessary but instead require actors to rely on training, experience, and more independent preparation than that required for stage performances. Compressed rehearsal time requires players to come to the set or location fully prepared, with a good understanding of their characters and a readiness to adjust that understanding to the director's vision as needed. Performers in leading roles must have their characters' physical and emotional journeys mapped out, so that even when scenes are shot out of sequence, they know how each scene fits into the story and their characters' development. Often required to portray moments of extreme emotion without rehearsal or without the presence of their scene partners, screen actors depend on the work they have done alone and in advance. They must also develop their ability to maintain concentration because the production process itself presents constant distractions. While stage acting requires physical awareness, acting in the cinema necessitates even greater awareness: movements must fit framing choices, and gestures must be modified to accommodate their magnification when projected. Because performance details are combined with a dense array of filmic elements, actors learn to home in on the essentials so that audiences can locate the meaningful qualities in movements, gestures, and expressions. From the standpoint of actors, stage work and screen work involve differences in degree rather than kind. This insight implicitly informs the book's respect for actors' craft and their potential to contribute to films.

As this volume comes to a close, it should be apparent that terminology drawn from the craft of acting, Prague school semiotics, and elsewhere can make acting choices visible. The terms and concepts provided by these resources should have clarified that performance details, whether on stage or screen, can influence audiences because qualities in actors' physical and vocal gestures are joined with other carefully crafted production elements within evolving aesthetic and cultural conventions understood by audiences. This point warrants consideration, because reframing established views on the way films join cinematic elements has relevance for screen performance and for cinema in general.

This book has suggested that composite art forms such as film and theater use combinations of interlocking, material details to direct audiences' attention to some but not all possible connotations embedded in the "ostensive signs" used at a particular moment in a production. Moment by moment, composite art forms become legible to audiences by using combinations of specific gestures, lighting choices, and so on that reinforce some connotations carried by the representational details while excluding others. Even brief filmic moments present viewers with a host of specific, interdependent, equally important cinematic details: tight framing might allow audiences to see a hand reaching tentatively toward and grasping another; the physicality of the hands would carry social significance; the speed and duration of the gesture would color impressions; lighting choices and sound elements could influence interpretations. Some viewers might attend closely to the energy that infuses the grasping hands; others might explore their physicality. However, unlike a linguistic phrase, which features strings of generic modifiers joined to abstract concepts (as in "the old, broken-down chair"), the actual details of the framing, gesture, and so forth in this or any moment of cinema will function not as modifiers or abstract concepts, but instead as pieces of concrete evidence that guide audiences' interpretations by confirming the various details' corresponding connotations, with a counterpoint to those connotations sometimes also highlighted.

Analyzing acting as a component of film can contribute to criticism because it leads one to examine performance details that inform impressions about characters and disclose the film's cultural-aesthetic influences. Analyzing acting as a component of film can also transform one's view of cinema. Exploring acting choices allows the reciprocal relations between framing, editing, and performance elements to come into view and shows that films create meaning through combinations of formal details that engage audience associations. Thus, giving performance elements their due can illuminate the simple and yet surprising idea that films are enriched by the expressivity of all their cinematic components.

APPENDIX

CASE STUDY OF *ROMEO AND JULIET*

ACTING CHOICES/FRAMING CHOICES: CONSIDERATIONS FOR FILMMAKERS AND FILM SCHOLARS

1. The *selection and combination* of gestures and vocal/facial expressions are mutually interactive elements in the *performance montage* that actors/directors create.
2. In any scene, the *selection and combination* of actors' movements, gestures, facial and vocal expressions have a mutually interactive relationship with the *selection and combination* of shots, editing patterns, design elements, and audio choices.
3. Choices about framing, editing, production and sound design are choices about performance; acting choices are also choices about other cinematic elements.

Romeo and Juliet (1936)

Irving Thalberg (producer), George Cukor (director), William H. Daniels (director of photograpy), Cedric Gibbons (art director)

42-year-old Leslie Howard (Romeo), 37-year-old Norma Shearer (Juliet)

Production/directorial vision: Romeo and Juliet reveal the sparkling radiance of pure souls whose chaste but passionate attraction is a fairy tale; like Mary Pickford heroines and Douglas Fairbanks heroes, their dreamlike affair is inspiring but fated to change.

Theatrical model: Long shots and long takes; speeches are presented in dramatic space.

Polished, choreographed performances draw audiences into fictional, otherworldly realm.

Sequence when lines changed during first kiss: one long take/three playing areas

Romeo and Juliet (1968)

Franco Zeffirelli (director), Pasqualino de Santis (director of photography), Lorenzo Mongaiardino (designer)

18-year-old Leonard Whiting (Romeo), 17-year-old Olivia Hussey (Juliet)

Directorial vision: Romeo and Juliet embody the purity of the May 1968 generation whose idealism is misunderstood by the older generation bent on endless bloodshed.

Cinematic model: Medium close-ups, close-ups, short and long takes; choreography of staging and framing to create close-ups; searching eyes and point-of-view shots place audience inside the scene; meaning created by interactions with props and combinations of voice, movement, gesture, and lighting design; close-miked vocal expressions overheard.

Performances are part of the film's overall "musical" composition; framing, editing, design, audio, and acting choices provide an audiovisual illustration of emotional beats.

Sequence when lines are exchanged during first kiss: 10 shots in curtained, offstage area

William Shakespeare's Romeo + Juliet (1996)

Baz Luhrman (director), Donald McAlpine (director of photography), Catherine Martin (art director)

22-year-old Leonardo Di Caprio (Romeo), 17-year-old Claire Danes (Juliet)

Directorial vision: Romeo and Juliet's desire to author their own images in a ready-made image world is ill fated because "authentic" expressions of personal desire are used as marketable commodities (e.g., in the film and its ancillary market releases).

Televisual model: Close-ups, extreme close-ups, very short takes; dialogue and interior thoughts overheard.

Facial expressions and hand gestures convey the characters' "authentic" emotions, while the excitement of the moment is shown by zip pans, quick cuts, twirling camera.

Sequence when lines are exchanged: 60 shots in sideline and elevator spaces

USING THE CASE STUDIES IN A CLASS OR WORKSHOP

1. Show the 3-minute segments discussed in chapter 5. In the 1936 film, it starts at 30 minutes; in the 1968 film, at 33 minutes; in the 1996 film, at 30 minutes.
2. Alternatively, show the entire 15-minute scene of the Capulet ball in each film. In the 1936 film, it begins at 23 minutes; in the 1968 film, at 22 minutes (chapter 5 on the DVD); in the 1996 film, at 24 minutes (chapter 7 on the DVD).
3. Alternatively, prior to watching the scenes of the Capulet ball, show the opening scene from each of the three adaptations.
4. Have students read the case study scene before or after watching the adaptations; do a staged reading of the scene in class; have students write their own treatment of the scene.
5. Ask students to locate two or three other films based on the same script

or story; have them outline their findings in class presentations, or writing assignments, or media-rich presentation documents.

6. Ask students to develop three different treatments of a scene they would like to tape or film; use the three adaptations of *Romeo and Juliet* (or three other films) as sample approaches.
7. Have students reproduce 10–30 seconds from one or more of the case study scenes.
8. Select exercises from Patrick Tucker's *Secrets of Screen Acting* (especially 192–94), for example, using a frame (wood, rolled newspapers, etc.) 4 by 3 units or 16 by 9 units:

    a. Hold up the frame; have someone watch from about 8 feet away; have students stand so that the observer sees them in long shot, medium shot, etc.
    b. Put the frame in front of someone doing an ordinary activity like drinking a glass of water; discuss the adjustments needed for the action to make sense at different distances; use the frame to create different framings of a person asking someone for directions; discuss the adjustments needed for each frame selection.

SUGGESTED READING

Anderegg, Michael. 2004. *Cinematic Shakespeare.*

Benedetti, Robert. 2001. *Action! Acting for Film and Television.*

Naremore, James. 1988. *Acting in the Cinema.*

Tucker, Patrick. 2003. *Secrets of Screen Acting.* 2nd ed.

Weston, Judith. 1996. *Directing Actors: Creating Memorable Performances for Film and Television.*

NOTES

Introduction

1. Walter Benjamin, "The Work of Art in the Age of Mechanical Reproduction," in *Illuminations,* trans. Harry Zohn, ed. Hannah Arendt (New York: Harcourt, Brace and World, 1968), 231.

2. See Richard Maltby, *Hollywood Cinema,* 2nd ed. (Malden, Mass.: Blackwell, 2003), 370; see 628 nn. 3–10. According to Maltby, writings by Vsevolod Pudovkin, Frank D. McConnell, Foster Hirsh, Richart Dyer, and James Naremore reveal "the paucity of the vocabulary" for critical analysis of film performance.

3. There are integral connections between the principles used to compose and analyze music and sequences of human movement in the performing and dramatic arts. Chapter 8 outlines some of those connections and shows that some structural studies of narration are also grounded in basic principles of music.

4. Kamilla Elliott, *Rethinking the Novel/Film Debate* (New York: Cambridge University Press, 2003), 119. See John L. Fell, *Film and the Narrative Tradition* (Norman: University of Oklahoma Press, 1974); A. Nicholas Vardac, *Stage to Screen: Theatrical Origins of Early Film: David Garrick to D. W. Griffith* (Cambridge: Harvard University Press, 1949).

5. Benjamin, "Work of Art," 229.

6. Ibid., 229–30.

7. See David Edelstein, "The Love Boat: James Cameron's *Titanic,*" *Slate,* 21 December 1997, http://www.slate.com/id/3240, consulted 22 January 2007.

8. See Edward Guthmann, "Sailing into Darkness: Dench Touchingly Captures Fading Mind in 'Iris,'" *San Francisco Chronicle,* 15 February 2002, http://www.sfgate.com, consulted 22 January 2007; Charles Taylor, *"Iris," Salon.com,* 14 December 2001, http://www.archive.salon.com, consulted 22 January 2007. Winslet received an Oscar nomination for Best Supporting Actress for her performance in *Iris.* Earlier, she had received a Best Supporting Actress nomination for her performance in *Sense and Sensibility* (Ang Lee, 1995). She has also received Oscar nominations for Best Actress for her performances in *Eternal Sunshine of the Spotless Mind* (Michel Gondry, 2004) and *Little Children* (Todd Field, 2006).

9. Growing respect for DiCaprio's performances is also reflected in his Academy Award nominations. While he received a nomination for Best Supporting Actor for his performance in *What's Eating Gilbert Grape* (Lasse Hallestróm, 1993), his nominations for Best Actor belong to the Scorsese era; they include his performances in *The Aviator* (Martin Scorsese, 2004) and *Blood Diamond* (Edward Zwick, 2006).

10. See Benjamin, "Work of Art," 230, 231, 247.

11. Ibid., 230.

12. David Edelstein, "Virginia Slim: *The Hours* Is a Depressive Closet Case," *Slate,* 31 December 2002, http://www.slate.com/id/2076194, consulted 22 January 2007. See Mark Caro, *"The Hours," Chicago Tribune,* n.d., http://metro mix.chicagotribune.com, consulted 22 January 2007; Mick LaSalle, "Film Proves to Be Book's Finests 'Hours,'" *San Francisco Chronicle,* 27 December 2002, http://sfgate.com, consulted 22 January 2007; Andrew O'Hehir, "Who's Afraid of Virginia Woolf?" *Salon.com,* 27 December 2002, http://dir.salon.com, consulted 22 January 2007.

13. Roget Ebert, *"Monster," Chicago Sun-Times,* 1 January 2004, http:// rogerebert.suntimes.com, consulted 22 January 2007. See David Edelstein, "Portraits of a Serial Killer: The Life and Death of Aileen Wuornos," *Slate,* 26 December 2003, http://www.slate.com/id/2093192, consulted 22 January 2007; Michael Wilmington, *"Monster," Chicago Tribune,* n.d., http://metro mix.chicagotribune.com, consulted 22 January 2007.

14. Benjamin, "Work of Art," 228.

15. See Christian Metz, *Film Language: A Semiotics of the Cinema,* trans. Michael Taylor (New York: Oxford University Press, 1974). See Robert Stam, Robert Burgoyne, and Sandy Flitterman-Lewis, *New Vocabularies in Film Semiotics* (New York: Routledge, 1992), 28–68. Part 2, "Cine-Semiology," provides a comprehensive account of film theory's focus on framing and editing. Theater scholar Patrice Pavis also adheres to the notion that framing and editing are cinema's defining features; see *Analyzing Performance: Theater, Dance, and Film,* trans. David Williams (Ann Arbor: University of Michigan Press, 2003), 130.

16. Michael L. Quinn, *The Semiotic Stage: Prague School Theater Theory* (New York: Peter Lang, 1995), 21.

17. Ibid., 73. Mukařovský's essay, "Chaplin in *City Lights:* An Attempt at a Structural Analysis of an Acting Phenomenon," can be found in *Structure, Sign and Function,* trans. John Burbank and Peter Steiner (New Haven: Yale University Press, 1978), 171–77.

18. Media's ability to increase visibility of human expression has prompted the mistaken impression that mediated performance is comparable to surveillance. Most notably, writing about the troubling effects of modern technology in Nazi Germany, Benjamin deftly identified the social and political dangers created by "the expansion of the field of the testable which mechanical equipment brings about" ("Work of Art," 246). Seventy years later, government actions continue to confirm the legitimacy of Benjamin's concerns. However, while Benjamin is right that gesture in film can lend "itself more readily to analysis" than gesture on stage, film performances are not simply captured, and filmic gestures require the same careful study that stage performances and other aspects of cinema do (236).

19. See Marvin Carlson, *Performance: A Critical Introduction* (New York: Routledge, 1996), 5; Graham F. Thompson, "Approaches to 'Performance': An

Analysis of Terms," *Screen* 26, no. 5 (1985): 78–90. In *Questions of Cinema,* Stephen Heath notes that since "all representation is performance," "film performance" includes the performance of the film as a whole (Bloomington: Indiana University Press, 1981), 115. Richard Maltby also finds that performance includes "the performance of the camera, the editing, and the mise-en-scène" (*Hollywood Cinema,* 370).

20. We are especially indebted to insights on acting expressed in the writings of film scholar Doug Tomlinson and theater scholar Michael Quinn, who both passed away as young men. Our work continues research published in a series of special issues on acting in *The Velvet Light Trap* (1972), *Sight and Sound* (1973), *Screen* (1978, 1985, 1999), *Quarterly Review of Film and Video* (1979), *Cinema Journal* (1980), *Wide Angle* (1984), *Journal of Film and Video* (1990, 2006), *Post Script* (1993), and *Cineaste* (2006).

Chapter 1

1. Carole Zucker, "The Concept of 'Excess' in Film Acting: Notes toward an Understanding of Non-naturalistic Performance," *Post Script* 12, no. 2 (1993): 56.

2. See Jacques Derrida, "Structure, Sign, and Play in the Discourse of the Human Sciences," in *Writing and Difference,* trans. Alan Bass (Chicago: University of Chicago Press, 1978), 278–93.

3. Bert O. States, *Great Reckonings in Little Rooms: On the Phenomenology of Theater* (Berkeley and Los Angeles: University of California Press, 1985), 119–20.

4. Bert O. States, *The Pleasure of the Play* (Ithaca, N.Y.: Cornell University Press, 1994), 30; States, *Great Reckonings,* 119. States identifies Christian Metz as the source of the position that actors are absent from film performance and that films lack the actual aspect of performance (see *Pleasure of the Play,* 30). Chapters 2 and 3 examine the pertinent oversights in Metz's work; chapter 4 provides an alternative to Metz's view of the cinema.

5. States, *Great Reckonings,* 201.

6. Benjamin, "Work of Art," 237.

7. Ibid., 230, 229.

8. States, *Great Reckonings,* 120.

9. See Maltby, *Hollywood Cinema,* 380–89.

10. Michael Kirby, "On Acting and Not-Acting," *Drama Review* 16, no. 1 (1972): 5. Kirby does not see film acting as "received acting," but other scholars have used that term or idea to describe film acting.

11. Kirby, "Acting and Not-Acting," 5.

12. James Naremore, *Acting in the Cinema* (Berkeley and Los Angeles: University of California Press, 1988), 17.

13. Ibid., 12.

14. James Quandt, introduction to *Robert Bresson,* ed. Quandt (Toronto: Toronto International Film Festival Group, 1998), 5.

15. T. Jefferson Kline, "Picking Dostoyevsky's Pocket: Bresson's Sl(e)ight of Screen," in Quandt, *Robert Bresson,* 242.

16. Ibid., 243.

17. Doug R. Tomlinson, "Studies in the Use and Visualization of Film Performance: Alfred Hitchcock, Robert Bresson, and Jean Renoir," Ph.D. diss., New York University, 1986, 218.

18. Quandt, introduction to *Robert Bresson,* 7.

19. Kline, "Picking Dostoyevsky's Pocket," 238.

20. See David A. Cook, *A History of Narrative Film,* 4th ed. (New York: Norton, 2004), 315–26. As Cook explains, Georges Sadoul used the term *poetic realism* to describe the style, mood, and themes central to French films produced between 1934 and 1940. Cook describes Renoir as "the greatest and most influential director to emerge from poetic realism" and points out that during this period "French films were generally regarded as the most important and sophisticated in the world" (318, 326).

21. Tomlinson, "Use and Visualization," 360.

22. Ibid., 363.

23. Ibid.

24. See Kirby, "Acting and Not-Acting," 5–8.

25. Ibid., 9.

26. Ibid.

27. Paul McDonald, "Why Study Film Acting? Some Opening Reflections," in *More Than a Method: Trends and Traditions in Contemporary Film Performance,* ed. Cynthia Baron, Diane Carson, and Frank P. Tomasulo (Detroit: Wayne State University Press, 2004), 29.

28. Ibid.

29. Ibid., 30.

30. Richard De Cordova, *Picture Personalities* (Urbana: University of Illinois Press, 1990), 98.

31. See Cynthia Baron, "Crafting Film Performances: Acting in the Hollywood Studio Era," in *Screen Acting,* ed. Alan Lovell and Peter Krämer (London: Routledge, 1999), 31–45.

32. Eric Ergenbright and Jack Smalley, "Star Factory," *Ladies Home Journal,* July 1937, 54.

33. Ibid.

34. Ibid., 14, 15, 54.

35. Ibid., 54.

36. Ibid.

37. Ibid., 55.

38. "Young Starlets Learn to Act," *Life,* 13 November 1937, 36.

39. That sort of information is documented in (but largely restricted to) oral histories. For example, in the Performing Arts Oral History Collection, the transcript of Ronald L. Davis's interview with Virginia Mayo reveals that she studied with Enright throughout her career. Mayo points out that Enright prepared the actress for her performance in *The Best Years of Our Lives* (1946) and that di-

rector William Wyler simply suggested a few pieces of business when she got to the set. See Virginia Mayo, interview, 30 November 1973, Performing Arts Oral History Collection, Southern Methodist University.

40. See "Terry Hunt's Job Is to Keep Movie Stars Thin and Healthy," *Life,* 15 July 1940, 55–57.

41. "The Big Build-Up: Hollywood Starts to Turn 'a Pretty Girl Next Door' into a Star," *Life,* 30 August 1948, 77.

42. Ibid., 80.

43. "Apprentice Goddesses," *Life,* 1 January 1951, 36.

44. Ibid.

45. Ibid., 41.

46. Ibid.

47. Universal International Collection, Talent School Files, Cinema-Television Library, University of Southern California.

48. Dana Andrews, Constance McCormick Collection, Cinema-Television Library, University of Southern California.

49. Stanley Frank, "Knockouts to Order," *Saturday Evening Post,* 3 January 1948, 12.

50. Ibid.

51. Even today evidence that certain actors do their own stunts helps to authenticate their performances; Jackie Chan's international star status actually depends in part on the fact that he performs his own remarkably dangerous stunts.

52. "The Strange Doings of Actress at Practice: Friends Help Natalie Wood Polish Dramatics," *Life,* 28 January 1957, 97.

53. Ibid.

54. Ibid.

55. Lillian Burns (Sidney), interview, 17 August 1986, Performing Arts Oral History Collection, Southern Methodist University; Sandra Shevey, "Lillian Burns Sidney—She's Drama," *Los Angeles Times,* 18 December 1977, Calendar 88.

56. Philip K. Scheuer, "Franchot Tone More Than Just 'Man Joan Married,'" *Los Angeles Times,* 24 November 1935, n.p.

57. "Meet the Madame," *Modern Screen,* November 1940, 89.

58. Maurice Zolotow, "The Stars Rise Here," *Saturday Evening Post,* 18 May 1957, 44.

59. See Cynthia Baron, "As Red as a Burlesque Queen's Garters: Cold War Politics and the Actors' Lab in Hollywood," in *Headline Hollywood: A Century of Film Scandal,* ed. David A. Cook and Adrienne McLean (New Brunwick, N.J.: Rutgers University Press, 2001), 143–62.

60. See Foster Hirsh, *A Method to Their Madness: The History of the Actors Studio* (New York: Da Capo, 1984); and Robert Lewis, *Method or Madness?* (New York: Samuel French, 1958).

61. See Robert Barton, *Acting Onstage and Off,* 4th ed. (Belmont, Calif.: Thomason-Wadsworth, 2006), 155–64; David Krasner, ed., *Method Acting Reconsidered* (New York: St. Martin's Press, 2000), 3–39; and David Krasner,

"Strasberg, Adler and Meisner: Method Acting," *Twentieth Century Actor Training,* ed. Alison Hodge (New York: Routledge, 2000), 129–50.

62. See Barton, *Acting Onstage and Off,* 110–45; and Sharon Marie Carnicke, *Stanislavsky in Focus* (Amsterdam: Harwood/Routledge, 1998).

63. See Carnicke, *Stanislavsky in Focus;* and Sharon Marie Carnicke, "Stanislavsky's System: Pathways for the Actor," in Hodge, *Twentieth Century Actor Training,* 11–36.

64. See Sharon Marie Carnicke, "Lee Strasberg's Paradox of the Actor," in Lovell and Krämer, *Screen Acting,* 75–87.

65. Lee Strasberg, *A Dream of Passion: The Development of the Method* (Boston: Little, Brown, 1987), 172.

66. See William H. Phillips, *Film: An Introduction,* 2nd ed. (Boston: Bedford/St. Martin's Press, 2002), 19–26.

67. Ibid., 23.

68. Ibid.

69. Christine Geraghty, "Re-examining Stardom: Questions of Texts, Bodies, and Performance," in *Reinventing Film Studies,* ed. Christine Gledhill and Linda Williams (London: Arnold, 2000), 192.

70. Ibid.

71. Ibid.; see also Philip Drake, "Reconceptualizing Screen Performance," *Journal of Film and Video* 58, nos. 1–2 (2006): 84–94.

72. De Cordova, *Picture Personalities,* 19.

73. Miriam Hansen, *Babel and Babylon: Spectatorship in American Silent Film* (Cambridge: Harvard University Press, 1991), 23.

74. See Vanessa R. Schwartz, "Cinematic Spectatorship before the Apparatus: The Public Taste for Reality in *Fin-de-Siècle* Paris," in *Cinema and the Invention of Modern Life,* ed. Leo Charney and Vanessa R. Schwartz (Berkeley and Los Angeles: University of California Press, 1995), 297–319.

75. See Richard Abel, *The Cine Goes to Town: French Cinema, 1896–1914* (Berkeley and Los Angeles: University of California Press, 1994); and Charles Musser, *Before the Nickelodeon: Edwin S. Porter and the Edison Manufacturing Company* (Berkeley and Los Angeles: University of California Press, 1991).

76. Abel, *Cine Goes to Town,* xiv.

77. De Cordova, *Picture Personalities,* 36.

78. See Cook, *History of Narrative Film,* 46–48.

79. Toby Cole and Helen Krich Chinoy, eds., *Actors on Acting* (New York: Crown, 1970), 203.

80. Ibid.

81. Ibid., 213.

82. Ibid., 214.

83. Ben Brewster and Lea Jacobs, *Theatre to Cinema: Stage Pictorialism and the Early Feature Film* (New York: Oxford University Press, 1997), 94.

84. Naremore, *Acting in the Cinema,* 30.

85. Ibid., 28.

Chapter 2

1. Kirby, "Acting and Not-Acting," 9.

2. Jeremy G. Butler, introduction to *Star Texts: Image and Performance in Film and Television,* ed. Butler (Detroit: Wayne State University Press, 1991), 7.

3. Ibid.

4. See Cook, *History of Narrative Film,* 118–22. The factors that have made it difficult to determine Kuleshov's actual views are comparable to those that have affected understanding of Stanislavsky's body of work; see Carnicke, *Stanislavsky in Focus.*

5. Lev Kuleshov, *Kuleshov on Film: Writings by Lev Kuleshov,* ed. and trans. Ronald Levaco (Berkeley and Los Angeles: University of California Press, 1974), 192.

6. Cook, *History of Narrative Film,* 119.

7. Ibid.

8. Maltby, *Hollywood Cinema,* 391; the quote is from Jay Leyda, *Kino: A History of the Russian and Soviet Film,* 3rd ed. (Princeton, N.J.: Princeton University Press, 1983), 165.

9. Cook, *History of Narrative Film,* 119.

10. Ibid. Commutation tests are often used in studies of images and spoken or written language. One uses substitution, transposition, addition, or deletion to assess how changes in the visual, audio, or written form affect the meaning images or words convey.

11. Ronald Levaco, introduction to *Kuleshov on Film,* 8.

12. Cook, *History of Narrative Film,* 119.

13. Kuleshov, *Kuleshov on Film,* 200.

14. Butler, introduction to *Star Texts,* 7.

15. Kuleshov, *Kuleshov on Film,* 192.

16. Ibid.

17. Ibid.

18. Ibid., 192–93.

19. Ibid., 193.

20. Ibid.

21. Ibid.

22. Ibid., 194.

23. Ibid.

24. Ibid., 194–95.

25. Ibid., 195.

26. Ibid.

27. Ibid., 102; see 99–115 for "the training of the actor."

28. Ibid., 102.

29. Ibid., 107.

30. Ibid., 108.

31. Ibid., 113.

32. Ibid.

33. Ibid., 115.

34. Ibid.

35. Naremore, *Acting in the Cinema,* 25.

36. Butler, introduction to *Star Texts,* 7.

37. Kuleshov, *Kuleshov on Film,* 193.

38. Ibid., 63.

39. Ibid., 63, 99–100.

40. Ibid., 195.

41. Kristin Thompson and David Bordwell, *Film History: An Introduction* (New York: McGraw-Hill, 1994), 583, 585.

42. Kirby, "Acting and Not-Acting," 9. While Kirby's essay suggests that, in a type of realism found in many films, actors do very little, it seems that more often actors are required to do very little that would convey emotion or intention in films that belong to modernist traditions.

43. Doug Tomlinson, "Performance in the Films of Robert Bresson: The Aesthetics of Denial," in Baron, Carson, and Tomasulo, *More Than a Method,* 76.

44. Ibid., 77.

45. Ibid.

46. Kirby, "Acting and Not-Acting," 9.

47. Tomlinson, "Performance in Bresson," 71.

48. Frank P. Tomasulo, "'The Sounds of Silence': Modernist Acting in Michelangelo Antonioni's *Blow-Up,*" in Baron, Carson, and Tomasulo, *More Than a Method,* 96.

49. Ibid., 102.

50. Ibid., 108.

51. Ibid., 115.

52. Ibid., 120.

53. Diane Carson, "Plain and Simple: Masculinity through John Sayles's Lens," in Baron, Carson, and Tomasulo, *More Than a Method,* 177.

54. Ibid.

55. Ibid.

56. Jonathan Rosenbaum, *Placing Movies: The Practice of Film Criticism* (Berkeley and Los Angeles: University of California Press, 1995), 159–60.

57. Ibid., 161.

58. Ivone Margulies, "John Cassavetes: Auteur Director," in *The New American Cinema,* ed. Jon Lewis (Durham, N.C.: Duke University Press, 1998), 294.

59. Ibid., 294.

60. Tomlinson, "Use and Visualization," 35.

61. Jean Renoir, *Directing the Film: Film Directors on Their Art,* ed. Eric Sherman (Los Angeles: Acrobat, 1976), 162–63.

62. Michelangelo Antonioni, *The Architecture of Vision: Writings and Interviews on Cinema,* ed. Carlo de Carlo, Giorgio Tinazzi, and Marga Cottino-Jones (New York: Marsillo, 1976), 175.

63. Henry Fonda, in *Playing to the Camera: Film Actors Discuss Their Craft,* ed. Bert Cardullo, Harry Geduld, Ronald Gottesman, and Leigh Woods (New Haven: Yale University Press, 1998), 212.

64. Robert Altman, *Robert Altman: Interviews,* ed. David Sterritt (Jackson: University Press of Mississippi, 2000), 129.

65. Fonda, in Cardullo et al., *Playing to the Camera,* 216.

66. Carnicke, "Screen Performances and Directors' Visions," in Baron, Carson, and Tomasulo, *More Than a Method,* 52.

67. Philip Auslander, *Liveness: Performance in a Mediatized Culture* (New York: Routledge, 1999), 29; Kirby, "Acting and Not-Acting," 4. Kirby does not see film acting as "nonmatrixed representation." Auslander acknowledges that he uses Kirby's term out of context to suit the point he wants to make about cinema.

68. Kuleshov, *Kuleshov on Film,* 195.

69. Maltby, *Hollywood Cinema,* 374.

70. Ibid.

71. Ibid.

72. Ibid.

73. Ronald E. Shields, "Acting Prima Donna Politics in Tomás Gutiérrez Alea's *Strawberry and Chocolate,*" in Baron, Carson, and Tomasulo, *More Than a Method,* 237.

74. Ibid.

75. Ibid.

76. Ibid., 237–38.

77. Kuleshov, *Kuleshov on Film,* 195.

78. Butler, introduction to *Star Texts,* 11.

79. Stam, Burgoyne, and Flitterman-Lewis, *New Vocabularies,* 151; see 151–54.

80. See Jean-Louis Oudart, "Suture and Cinema," *Screen* 18, no. 4 (1977–78): 35–47; and Daniel Dayan, "The Tutor-Code of Classical Cinema," in *Film Theory and Criticism,* 5th ed., ed. Leo Braudy and Marshall Cohen (New York: Oxford University Press, 1999), 118–29.

81. Stam, Burgoyne, and Flitterman-Lewis, *New Vocabularies,* 169.

82. Ibid.

83. Ibid.

84. William Rothman, "Against 'The System of Suture,'" in Braudy and Cohen, *Film Theory and Criticism,* 131.

85. Kuleshov, *Kuleshov on Film,* 195.

86. Sergei Eisenstein, *Film Form: Essays in Film Theory,* ed. and trans. Jay Leyda (New York: Harcourt, Brace and World, 1949), 40.

87. Ibid., 41.

88. Ibid., 40.

89. Ibid., 41.

90. Ibid.

91. Jonathan Crary, *Suspensions of Perception: Attention, Spectacle, and Modern Culture* (Cambridge: MIT Press, 1999), 1.

92. Ibid.

93. Ibid.

94. Ibid., 1–2.

95. Ibid., 1.

96. Ibid., 5.

97. Ibid., 1.

98. Ibid., 2.

99. Ibid., 3.

100. Pavis, *Analyzing Performance,* 130. One should note that Pavis feels qualified to define cinema even though his work reveals limited knowledge of film practice and contempt for the art form. He notes, for example, that "the processes of film actors remain relatively unfamiliar to us," and he finds it appropriate to refer to the "incontinent flow of film (its *micturition*)" (116, 130).

101. Alan T. Bates, Tina P. Patel, and Peter F. Liddle, "External Behavior Monitoring Mirrors Internal Behavior Monitoring," *Journal of Psychophysiology* 19, no. 4 (2005): 281.

102. See Giacomo Rizzolatti and Laila Craighero, "The Mirror Neuron System," *Annual Review of Neuroscience* 27 (2004): 169–92.

103. Kirby, "Acting and Not-Acting," 9.

104. Auslander, *Liveness,* 29.

105. Quinn, *The Semiotic Stage,* 22, 18.

106. Kirby, "Acting and Not-Acting," 9.

107. See ibid., 8.

Chapter 3

1. Butler, introduction to *Star Texts,* 11; see 15–16.

2. Ibid., 10.

3. Ibid., 11.

4. Stam, Burgoyne, Flitterman-Lewis, *New Vocabularies,* 72.

5. Ibid., 71.

6. The confusion between characters and performance elements is so pervasive that even Francesco Casetti will slip sometimes and say that elements "such as the play of characters, décor, and other aspects of mise-en-scène . . . concern problems of appropriateness" (*Inside the Gaze: The Fiction Film and Its Spectator,* trans. Nell Andrew with Charles O'Brien [Bloomington: Indiana University Press, 1988], 29). While décor is an observable aspect of mise-en-scène, characters are not. Audiences make inferences about "the play of characters" based on the details of gestures, expressions, framing, music, editing, sound effects, and so on.

7. Kuleshov, *Kuleshov on Film,* 115, 195.

8. Butler, introduction to *Star Texts,* 11.

9. Paul McDonald, "Supplementary Chapter: Reconceptualising Stardom," in Richard Dyer, *Stars,* new ed. (London: British Film Institute, 1998), 182.

10. See Hansen, *Babel and Babylon.*

11. Paul McDonald, "Stars in the Online Universe: Promotion, Nudity, Reverence," in *Contemporary Hollywood Stardom,* ed. Thomas Austin and Martin Barker (London: Arnold, 2003), 38–42.

12. Geraghty, "Re-examining Stardom," 187.

13. Ibid., 189.

14. Ibid.

15. Ibid., 191–99.

16. See Gérard Genette, *Narrative Discourse: An Essay in Method,* trans. Jane E. Lewin (Ithaca, N.Y.: Cornell University Press, 1980); and Gérard Genette, *Narrative Discourse Revisited,* trans. Jane E. Lewin (Ithaca, N.Y.: Cornell University Press, 1988).

17. Stephen Heath is the author of *Questions of Cinema.* He is also coeditor of *The Cinematic Apparatus* (London: Macmillan, 1980); and of *Cinema and Language* (Frederick, Md.: University Publications of America, 1983). His essays on ideology and film semiotics in *Screen* in the 1970s enhanced the influence French theorists Louis Althusser and Christian Metz would have on cinema studies in the United Kingdom and the United States. See Heath, "Comment on 'The Idea of Authorship,'" *Screen* 14, no. 3 (1973): 86–91; Heath, "Film and System: Terms of Analysis, Part I," *Screen* 16, no. 1 (1977): 7–77. French film theory turned attention away from "creative auteurs, or authors, to focus on the ideological and political content of film [and] the specific cinematic mechanisms which helped produce meaning" (Douglas Kellner, "Hollywood Film and Society," in *The Oxford Guide to Film Studies,* ed. John Hill and Pamela Church Gibson [New York: Oxford University Press, 1998], 356).

18. Stephen Heath, "Body, Voice," in *Questions of Cinema,* 178. Barry King touches on several aspects of Heath's taxonomy in "Articulating Stardom," *Screen* 26, no. 5 (1985): 27–50. However, given his focus on stardom, King does not consider Heath's final two categories: *typage* and performance elements.

19. Paul McDonald, "Film Acting," in Hill and Gibson, *Oxford Guide to Film Studies,* 31.

20. Ibid., 32.

21. Heath, "Body, Voice," 183.

22. Ibid., 179.

23. Ibid., 180.

24. Ibid. As Heath notes, he draws this phrase from Sylvie Pierre, "Éléments pour une théorie du photogramme," *Cahiers du cinema* 226–27 (1971): 81.

25. See Cynthia Baron, "*The Player*'s Parody: A Different Kind of Suture," in *Postmodernism in the Cinema,* ed. Cristina Degli-Esposti (New York: Berghahn Books, 1998), 20–43. Altman's interest in character as social type represents a departure from norms established in classical Hollywood cinema. Rather than employ characters as psychological essences that symbolize transcendent moral categories, he examines characters indigenous to an environment. The defining role of social milieu is highlighted throughout the film, and even simple moments remind one that characters are thoroughly shaped by their lives at the

studios. For example, at lunch with other members of the story department, Griffin suggests that they talk about something other than work but "an uncomfortable silence follows, then laughter—there is nothing else for them to discuss" (Baron, "*The Player's* Parody," 32).

26. Heath, "Body, Voice," 182.

27. Ibid.

28. Ibid.

29. Ibid., 183.

30. Ibid.

31. Ibid. Heath finds the "strategy of personification" used most clearly in the "Mademoiselle 19 ans" segment in *Masculine Feminine.* Typecasting that illuminates the operations of ideology and psychology can also be found in films by Tomás Gutiérrez Alea such as *Memories of Underdevelopment* (1968).

32. Ibid.

33. Ibid.

34. Ibid.

35. Ibid.

36. Ibid., 184.

37. William Graver, "The Actor's Bodies," *Text and Performance Quarterly* 17, no. 3 (1997): 221; see also 221–35.

38. Kirby, "Acting and Not-Acting," 4.

39. While the 1985 reprint of Kirby's article is the same as the 1972 version, the 2002 reprint has revisions that allow performers to be described in gender-neutral terms. In addition, the 1972 essay describes the second step on the continuum as "nonmatrixed representation," whereas the 2002 reprint refers to it as performing in a "symbolized matrix." Thus, by using "nonmatrixed representation" to describe screen acting, Auslander not only misrepresents Kirby's brief comments on film acting, namely, that it often features "simple acting," he also employs terminology that fails to capture Kirby's evolving perspective.

40. Kirby, "Acting and Not-Acting," 5. While it can be useful to delineate distinctions among a range of performance modes by considering the question of intention—because that is how those distinctions have been made—one should note that assessments about art based on notions of intention have been called into question. Structural analyses of literature persuasively argued for a "pitiless divorce . . . between the producer of the text and its user; between its owner and its customer; between its author and its reader" (Roland Barthes, *S/Z: An Essay,* trans. Richard Miller [New York: Hill and Wang, 1974], 4). Scholars pushed for that divorce for two related reasons. First, the connection between author and text was one that served "the literary institution" rather than the reader (Barthes, *S/Z,* 4). Second, it was believed that reliable insights and evaluation could "be linked only to a practice" (Barthes, *S/Z,* 4), and thus based only on evidence directly available to the reader, namely, the work of literature itself. Momentarily setting aside questions of intention can facilitate understanding of the role performance elements play in film, especially given that some observers have, without analysis, decided that screen performance involves very little intention.

41. Kirby, "Acting and Not-Acting," 5.
42. Ibid.
43. Ibid., 6.
44. Ibid.
45. Ibid., 7.
46. Cynthia Baron, "The Cybernetic Logic of the Lumière Actualities, 1895–1897," *Quarterly Review of Film and Video* 18, no. 2 (2001): 179.
47. Ibid.
48. Ibid.
49. Ibid., 180.
50. Kirby, "Acting and Not-Acting," 8.
51. Ibid., 9.
52. Ibid.
53. See Naremore, *Acting in the Cinema,* 9–17.
54. Kirby, "Acting and Not-Acting," 4.
55. Naremore, *Acting in the Cinema,* 15.
56. Ibid., 12.
57. Ibid.
58. Ibid.
59. Kirby, "Acting and Not-Acting," 9.
60. Maltby, *Hollywood Cinema,* 388.
61. Ibid., 389.
62. Kirby, "Acting and Not-Acting," 3–4.
63. Ibid., 6.
64. Ibid., 7.
65. Ibid., 9.
66. Auslander, *Liveness,* 29. Auslander does not consider performance from the vantage point of reception but instead seems to have developed his characterization of screen performance from anecdotal remarks by actors such as Willem Dafoe, who once noted that from the point of view of the performer, avant-garde theatrical performing and film acting were both "primarily nonmatrixed, task-based performing" (29).
67. Kirby, "Acting and Not-Acting," 5.
68. Ibid.
69. Eli Rozik, *The Roots of Theatre: Rethinking Ritual and Other Theories of Origin* (Iowa City: University of Iowa Press, 2002), xi.
70. Heath, "Body and Voice," 180; Rozik, *The Roots of Theatre,* 21.
71. Rozik, *The Roots of Theatre,* 74.
72. Ibid.
73. See Christopher D. Frith and Daniel M. Wolpert, eds., *The Neuroscience of Social Interaction: Decoding, Imitating, and Influencing the Actions of Others* (New York: Oxford University Press, 2004); Robert Sylwester, "Mirror Neurons," August 2002, http://www.brainconnection.com/content/181, consulted 10 March 2005; "Nova Science NOW: PBS Airdate 25 January 2005," http://www.pbs.org/wgbh/nova/transcripts/3204_science.html, consulted 10 March 2005.

Chapter 4

1. Butler, introduction to *Star Texts*, 11.

2. Ibid.

3. Saussure's structural linguistics has provided a model for analyses that see film as a language and as a form of written text. That linguistic orientation has carried over into psychoanalytic studies of film language and spectator positioning. While film scholarship has rarely drawn on Prague semiotics, Mikhail Bakhtin's work, which suggests a parallel with Prague school semiotics insofar as they both represent a "critique of the underlying premises of first-phase Russian Formalism," has been brought into film studies (Stam, Burgoyne, and Flitterman-Lewis, *New Vocabularies*, 14). James Naremore's *Acting in the Cinema* also touches on selected insights offered by "the early semiotic theorists in the Prague Circle" (14; see 84, 139). For example, explaining that disparities among performance elements contribute to the meaning conveyed, Naremore notes that actors reveal characters' conflicting emotions by showing us a succession of contradictory facial expressions or by using gestures that contradict their concomitant facial or vocal expressions.

4. Quinn, *The Semiotic Stage*, 1. Following work by Prague school theorists, other scholars have explored semiotic approaches to the actor's means of expression. In the 1960s, Polish semiotician Tadeusz Kowzan identified eight components of the actor's means of expression: word, tone, mime, gesture, movement, makeup, hairstyle, costume (see Elaine Aston and George Savona, *Theatre as Sign-System: A Semiotics of Text and Performance* [New York: Routledge, 1991], 108). One could argue that Kowzan's work represents a point of departure for Patrice Pavis, Keir Elam, Martin Esslin, and others.

5. Ladislav Matejka and Irwin R. Titunik, preface to *Semiotics of Art: Prague School Contributions*, ed. Matejka and Titunik (Cambridge: MIT Press, 1976), x.

6. Ibid.

7. Ladislav Matejka, "Postscript: Prague School Semiotics," in Matejka and Titunik, *Semiotics of Art*, 272.

8. See Peter Steiner, "Jan Mukařovský's Structural Aesthetics," in Mukařovský, *Structure, Sign, and Function*, xvi.

9. Ibid., xiv.

10. Ibid.

11. Quinn, *The Semiotic Stage*, 18, 19.

12. Matejka and Titunik, preface to *Semiotics of Art*, ix.

13. Matejka, "Postscript," 282.

14. Ibid., 282, 283.

15. Ibid., 265.

16. See Steiner, "Jan Mukařovský's Structural Aesthetics," xii.

17. Matejka, "Postscript," 266.

18. Ibid. In the last part of the citation, Matejka is quoting from Vilém Mathesius, "On the Potentiality of the Phenomena of Language," in *Prague School Reader in Linguistics*, ed. J. Vachek (Bloomington: Indiana University Press,

1964), 1–32. Mathesius was a student of Masaryk and the first chairman of the Prague Linguistic Circle.

19. Matejka, "Postscript," 280.

20. Steiner, "Jan Mukařovský's Structural Aesthetics," xiii; see Matejka, "Postscript," 280.

21. Steiner, "Jan Mukařovský's Structural Aesthetics," xv; Quinn, *The Semiotic Stage,* 20.

22. Quinn, *The Semiotic Stage,* 20.

23. Stam, Burgoyne, and Flitterman-Lewis, *New Vocabularies,* 37.

24. Ibid., 40.

25. Steiner, "Jan Mukařovský's Structural Aesthetics," xiv.

26. Quinn, *The Semiotic Stage,* 73. Mukařovský's essays on film include "Chaplin in *City Lights:* An Attempt at a Structural Analysis of a Dramatic Figure" (1931), "Time in Film" (late 1930s), and "A Note on the Aesthetics of Film" (1933); they can be found in *Structure, Sign, and Function.* His essay on time in film shows that film is best understood as a cultural and aesthetic form that exists "between" literature and theater. His essay on the aesthetics of film also establishes connections between film, literature, music, painting, and theater. In *Aesthetic Function: Norm and Value as Social Facts,* trans. Mark E. Suino (Ann Arbor: University of Michigan Press, 1970), Mukařovský also notes connections between film, epic poetry, drama, and painting (12).

Mukařovský's essay on aesthetics in film also provides an alternative perspective on shots and shot-to-shot relations. Analyzing cinematic space, he notes that films sometimes use conventional strategies for creating depth by directing viewers' attention toward the background, but that films also often reverse that conception by directing viewers' attention outward from the picture. Mukařovský sees antecedents for those multidimensional strategies in the methods that seventeenth-century baroque painters used to create dynamic pictorial space (*Structure, Sign, and Function* 181). By making that connection, Mukařovský anticipates the work of scholars who see connections between contemporary entertainment and the way baroque paintings counter the limitations of the frame by creating a "coextensive space . . . that can appear to extend *both* into the material confines of the two-dimensional surface *and* into the space of the audience" (Angela Ndalianis, *Neo-Baroque Aesthetic and Contemporary Entertainment* [Cambridge: MIT Press, 2004], 163).

Mukařovský also recognized that shots are the basis of cinematic space, yet his analysis is entirely different from work that identifies the suturing effect of shot/reverse shot pairs as the dominant feature of mainstream cinema. Rather than giving priority to one, isolated shot combination, Mukařovský argued that audiences encounter film space through and in terms of the interactions between all of the shots in a scene. While movements in the film are often subordinated to the plot so that they function to convey characters' movements, Mukařovský's concern with the evolving structure of components in cinematic space leads him to discuss actors' movements in relationship to the cinematic "stage" space created by the cinematic frame.

27. Quinn, *The Semiotic Stage,* 13.
28. Steiner, "Jan Mukařovský's Structural Aesthetics," vii.
29. See ibid.
30. Ibid., viii.
31. Quinn, *The Semiotic Stage,* 22. The first part of the citation is a quote from an unpublished letter by Jirí Veltruský; see Quinn, 39 n. 35.
32. Ibid., 21. Rather than setting out criteria for identifying, delimiting, and defining autonomous segments in narrative film, Prague semiotics anticipates studies in film history that examine aspects of cinema in relation to adherence to or divergence from aesthetic or cultural norms (see Robert C. Allen and Douglas Gomery, *Film History: Theory and Practice* [New York: McGraw-Hill, 1985], 4–5, 76–80).
33. Ibid., 82.
34. Stam, Burgoyne, and Flitterman-Lewis, *New Vocabularies,* 14–15.
35. Mukařovský, *Aesthetic Function,* 4.
36. Matejka, "Postscript," 280.
37. Quinn, *The Semiotic Stage,* 71.
38. Ibid., 23.
39. Ibid.
40. Mukařovský, *Structure, Sign, and Function,* 172.
41. See Maltby, *Hollywood Cinema,* 271.
42. Mukařovský, *Structure, Sign, and Function,* 173; see Mukařovský, *Aesthetic Function,* 12.
43. See Maltby, *Hollywood Cinema,* 389.
44. Mukařovský, *Structure, Sign, and Function,* 174.
45. Steiner, "Jan Mukařovský's Structural Aesthetics," xv.
46. Ibid.
47. Explicitly recognizing distinctions between the actor, the perceptible elements of the performance, and the immaterial dramatic character, Mukařovský notes that one can examine characters in dramatic literature (plays and screenplays) to see how texts are shaped by their period and milieu, to study interrelationships between characters, and to see if characters are organized so that one character dominates the dramatic action or if there is equilibrium in the way characters are integrated into the dramatic action (see *Structure, Sign, and Function,* 172).
48. Mukařovský, *Structure, Sign, and Function,* 172.
49. Ibid.
50. Ibid., 172, 173.
51. Ibid., 173.
52. Ibid.
53. Ibid., 174.
54. Ibid., 173. Mukařovský refers to the tableaux as "pointes."
55. Ibid.
56. Ibid., 172.

57. Ibid.
58. Ibid., 173.
59. Ibid., 174.
60. See Eisenstein, *Film Form,* 52, 82.
61. Mukařovský, *Structure, Sign, and Function,* 175.
62. Quinn, *The Semiotic Stage,* 73.
63. Mukařovský, *Structure, Sign, and Function,* 173, 174.
64. Ibid., 174–75.
65. Ibid., 175.
66. Quinn, *The Semiotic Stage,* 73.
67. Mukařovský, *Aesthetic Function,* 39.
68. Ibid.
69. Ibid., 40.
70. Ibid.
71. Ibid.
72. Mukařovský, *Structure, Sign, and Function,* 175.
73. McDonald, "Film Acting," 34.

Chapter 5

1. See Rudolf Laban, *The Mastery of Movement,* 4th ed., revised by Lisa Ullmann (London: Macdonald and Evans, 1980). The analysis in chapter 8 of this volume draws on Laban Movement Analysis.
2. Eisenstein, *Film Form,* 75.
3. Ibid., 76.
4. Mukařovský, *Structure, Sign, and Function,* 173.
5. The Odessa Steps sequence is parodied in films such as *The Untouchables* (Brian de Palma, 1987) and *The Witches* (Nicholas Roeg, 1990).
6. See Eisenstein, *Film Form,* 48–49.
7. See the case study of *Romeo and Juliet* in the appendix.
8. George Cukor had been entrusted with MGM prestige ensemble films such as *Dinner at Eight* (1933) and literary adaptations such as *David Copperfield* (1935). Later, he would direct vehicles for some of the studio's top female stars, Katharine Hepburn in *Sylvia Scarlet* (1937) and Greta Garbo in *Camille* (1937).
9. See Anthony Davies, *Filming Shakespeare's Plays* (New York: Cambridge University Press, 1988), 14.
10. Thalberg's casting for the characters of Romeo and Juliet determined that all other roles would be played by actors older than the leads. Thus, a visibly aging John Barrymore was cast as Romeo's friend, Mercutio. As a member of the famous royal family of Broadway, Barrymore's inclusion further legitimized the film's connection to great theatrical art.
11. Even though the play is rendered more faithfully in the 1936 film, at the time theater director Harley Granville-Barker complained that the film drew too much attention to the visual ("Alas, Poor Will!" *The Listener,* 3 March 1936,

387–89). In the 1970s, critic Roger Manvell objected that the MGM film emphasized the "Italianate setting of the play, often at the expense of Shakespeare's poetic arias and recitative" (*Shakespeare on Film* [New York: Praeger, 1971], 9).

12. Stephen M. Buhler, "Reviving Juliet, Repacking Romeo," in *Shakespeare after Mass Media,* ed. Richard Burt (New York: Palgrave, 2002), 245.

13. Ibid.

14. Peter Holland, "Two-Dimensional Shakespeare: *King Lear* on Film," in *Shakespeare and the Moving Image,* ed. Anthony Davies and Stanley Wells (New York: Cambridge University Press, 1994), 53. Zeffirelli was not the first to bring a realistic rendering of Verona to the screen. In 1954, Renato Castellani did so by capturing the architecture and atmosphere of Verona. Yet "Castellani paralyzed theatrical expression in the interests of realism," while Zeffirelli found theatricalism within the realistic aesthetic by using Verona's piazza as a stage and by emphasizing Mercutio as a "theatrical personality" with a "neurotic compulsion to attract and play to an audience" (Davies, *Filming Shakespeare's Plays,* 16). As a result, Zeffirelli's realistic prism for Shakespeare's play seems so appropriate and effective that future adaptations often borrow his strategy. Baz Luhrman, for example, sets the central fight in his 1996 adaptation on an abandoned stage and pushes Mercutio's self-dramatization further into drag performance.

15. Olivia Hussey and Leonard Whiting received popular acclaim for their performances in the title roles. Both actors won Golden Globe Awards for the most promising newcomers; the film won the Golden Globe for Best English Language Foreign Film.

16. Zeffirelli's casting of teenagers in the roles of lovers and the much-touted bedroom scene that presents them as sexual beings also reflected changing cultural mores. By the 1960s, sociologists had created "a new conception of the adolescent—the teenager" who struggles through a liminal phase of growth between childhood and maturity, during which sexual urgings and adult concerns emerge (Buhler, "Reviving Juliet, Repacking Romeo," 247). That conception did not belong to Shakespeare's original play. Moreover, whereas the adult actors in Cukor's film accessed the world of childhood in their portrayals of Romeo and Juliet, Zeffirelli's young actors portray the conflicting tensions of adolescence, as Whiting does when his adult lovemaking is juxtaposed to the childish sobs that mark his response to news of his imminent exile.

17. Buhler, "Reviving Juliet, Repackaging Romeo," 252. The film's operatic impression can be traced to Zeffirelli, who moved from designing opera costumes and sets to directing operas. He learned filmmaking as an assistant to director Lucino Visconti, whose neorealist films have been described as epic and operatic. As with Zeffirelli's apprenticeship with Visconti, cinematographer Pasqualino de Santis learned his craft as an assistant to Gianni de Venanzo, the director of photography who contributed to the opulent and surreal design of Federico Fellini's *8½* (1963) and *Juliet of the Spirits* (1965).

18. Peter S. Donaldson, "'In Fair Verona': Media, Spectacle, and Performance in *William Shakespeare's Romeo + Juliet,*" in Burt, *Shakespeare after Mass Media,* 61.

19. Ibid., 62.
20. Ibid., 63.
21. See ibid., 72.
22. Francisco Menendez, "Redefining Originality: Pearce and Luhrman's Conception of Romeo and Juliet," *Creative Screenwriting* 5, no. 2 (1998): 39.
23. Eric Bauer, "Re-revealing Shakespeare: An Interview with Baz Luhrman," *Creative Screenwriting* 5, no. 2 (1998): 34.
24. Menendez, "Redefining Originality," 39.
25. Bauer, "Re-revealing Shakespeare," 32.
26. Brenda Cross, ed., *The Film Hamlet: A Record of Its Production* (London: Saturn Press, 1948), 12.
27. Foster Hirsh, *Laurence Olivier on Screen* (New York: Da Capo Press, 1984), 90–91.
28. See Neil Taylor, "The Films of Hamlet," in Davies and Wells, *Shakespeare and Moving Image,* 180, 188.
29. Ibid., 188.
30. Ibid.
31. Alasdair Brown, *Hamlet* (London: Warner Bros., 1990), 8. Brown's booklet accompanied the video release of Zeffirelli's film; see Taylor, "The Films of Hamlet," 191, 195.
32. Taylor, "The Films of Hamlet," 192.
33. Michael Caine, *Acting in Film* (New York: Applause Books, 1990), 63.
34. Patrick Tucker, *Secrets of Screen Acting,* 2nd ed. (New York: Routledge, 2003), 32.
35. Caine, *Acting in Film,* 59.
36. See Tucker, *Secrets of Screen Acting,* 70.
37. Ibid., 158.
38. Conrad Buff, interview, *Antwone Fisher,* DVD: Special Screening Copy, Twentieth Century Fox, 2003.
39. Ibid.
40. Cross, *The Film Hamlet,* 33.
41. Ibid., 34.
42. Ibid., 35.
43. Ibid.
44. Bernice W. Kliman, *Hamlet: Film, Television, and Audio Performance* (London: Associated University Presses, 1988), 27, 28.
45. Taylor, "The Films of Hamlet," 189.
46. Ibid.
47. Kliman, *Hamlet,* 171.
48. Ibid.
49. See Tucker, *Secrets of Screen Acting,* 143.
50. Ace Pilkington, "Zeffirelli's Shakespeare," in Davies and Wells, *Shakespeare and Moving Image,* 175.
51. Strasberg's reinterpretation of Stanislavsky's System provides methods for working in isolation. See Carnicke, "Strasberg's Paradox." Sharon Carnicke

would like to thank Setrak Bronzian, director and actor, for assistance in the analysis of the *Hamlet* adaptations.

Chapter 6

1. As noted in chapter 4, the various aspects of an actor's means of expression have been succinctly outlined by Prague school theorists and scholars such as Tadeusz Kowzan. This chapter's analysis of acting and cultural-aesthetic traditions benefits from our collaboration with Diane Carson, who contributed to the Society for Cinema Studies workshop, "Teaching Cross-Cultural Analysis of Film Performance," in 1999.

2. J. L. Anderson, "Spoken Silents in the Japanese Cinema; or, Talking to Pictures: Essaying the *Katsuben,* Contexturalizing the Texts," in *Reframing Japanese Cinema: Authorship, Genre, History,* ed. Arthur Nolletti, Jr., and David Desser (Bloomington: Indiana University Press, 1992), 261.

3. Keiko I. McDonald, *Japanese Classical Theater in Films* (Cranbury, N.J.: Associated University Presses, 1994), 11.

4. See David Desser, "Narrating the Human Condition: *High and Low* and Story-Telling in Kurosawa's Cinema," in *Perspectives on Akira Kurosawa,* ed. James Goodwin (New York: G. K. Hall, 1994), 157.

5. Joanne Bernardi, *Writing in Light: The Silent Scenario and the Japanese Pure Film Movement* (Detroit: Wayne State University Press, 2001), 33, 36.

6. Donald Richie, *Japanese Cinema: An Introduction* (New York: Oxford University Press, 1990), 3, 1.

7. Brian Powell, *Japan's Modern Theatre: A Century of Change and Continuity* (London: Japan Library, 2002), 27–33.

8. See Richie, *Japanese Cinema,* 11.

9. See Powell, *Japan's Modern Theatre,* 31.

10. See Powell, *Japan's Modern Theatre,* 31; see Bernardi, *Writing in Light,* 15.

11. Richie, *Japanese Cinema,* 12; Benito Ortolani, *The Japanese Theatre: From Shamanistic Ritual to Contemporary Pluralism,* rev. ed. (Princeton, N.J.: Princeton University Press, 1995), 247.

12. Ortolani, *The Japanese Theatre,* 253.

13. See Cook, *History of Narrative Film,* 732–36.

14. Ortolani, *The Japanese Theatre,* 257, 263, 264.

15. See McDonald, *Japanese Classical Theater in Films,* 11, 125–44, 170–80.

16. Akira Kurosawa, "Notes on Filmmaking," in Goodwin, *Perspectives on Akira Kurosawa,* 63.

17. Ibid.

18. Tadao Sato, "Akira Kurosawa Talks about *Throne of Blood,*" in Goodwin, *Perspectives on Akira Kurosawa,* 52.

19. Ibid.

20. Ibid.

21. Tony Rayns, "The 1930s and the 1940s," in Goodwin, *Perspectives on Akira Kurosawa,* 47.

22. Donald Richie, *The Films of Akira Kurosawa* (Berkeley and Los Angeles: University of California Press, 1965), 191.

23. Ibid.

24. Ibid.

25. Peter Grilli, "Kurosawa Directs a Cinematic *Lear*," in Goodwin, *Perspectives on Akira Kurosawa,* 60.

26. Ibid.

27. Ortolani, *The Japanese Theatre,* 167; Richie, *Japanese Cinema,* 8.

28. Oscar G. Brockett, *History of the Theatre,* 5th ed. (Boston: Allyn and Bacon, 1987), 305.

29. Ibid., 307.

30. Powell, *Japan's Modern Theatre,* xxix.

31. Ibid., xxx.

32. Ibid., xxviii.

33. Brockett, *History of the Theatre,* 297, 298; James R. Brandon, introduction to *No and Kyogen in the Contemporary World,* ed. Brandon (Honolulu: University of Hawaii Press, 1997), 6.

34. See Ortolani, *The Japanese Theatre,* 151.

35. Brockett, *History of the Theatre,* 298, 300.

36. Brandon, introduction to *No and Kyogen,* 4.

37. Richard Emmert, "Expanding *No*'s Horizons: Considerations for a New *No* Perspective," in Brandon, *No and Kyogen,* 25.

38. Ibid.

39. Ibid.

40. Ibid.

41. Ibid.

42. Ibid., 26.

43. Ibid.

44. Ibid., 27.

45. Tadashi Suzuki, *The Way of Acting,* trans. J. Thomas Rimer (New York: Theatre Communications Group, 1986), 5.

46. Ortolani, *The Japanese Theatre,* 153.

47. Ibid.

48. As the comparative study reveals, performances are grounded in specific conceptions of character, person, and identity. Describing those conceptions can be difficult because characters also exist on a continuum defined by degrees of typicality and individuality; within a single film characters can have plot functions that range from extra to messenger boy to confidant to antagonist to hero.

49. See Lillian Ross and Helen Ross, "Vladimir Sokoloff," in *The Player: A Profile of an Art* (New York: Limelight Editions, 1984), 310–15.

50. Naremore, *Acting in the Cinema,* 60.

51. Ibid., 63.

52. Ibid., 63; see 64.

53. Ibid., 51.

54. Ibid., 53.

55. Ibid., 56, 53.

56. Ibid., 53.

57. Ibid.; see James H. McTeague, *Before Stanislavsky: American Professional Acting Schools and Acting Theory, 1875–1925* (Metuchen, N.J.: Scarecrow Press, 1993).

58. Naremore, *Acting in the Cinema,* 54.

59. See ibid., 55.

60. See Elaine Aston, *An Introduction to Feminism and Theater* (New York: Routledge, 1995), 65–66; Gay Gibson Cima, *Performing Women: Female Characters, Male Playwrights, and the Modern Stage* (Ithaca, N.Y.: Cornell University Press, 1993), 7–8; Lauren Love, "Rejecting the Organic: A Feminist Actor's Approach," in *Acting (Re)Considered: A Theoretical and Practical Guide,* 2nd ed., ed. Phillip B. Zarilli (New York: Routledge, 2002), 278.

61. See Aston, *Feminism and Theater,* 66; Cima, *Performing Women,* 7–8; Elin Diamond, "Brechtian Theory/ Feminist Theory: Toward a Gestic Feminist Criticism," *Drama Review* 32, no. 1 (1988): 83–86. Stanislavsky's System suggests ways to analyze scripts in terms of (1) the problems characters need to solve to reach their goals, (2) the specific actions characters will use to reach their goals, and (3) the structure of scenes that arises from the actions characters take in pursuit of their goals. The nearly exclusive identification of Stanislavsky with realism ignores much of his career; his Chekhov productions, which used naturalism as their theatrical style, represent a phase of his work that precedes his most concentrated efforts to develop an acting system. He also directed stylized operas, symbolist plays, and verse dramas by Pushkin, Shakespeare, and Molière. His System, which turned away from emotional memory as a lure to the actor's work, articulates methods for utilizing imagination, physical and mental exercises from yoga, modern dance, the Soviet interpretation of the Method of Physical Actions, and his last, most innovative approach, Active Analysis, through which the text is viewed as a dynamic structure of actions and counteractions that produce chains of events. See Carnicke, *Stanislavsky in Focus,* 154–62; Carnicke, "Stanislavsky's System," 11–36; Carnicke, "Screen Performances," 46–47.

62. See Diamond, "Brechtian Theory/Feminist Theory," 83–86.

63. Ellen Gainor, "Rethinking Feminism, Stanislavsky, and Performance," *Theatre Topics* 12, no. 2 (2002): 167–68.

64. Ibid., 172.

65. Cima, *Performing Women,* 7–8.

Chapter 7

1. Laurence Olivier, "The Art of Persuasion," in Cole and Chinoy, *Actors on Acting,* 410.

2. Ibid.

3. Geraldine Page, "The Bottomless Cup," in Cole and Chinoy, *Actors on Acting,* 639.

4. Josephine Dillon, *Modern Acting: A Guide for Stage, Screen, and Radio* (New York: Prentice-Hall, 1940), 18.

5. Patsy Ann Hecht, "Kinetic Techniques for the Actor," Ph.D. diss., Wayne State University, 1971, 88.

6. Jerzy Grotowski, *Towards a Poor Theatre,* ed. Eugenio Barba (London: Methuen, 1975), 21.

7. Ibid., 17.

8. François Delsarte, "Elements of the Delsarte System," in Cole and Chinoy, *Actors on Acting,* 188.

9. Antonin Artaud, "Athlete of the Heart," in Cole and Chinoy, *Actors on Acting,* 235.

10. Strasberg, *A Dream of Passion,* 60.

11. Ibid., 94.

12. Aulus Gellius, "The Grief of Polus," in Cole and Chinoy, *Actors on Acting,* 15.

13. See Carnicke, *Stanislavsky in Focus,* 136–37.

14. See ibid., 128. See Strasberg, *A Dream of Passion,* 152–55.

15. Aristotle, "Management of the Voice," in Cole and Chinoy, *Actors on Acting,* 12.

16. Carnicke, "Stanislavsky's System," 26.

17. Ibid., 26.

18. Lisa Wolford, "Grotowski's Vision of the Actor: The Search for Contact," in Hodge, *Twentieth Century Actor Training,* 193.

19. Ibid., 198.

20. Ibid., 199, 193.

21. Ibid., 197.

22. As Wolford explains, "Grotowski cited Stanislavsky's work with physical actions, Meyerhold's biomechanics and the Delsarte system as particularly fruitful in the development of his own practice, along with the work of Vakhtangov and Dullin. He [also] acknowledged having been inspired by the training methods of Kathakali, Peking Opera, and Noh Theatre" (ibid., 200).

23. Ibid., 200, 199.

24. Robert Leach, "Meyerhold and Biomechanics," in Hodge, *Twentieth Century Actor Training,* 38.

25. Ibid., 39.

26. Ibid., 39–40, 43.

27. Suzuki, *The Way of Acting,* 8.

28. Denis Diderot, *The Paradox of the Actor* (New York: Hill and Wang, 1957), 32–33.

29. François Delsarte, *The Delsarte System of Oratory* (New York: Edgar S. Werner, 1893), 460.

30. Ibid., 39–40.

31. Ibid., 409.

32. John Delman, Jr., *The Art of Acting* (New York: Harper, 1949), 241.

33. Ted Shawn, *Every Little Movement* (New York: Dance Horizons, 1963), 11.

34. Ibid.

35. See Hecht, "Kinetic Techniques," 41–132; 74–75 for calculation of gestures.

36. Anna Morgan, *An Hour with Delsarte* (Boston: Lee and Shephard, 1891), 58–59.

37. Hecht, "Kinetic Techniques," 81.

38. Rhona Blair, "Reconsidering Stanislavsky: Feeling, Feminism and the Actor," *Theatre Topics* 12, no. 2 (2002): 178. Chapter 2 points out that research on mirror neurons and their role in cognition, emotion, self-construction, and cultural transmission has profound implications for studies of gesture and expression in (screen) performance because it promises to illuminate the neurological dimension of human perception. Looking at the production rather than the reception side of human expression, neuropsychologist Susana Bloch has helped to clarify the physiological aspect of human expression. Bloch has isolated patterns of breathing, muscle tension, posture, gesture, and vocalization that are related to the human expression of six basic emotions: joy, sexual arousal, tenderness, grief, fear, and anger. The research conducted by Bloch and others demonstrates that emotions are manifested through discernable physical changes. For each of the six basic emotions, Bloch has located a unique breathing pattern that is "characterized by amplitude and frequency of modulation, and whether [a person inhales or exhales] through the nose or mouth" (Barton, *Acting On Stage and Off*, 299). She has determined that each of the six basic emotions is also distinguished by "a muscular activation characterized by a set of contracting or relaxing muscles, particularly those of the abdomen, and defined by a particular posture" (ibid., 299). Bloch has also identified "facial muscle patterns" unique to each of the six basic, global emotions. Echoing Stanislavsky's finding on physical action, Bloch's techniques of "Alba Emoting" involve using the breathing pattern and muscle tension associated with one of the basic emotions to create that feeling and to present that emotion to audiences without being overwhelmed by the feeling (Barton, 300; see Pamela D. Chabora, "Emotion Training and the Mind/Body Connection: Alba Emoting and the Method," in Krasner, *Method Acting Reconsidered*, 229–43).

39. Paul Ekman, "Biological and Cultural Contributions to Body and Facial Movement in the Expression of Emotion," in *Explaining Emotions* (Berkeley and Los Angeles: University of California Press, 1980), 91.

40. Ibid., 93.

41. Ibid., 74–76.

42. Ibid., 85.

43. Delman, *The Art of Acting*, 241.

44. See McTeague, *Before Stanislavsky*, 1–43; Steele MacKaye's assistant, Franklin H. Sargent, became head of the Lyceum Theatre and School of Acting in 1885, when MacKaye severed his ties with the Lyceum a year after establishing it. In 1892, Sargent renamed the school, the American Academy of Dra-

matic Arts and continued as head of the school until his death in 1924 (ibid., 45–93).

45. See Naremore, *Acting in the Cinema,* 53–67.

46. See Dillon, *Modern Acting,* 3–19.

47. McDonald, "Film Acting," 30.

48. Geoff Andrew, *Stranger Than Paradise: Maverick Film-makers in Recent Amercian Cinema* (New York: Limelight, 1999), 111.

49. Scott McKenzie, "Wayne Wang," in *Fifty Contemporary Filmmakers,* ed. Yvonne Tasker (New York: Routledge, 2002), 370.

50. Ibid., 370, 372.

51. After reading Auster's "Auggie Wren's Christmas Story" in the Christmas 1990 edition of the *New York Times,* Wang initiated the collaboration with Auster and wrote the first treatment for *Smoke.*

52. Morgan, *An Hour with Delsarte,* 96–97.

53. Ibid., 47.

54. Ibid., 48.

55. Ibid., 55–56.

56. John Zorn, ed., *The Essential Delsarte* (Metuchen, N.J.: Scarecrow Press, 1968), 109; see Delsarte, *Delsarte System of Oratory,* 430.

57. Morgan, *An Hour with Delsarte,* 54.

58. Suzanne K. Langer, *Feeling and Form* (New York: Charles Scribner's Sons, 1953), 59–60; see Bernard Beckerman, *Dynamics of Drama: Theory and Methods of Analysis* (New York: Knopf, 1970), 31.

59. See Naremore, *Acting in the Cinema,* 17. Nonnaturalistic productions prompt audiences to acknowledge the crafted nature of performances. Work inspired by Bertolt Brecht and his collaborators, for example, often draws attention to the observable elements of performance by inviting the audience to measure the distance between actor and character. Actors' gestures and vocal expressions are presented in spatial and/or temporal counterpoint to other performance and cinematic elements; dramatic, visual, and aural/musical elements are placed in counterpoint to emphasize the opaque dimension of the entire production. Disparate elements do not cohere to produce a seamless picture of "the world" made visible through transparent production elements. Jean-Luc Godard's *Weekend* contains many scenes with Brechtian performances; one occurs in the aftermath of the collision between the sports car and the tractor when the young woman rants at the dumbstruck farmer as the townspeople look on in amusement.

60. Ibid.

61. Ibid., 76.

62. Ibid., 51. Postmodern productions sometimes feature performances that use stylized "movement vocabulary" as a response to performing art traditions influenced by the emphasis on natural behavior in "modern dramatic literature."

63. See Joseph R. Roach, *The Player's Passion: Studies in the Science of Acting* (Newark: University of Delaware Press, 1985), 69–74.

64. David Richard Jones, *Great Directors at Work: Stanislavski, Brecht,*

Kazan, Brook (Berkeley and Los Angeles: University of California Press, 1986), 149.

65. Ibid.

66. Grotowski, *Towards a Poor Theatre,* 21; see Robert Cohen, *Theatre* (Mountain View, Calif.: Mayfield, 1994), 351–54.

67. Naremore, *Acting in the Cinema,* 34.

68. Mario Falsetto, *Stanley Kubrick: A Narrative and Stylistic Analysis* (Westport, Conn.: Praeger, 1994), 165, 171.

69. Dennis Bingham, *Acting Male: Masculinities in the Films of James Stewart, Jack Nicholson, and Clint Eastwood* (New Brunswick, N.J.: Rutgers University Press, 1994), 111.

70. Leslie Felperin, "Smoke Opera," *Sight and Sound* 6, no. 4 (1996): 6.

71. Andrew, *Stranger Than Paradise,* 129. Our understanding of *Smoke* owes a great deal to Owen Shapiro and Frank P. Tomasulo, who were members of our panel on performances in the film at the Society for Cinema Studies conference in 2000.

Chapter 8

1. Hillel Schwartz, "Torque: The New Kinaesthetic of the Twentieth Century," in *Incorporations,* ed. Jonathan Crary and Sanford Kwinter (New York: Zone, 1992), 101.

2. Ibid.

3. Ibid.

4. Ibid., 71.

5. Ibid.

6. See Isa Partsch-Bergsohn, *Modern Dance in Germany and the United States: Crosscurrents and Influences* (Chur, Switzerland: Harwood, 1994), 63.

7. Ibid., 44.

8. Ibid., 68.

9. See ibid., 81.

10. Schwartz, "Torque," 72.

11. Ibid., 74.

12. Partsch-Bergsohn, *Modern Dance,* 28. Laban's work also led to a complex notation system for transcribing dance choreography. Albert Knust is the Laban protégé most responsible for developing Labanotation. John Hodgson explains that even before Knust's *Encyclopedia of Kinetography* was published in 1948, "Knust knew more about the method of notation than the master who formulated the script" (*Mastering Movement: The Life and Work of Rudolf Laban* [New York: Routledge, 2001], 104). Carol-Lynne Moore and Kaoru Yamamoto discuss various types of notation in *Beyond Words: Movement Observation and Analysis* (New York: Gordon and Breach, 1988), 228–41. Laban Movement Analysis is also just "one observational framework widely used in movement study" (Moore and Yamamoto, 181). Ray Birdwhistell, William Condon, Albert Scheflen, and others have developed rubrics for studying human movement.

Working in the area of body therapy, Irmgard Bartenieff, F. M. Alexander, Moshe Feldenkrais, and others have developed systems for analyzing human movement. Important contributions to movement analysis have been made by Warren Lamb and other analysts who are members of Action Profilers International. Joan Herrington provides a concise overview of Anne Bogart's movement-centered directorial approach in "Directing with the Viewpoints," *Theatre Topics* 10, no. 2 (2000): 155–68.

13. Schwartz, "Torque," 91–92.

14. Ibid., 92.

15. Ibid.

16. See ibid., 80.

17. Irmgard Bartenieff with Doris Lewis, *Body Movement: Coping with the Environment* (New York: Gordon and Breach, 1980), ix.

18. Hodgson, *Mastering Movement,* 5.

19. Ibid., 42.

20. Clive Barker, "Joan Littlewood," in Hodge, *Twentieth Century Actor Training,* 115.

21. Ibid., 119.

22. Valerie Preston-Dunlap, *Rudolf Laban: An Extraordinary Life* (London: Dance Books, 1998), 273.

23. Carnicke, "Stanislavsky's System," 26; see Valentina Litvinoff, "The Natural and the Stylized: In Conflict or Harmony?" in *Movement for the Actor,* ed. Lucille S. Rubin (New York: Drama Book Specialists, 1980), 106.

24. Litvinoff, "Natural and Stylized," 104.

25. Ibid., 107.

26. *Training Day* received three major honors in the 2002 Black Reel Award theatrical release competition. Exemplifying the verve and emotional gravity of New African American Cinema, *Training Day* was named Best Film, Antoine Fuqua was named Best Director, and Denzel Washington received the award for Best Actor. Fuqua would subsequently receive Black Reel Award nominations for his direction of *Tears of the Sun* (2003) and *Lightning in a Bottle* (2004). A director respected by his peers but not well known in mainstream culture, Fuqua can perhaps be compared to directors such as Charles Burnett, Bill Duke, Carl Franklin, Allen and Albert Hughes, and John Singleton. Fuqua's transition "into feature films resembles the professional track followed by his contemporaries Hype Williams and F. Gary Gray" because he also made his reputation directing award-winning music videos and high-profile commercials before moving into feature films (Melvin Donalson, *Black Directors in Hollywood* [Austin: University of Texas Press, 2003], 319).

27. Donald Bogle, *Toms, Coons, Mulattoes, Mammies, and Bucks: An Interpretive History of Blacks in American Films,* 4th ed. (New York: Continuum, 2001), 423.

28. Bob Graham, "Denzel Gets Dangerous," *San Francisco Chronicle,* 5 October 2001, C1.

29. Ibid.

30. Jean Newlove, *Laban for Actors and Dancers* (New York: Routledge, 1993), 61.

31. Ibid., 48.

32. See ibid.

33. Ibid.

34. See ibid.

35. See Vera Maletic, *Body Space Expression: The Development of Rudolf Laban's Movement and Dance Concepts* (New York: Mouton de Gruyter, 1987), 100.

36. See Newlove, *Laban,* 105. The Laban system is so comprehensive that there are entire areas of inquiry not considered in our discussion. For example, future studies could examine performances in a film in light of what Laban termed "incomplete efforts," which provide frameworks for analyzing characters (who have needs or problems) who must perform actions in order to achieve their objective in a scene and/or narrative. Jean Newlove explains that incomplete efforts are revealed by actions "in which two motion factors are stressed, one of which may be flow" (128). Actions with identifiable space and time dimensions are opposed to those with identifiable flow and weight qualities; those with discernable space and flow qualities are opposed to actions with identifiable weight and time qualities; those with clear space and weight qualities are opposed to ones in which qualities of time and flow are discernable. Laban proposed that the incomplete efforts are indicative of inner attitudes. For instance, he suggested "the characteristics of the incomplete effort Space-Time were representative of an AWAKE attitude" (Newlove, 131).

37. Laban, *The Mastery of Movement,* 21. Some terms can be applied to the motion of objects and the movement of humans. It makes sense to say that "a car is ascending the hill" and that "a person is ascending the staircase." Yet even that phrase shows that there are crucial differences between motion and movement—the word "ascending" carries entirely different connotations when applied to inanimate motion and human movement. To say that the car is ascending the hill means the car is going up the hill; to say that a person is ascending the staircase indicates that he or she is going up the stairs with a certain dignity, grace, and composure.

38. Ibid., 169.

39. Ibid., 21.

40. Ibid., 169.

41. Moore and Yamamoto, *Beyond Words,* 55.

42. Warren Lamb and Elizabeth Watson, *Body Code: The Meaning in Movement* (London: Routledge, 1979), 7.

43. Maletic, *Body Space Expression,* 162.

44. Ibid., 163.

45. See ibid., 190.

46. See Genette, *Narrative Discourse.*

47. Jean Sabatine, *Movement Training for the Stage and Screen* (New York: Back Stage Books, 1995), 141.

48. Eden Davies, *Beyond Dance: Laban's Legacy of Movement Analysis* (London: Brechin Books, 2001), 66.

49. Moore and Yamamoto, *Beyond Words,* 121.

50. See ibid., 120.

51. Ibid., 121.

52. See ibid.

53. Ibid. Eisenstein's speculations about five "methods of montage" touch on the five structural features of music composition, narrative design, and human movement. Order and duration are central to "metric montage" that is based on simple, "metric" intervals. Acceleration is achieved by using increasingly shorter lengths of film; sequences are edited according to march time, waltz time, or three-quarter time. Order, duration, and frequency become more complicated in "rhythmic montage," an approach used in most film practice, for "the content within the frame is a factor possessing equal rights to consideration" (Eisenstein, *Film Form,* 73). Chapter 5's comparative analysis of the Shakespeare adaptations illustrates different uses of "rhythmic montage." Like the use of voice in literature and dominant movements in a movement phrase, "tonal montage" involves arrangement of filmic elements to express a single "emotional sound," tone, accent, or voice. In *Far From Heaven,* the filmmaker's use of periwinkle blue in lighting, costuming, and set design is an example of "tonal montage." As Eisenstein explains, "Working with combinations of varying degrees of soft-focus or varying degrees of 'shrillness' would be a typical use of tonal montage" (*Film Form,* 76). Like characters who disclose a narrative's underlying mood or the use of contrasting time elements in movement, "overtonal montage" creates a mood that exists in counterpoint to the dominate tone or accent of a sequence. Similarly, "intellectual montage" creates a counterpoint to a scene's dominant tone, but in this case the shot combinations convey ideas rather than moods or feelings.

54. Moore and Yamamoto, *Beyond Words,* 123.

55. Ibid., 285; see 116.

56. Ibid., 85.

57. Ibid., 184. Cynthia Baron would like to thank Michael Ellison for sharing information about physical approaches to performance.

Chapter 9

1. The terms used here are those most commonly employed by actors in the United States; they do not necessarily reflect accurate translations of Stanislavsky's Russian terminology. In particular, contemporary actors tend to confuse "objectives" with "actions," often using these two discrete terms as if they were synonyms. In fact, Stanislavsky sees "objectives" as the "problems" posed by the given circumstances that characters must solve through their "actions." See the glossary in Carnicke, *Stanislavsky in Focus,* for more on each of these terms.

2. Roland Barthes, *Image-Music-Text,* trans. Stephen Heath (New York: Hill and Wang, 1997), 107. Barthes sees a story as an argument that depends on "a logic of actions and a 'syntax' of characters" (87). He notes that theorists from Aristotle to his contemporary Claude Bremond see characters' choices as more significant than other aspects of narrative because they lead to actions undertaken. Barthes argues that actions themselves can be seen as the central organizing principle in narratives and explains that "paradigmatic" oppositions (of contrasting selections) have also been identified as a central organizing principle in narrative (see 99–100). Barthes establishes the importance of character actions by identifying the action or "proairetic" code one of the five key areas of consideration in studies of narrative logic. He argues that "what sustains, flows in a regular way, brings everything together, like the strings, are the proairetic sequences, the series of actions, the cadence of familiar gestures" (*S/Z,* 29). Barthes also acknowledges the importance of the hermeneutic code, the rubric for considering enigmas posed and finally answered; the "tonal unity" in most works of literary fiction is dependent on the two sequential codes (the hermeneutic and proairetic codes) that make possible "the revelation of truth and the coordination of the actions represented" (*S/Z,* 30). That small groups of actions can be identified as forming distinct sequences shows that characters' actions are fundamental, for characters' actions alone determine whether or not a sequence will be one of "desire, communication [or] struggle" (*Image-Music-Text,* 107). Stanislavsky is sometimes seen as a "structuralist." See Marvin Carlson, *Theories of the Theatre: A Historical and Critical Survey from the Greeks to the Present* (Ithaca, NY: Cornell University Press, 1993), 491.

3. Carnicke, *Stanislavsky in Focus,* 169.

4. Judith Weston, *Directing Actors: Creating Memorable Performances for Film and Television* (Studio City, Calif.: Michael Wiese Productions, 1996), 219.

5. Denny Martin Flinn, *How Not to Write a Screenplay* (Hollywood: Lone Eagle Publishing, 1999), 68.

6. Ibid.

7. See Carnicke, *Stanislavsky in Focus,* 169.

8. See ibid., 154–69. For both types of analysis, see also Carnicke, "Stanislavsky's System," 11–36.

9. Adler's lectures on script analysis were edited by Barry Paris as *Stella Adler on Ibsen, Strindberg, and Chekhov* (New York: Knopf, 1999); her master class notes were compiled and edited by Howard Kissel in *The Art of Acting* (New York: Applause, 2000).

10. See Carnicke, *Stanislavsky in Focus,* 64.

11. For example, commentaries on the DVDs for *Training Day* and *The Grifters* reveal that these productions are grounded in extensive "homework" and script analysis.

12. Moore and Yamamoto, *Beyond Words,* 185.

13. Litvinoff, "Natural and Stylized," 107.

14. See also popular books on acting such as Ivana Chubbuck, *The Power of the Actor: The Chubbuck Technique* (New York: Gotham Books, 2004); William

Ball, *A Sense of Direction: Some Observations on the Art of Directing* (New York: Drama Book Publishers, 1984); and Doug Moston, *Coming to Terms with Acting: An Instructive Glossary* (New York: Drama Book Publishers, 1993).

15. Robert Benedetti, *Action! Acting for Film and Television* (Boston: Allyn and Bacon, 2001), 82.

16. Ibid.

17. Weston, *Directing Actors,* 98.

18. Benedetti, *Action!* 90.

19. Ibid.

20. Ibid., 95.

21. Ibid.

22. Weston, *Directing Actors,* 107.

23. Benedetti, *Action!* 95–96.

24. Ibid., 96.

25. Ibid., 99.

26. Ibid. In this sensitivity to the interactive dynamics of a scene, Weston and Benedetti stop just short of fuller incorporation of Active Analysis, which treats such dynamics with even greater clarity and precision.

27. Ibid., 84.

28. Weston, *Directing Actors,* 92.

29. Ibid., 32.

30. Ibid. Weston provides lists of action verbs in appendix C, 302–7.

31. Ibid., 30.

32. Ibid., 137.

33. Ibid.

34. Ibid.

35. Ibid., 219.

36. Ibid.

37. Ibid., 211.

38. Ibid., 225.

39. Robert Cohen, *Acting Power* (Palo Alto, Calif.: Mayfield, 1978), 72.

40. Ibid.

41. Ibid.

42. Ibid., 72–73.

43. Ibid., 73.

44. Ibid., 74.

45. Ibid.

46. Ibid.

47. Ibid., 76.

48. Ibid., 79.

49. Ibid., 77.

50. Ibid.

51. Ibid.

52. Ibid.

53. Ibid.

54. Ibid., 77–78.
55. Ibid., 78.
56. Ibid.
57. Ibid.
58. Ibid., 79.
59. Ibid., 71.
60. See Jonathan Hacker and David Price, *Take Ten: Contemporary British Film Directors* (New York: Oxford University Press, 1991), 169. Useful insights into Frears's style can be found in James Saynor, "Accidental Auteur," *Sight and Sound* 3, no. 4 (1993): 3–8.
61. See ibid., 172–74. The film's smart script, stylish design, captivating performances, and acerbic insights into the complexity of human relations have caused *The Grifters* to become an increasingly respected work of cinema. Its merits were recognized at the time of its release. Screenwriter Donald Westlake received an Academy Award nomination for his adaptation of Jim Thompson's novel. Anjelica Huston received an Academy Award nomination for Best Actress and Annette Bening was nominated for Best Supporting Actress. British director Stephen Frears received an Academy Award nomination for Best Director. For Frears, *The Grifters* contributed to the growing respect of his work among film professionals. Following several years of directing in British television, Frears had gained notice for directing *My Beautiful Laundrette* (1985) and *Sammy and Rosie Get Laid* (1987). During that same period, he was nominated for a Golden Palm Award at Cannes for his direction of *Prick Up Your Ears* (1987). From there, Frears was called on to direct *Dangerous Liaisons* (1988), his first piece with American film stars.
62. Commentary on the DVD reveals that Huston, Cusack, Frears, and the screenwriter Donald Westlake all saw the last scene as a boxing match. Cusack points out that this last confrontation is where the whole film had been heading and that he knew he had to be completely engaged in the scene for it to work. Huston concurs and explains that the connection between the characters' actions and her actions in relation to Cusack were so strong that at the end of the scene she left the sound stage and the lot with the briefcase of money. Frears explains that during rehearsal, Cusack and Huston began by being so determined to achieve their characters' objectives they could not get through the scene. Frears cleared the set and collaborated with Huston and Cusack to find ways to structure give-and-take into the scene so that it could develop through the escalating stages of the confrontation.
63. Rozik, *The Roots of Theatre*, 21.

Conclusion

1. Heath, *Questions of Cinema*, 183.
2. Steiner, "Jan Mukařovský's Structural Aesthetics," xv.
3. Their insights confirm that filmic gestures and expressions, entirely distinct from characters, actors, and star images, interact with other observable aspects of cinematic representations. Practitioners from François Delsarte to

Jerzy Grotowski recognize that performances are composed of physical/vocal signs. Laban Movement Analysis highlights the material aspect of acting by focusing on "actual movement, rather than its completed result" (Lamb and Watson, *Body Code,* 7). The concrete dimension of performance also comes into view when one draws on principles of script analysis, for the terms and concepts developed by Stanislavsky can clarify the way actors' physical and vocal choices illuminate character.

BIBLIOGRAPHY

Abel, Richard. *The Cine Goes to Town: French Cinema, 1896–1914.* Berkeley and Los Angeles: University of California Press, 1994.

Acting in the Cinema: A *Cineaste* Supplement (published with support from the Academy of Motion Picture Arts and Sciences), 31, no. 4 (2006): 18–79.

Adler, Stella. *The Art of Acting.* Ed. Howard Kissel. New York: Applause, 2000.

Adler, Stella. *Stella Adler on Ibsen, Strindberg and Chekhov.* Ed. Barry Paris. New York: Knopf, 1999.

Affron, Charles. "Performing Performing: Irony and Affect." *Cinema Journal* 20, no. 1 (1980): 42–52.

Albertson, Lillian. *Motion Picture Acting.* New York: Funk and Wagnalls, 1947.

Allen, Robert C., and Douglas Gomery. *Film History: Theory and Practice.* New York: McGraw-Hill, 1985.

Amosy, Ruth. "Semiology and Theater: By Way of Introduction." *Poetics Today* 2, no. 3 (1981): 5–9.

Anderegg, Michael. *Cinematic Shakespeare.* Lanham, Md.: Rowman and Littlefield, 2004.

Anderegg, Michael. *Orson Welles, Shakespeare, and Popular Culture.* New York: Columbia University Press, 1999.

Anderson, J. L. "Spoken Silents in the Japanese Cinema; or, Talking to Pictures: Essaying the *Katsuben*, Contexturalizing the Texts." In *Reframing Japanese Cinema: Authorship, Genre, History,* ed. Arthur Nolletti, Jr., and David Desser, 259–310. Bloomington: Indiana University Press, 1992.

Andrew, Geoff. *Stranger Than Paradise: Maverick Film-makers in Recent American Cinema.* New York: Limelight, 1999.

Andrews, Dana. Interview. Constance McCormick Collection. Cinema-Television Library, University of Southern California.

"Apprentice Goddesses." *Life,* 1 January 1951, 36–41.

Aston, Elaine. *An Introduction to Feminism and Theater.* New York: Routledge, 1995.

Aston, Elaine, and George Savona. *Theatre as Sign-System: A Semiotics of Text and Performance.* London: Routledge, 1991.

Aubert, Charles. *The Art of Pantomime.* Trans. Edith Sears. New York: Henry Holt, 1927.

Auslander, Philip. *Liveness: Performance in a Mediatized Culture.* New York: Routledge, 1999.

Austin, Thomas, and Martin Barker, eds. *Contemporary Hollywood Stardom.* London: Arnold, 2003.

Bakhtin, M. M. *The Dialogic Imagination.* Ed. Michael Holquist, trans. Caryl Emerson and Michael Holquist. Austin: University of Texas Press, 1981.

Ball, William. *A Sense of Direction: Some Observations on the Art of Directing.* New York: Drama Book Publishers, 1984.
Barish, Jonas. *The Antitheatrical Prejudice.* Berkeley and Los Angeles: University of California Press, 1981.
Barker, Clive. "Joan Littlewood." In *Twentieth Century Actor Training,* ed Alison Hodge, 113–28. New York: Routledge, 2000.
Baron, Cynthia. "As Red as a Burlesque Queen's Garters: Cold War Politics and the Actors' Lab in Hollywood." In *Headline Hollywood: A Century of Film Scandal,* ed. David A. Cook and Adrienne McLean, 143–62. New Brunwick, N.J.: Rutgers University Press, 2001.
Baron, Cynthia. "Crafting Film Performances: Acting in the Hollywood Studio Era." In *Screen Acting,* ed. Alan Lovell and Peter Krämer, 31–45. London: Routledge, 1999.
Baron, Cynthia. "The Cybernetic Logic of the Lumière Actualities, 1895–1897." *Quarterly Review of Film and Video* 18, no. 2 (2001): 169–89.
Baron, Cynthia. "*The Player*'s Parody: A Different Kind of Suture." In *Postmodernism in the Cinema,* ed. Cristina Degli-Esposti, 21–43. New York: Berghahn Books, 1998.
Baron, Cynthia, and Diane Carson, eds. Special issue on Screen Performance, *Journal of Film and Video* 58, nos. 1–2 (2006): 1–107.
Baron, Cynthia, Diane Carson, and Frank P. Tomasulo, eds. *More Than a Method: Trends and Traditions in Contemporary Film Performance.* Detroit: Wayne State University Press, 2004.
Barr, Tony. *Acting for the Camera.* New York: Harper and Row, 1986.
Bartenieff, Irmgard with Doris Lewis. *Body Movement: Coping with the Environment.* New York: Gordon and Breach, 1980.
Barthes, Roland. *Image-Music-Text.* Trans. Stephen Heath. New York: Hill and Wang, 1977.
Barthes, Roland. *S/Z: An Essay.* Trans. Richard Miller. New York: Hill and Wang, 1974.
Barton, Robert. *Acting Onstage and Off.* 4th ed. Belmont, Calif.: Wadsworth/Thomas, 2006.
Bates, Alan T., Tina P. Patel, and Peter F. Liddle. "External Behavior Monitoring Mirrors Internal Behavior Monitoring." *Journal of Psychophysiology* 19, no. 4 (2005): 281–88.
Battock, Gregory, and Robert Nickas, eds. *The Art of Performance: A Critical Anthology.* New York: Dutton, 1984.
Bauer, Eric. "Re-revealing Shakespeare: An Interview with Baz Luhrman." *Creative Screenwriting* 5, no. 2 (1998): 32–35.
Bazin, André. *What Is Cinema?* 2 vols. Trans. Hugh Gray. Berkeley and Los Angeles: University of California Press, 1967.
Beck, Dennis C. "The Paradox of the Method Actor: Rethinking the Stanislavsky Legacy." In *Method Acting Reconsidered: Theory, Practice, Future,* ed. David Krasner, 261–82. New York: St. Martin's Press, 2000.

Beckerman, Bernard. *Dynamics of Drama: Theory and Method of Analysis.* New York: Knopf, 1970.

Benedetti, Robert. *Action! Acting for Film and Television.* Boston: Allyn and Bacon, 2001.

Benjamin, Walter. "The Work of Art in the Age of Mechanical Reproduction." In *Illuminations,* trans. Harry Zohn, ed. and intro. Hannah Arendt, 217–51. New York: Harcourt, Brace and World, 1968.

Bernardi, Joanne. *Writing in Light: The Silent Scenario and the Japanese Pure Film Movement.* Detroit: Wayne State University Press, 2001.

"The Big Build-Up: Hollywood Starts to Turn 'a Pretty Girl Next Door' into a Star." *Life,* 30 August 1948, 77–80.

Bingham, Dennis. *Acting Male: Masculinities in the Films of James Stewart, Jack Nicholson, and Clint Eastwood.* New Brunswick, N.J.: Rutgers University Press, 1994.

Bisplinghoff, Gretchen. "On Acting: A Working Bibliography." *Cinema Journal* 20, no. 1 (1980): 79–85.

Blair, Rhonda. "Reconsidering Stanislavsky: Feeling, Feminism, and the Actor." *Theatre Topics* 12, no. 2 (2002): 177–90.

Bloch, Susana. "Alba Emoting: A Psychophysiological Technique to Help Actors Create and Control Real Emotions." *Theatre Topics* 3, no. 2 (1993): 121–38.

Bogle, Donald. *Toms, Coons, Mulattoes, Mammies, and Bucks: An Interpretive History of Blacks in American Films,* 4th ed. New York: Continuum, 2001.

Brandon, James R. Introduction to *No and Kyogen in the Contemporary World,* ed. Brandon, 3–15. Honolulu: University of Hawaii Press, 1997.

Brewster, Ben, and Lea Jacobs. *Theatre to Cinema: Stage Pictorialism and the Early Feature Film.* New York: Oxford University Press, 1997.

Brockett, Oscar G. *History of the Theatre.* 5th ed. Boston: Allyn and Bacon, 1987.

Bryer, Jackson R., and Richard A. Davison, eds. *The Actor's Art: Conversations with Contemporary American Stage Performers.* New Brunswick, N.J.: Rutgers University Press, 2001.

Buchanan, Judith. *Shakespeare on Film.* New York: Pearson Education, 2005.

Buckland, Warren. *The Cognitive Semiotics of Film.* New York: Cambridge University Press, 2000.

Buff, Conrad. Interview. *Antwone Fisher.* DVD: Special Screening Copy. Twentieth Century Fox, 2003.

Buhler, Stephen M. "Reviving Juliet, Repackaging Romeo." In *Shakespeare after Mass Media,* ed. Richard Burt, 243–64. New York: Palgrave, 2002.

Burns, Lillian (Sydney). Interview. 17 August 1986. Performing Arts Oral History Collection, Southern Methodist University.

Butler, Jeremy G., ed. *Star Texts: Image and Performance in Film and Television.* Detroit: Wayne State University Press, 1991.

Caine, Michael. *Acting in Film.* New York: Applause, 1990.

Cardullo, Bert, Harry Geduld, Ronald Gottesman, and Leigh Woods, eds. *Play-*

ing to the Camera: Film Actors Discuss Their Craft. New Haven: Yale University Press, 1998.

Carlson, Marvin. *Performance: A Critical Introduction.* New York: Routledge, 1996.

Carlson, Marvin. *Theatre Semiotics: Signs of Life.* Bloomington: Indiana University Press, 1990.

Carlson, Marvin. *Theories of the Theatre: A Historical and Critical Survey from the Greeks to the Present.* Expanded ed. Ithaca, N.Y.: Cornell University Press, 1993.

Carnicke, Sharon Marie. "Lee Strasberg's Paradox of the Actor." In *Screen Acting,* ed. Alan Lovell and Peter Krämer, 75–87. London: Routledge, 1999.

Carnicke, Sharon Marie. "Screen Performances and Directors' Visions." In *More Than a Method: Trends and Traditions in Contemporary Film Performance,* ed. Cynthia Baron, Diane Carson, and Frank P. Tomasulo, 42–67. Detriot: Wayne State University Press, 2004.

Carnicke, Sharon Marie. *Stanislavsky in Focus.* Amsterdam: Harwood/Routledge, 1998.

Carnicke, Sharon Marie. "Stanislavsky's System: Pathways for the Actor." In *Twentieth Century Actor Training,* ed. Alison Hodge, 11–36. New York: Routledge, 2000.

Carson, Diane. "Plain and Simple: Masculinity through John Sayles's Lens." In *More Than A Method: Trends and Traditions in Contemporary Film Performance,* ed. Cynthia Baron, Diane Carson, and Frank P. Tomasulo, 1–19. Detroit: Wayne State University Press, 2004.

Casetti, Francesco. *Inside the Gaze: The Fiction Film and Its Spectator.* Trans. Nell Andrew with Charles O'Brien. Bloomington: Indiana University Press, 1998.

Cawelti, John G. "Performance and Popular Culture." *Cinema Journal* 20, no. 1 (1980): 4–13.

Chabora, Pamela D. "Emotion Training and the Mind/Body Connection: Alba Emoting and the Method." In *Method Acting Reconsidered,* ed. David Krasner, 229–43. New York: St. Martin's Press, 2000.

Chubbuck, Ivana. *The Power of the Actor: The Chubbuck Technique.* New York: Gotham Books, 2004.

Cima, Gay Gibson. *Performing Women: Female Characters, Male Playwrights, and the Modern Stage.* Ithaca, N.Y.: Cornell University Press, 1993.

Clark, Danae. *Negotiating Hollywood: The Cultural Politics of Actors' Labor.* Minneapolis: University of Minnesota Press, 1995.

Cohen, Robert. *Acting Power.* Palo Alto, Calif.: Mayfield, 1978.

Cohen, Robert. *Theatre.* Mountain View, Calif.: Mayfield, 1994.

Cole, Toby, and Helen Krich Chinoy, eds. *Actors on Acting.* New York: Crown, 1970.

Comey, Jeremiah. *The Art of Film Acting: A Guide for Actors and Directors.* New York: Focal, 2002.

Comolli, Jean-Louis. "Historical Fiction: A Body Too Much." *Screen* 19, no. 2 (1978): 41–54.

Cook, David A. *A History of Narrative Film.* 4th ed. New York: Norton, 2004.
Creed, Barbara. "The Cyberstar: Digital Pleasures and the End of the Unconscious." *Screen* 40, no. 2 (1999): 79–86.
Cross, Brenda, ed. *The Film Hamlet: A Record of Its Production.* London: Saturn Press, 1948.
Davies, Anthony. *Filming Shakespeare's Plays.* New York: Cambridge University Press, 1988.
Davies, Eden. *Beyond Dance: Laban's Legacy of Movement Analysis.* London: Brechin Books, 2001.
Dayan, Daniel. "The Tutor-Code of Classical Cinema." In *Film Theory and Criticism,* 5th ed., ed. Leo Braudy and Marshall Cohen, 118–29. New York: Oxford University Press, 1999.
Deák, Frantisek. "Structuralism in Theatre: The Prague School Contribution." *Drama Review* 20, no. 4 (1976): 83–94.
De Carlo, Carlo, Giorgio Tinazzi, and Marga Cottino-Jones, eds. *The Architecture of Vision: Writings and Interviews on Cinema.* New York: Marsillo, 1976.
De Cordova, Richard. *Picture Personalities: The Emergence of the Star System in America.* Urbana: University of Illinois Press, 1990.
De Lauretis, Teresa, and Stephen Heath, eds. *The Cinematic Apparatus.* New York: St. Martin's Press, 1980.
Delman, John, Jr. *The Art of Acting.* New York: Harper, 1949.
Delsarte, François. *The Delsarte System of Oratory.* New York: Edgar S. Werner, 1893.
Derrida, Jacques. "Structure, Sign, and Play in the Discourse of the Human Sciences." In *Writing and Difference,* trans. Alan Bass, 278–93. Chicago: University of Chicago Press, 1978.
Desser, David. "Toward a Structural Analysis of the Postwar Samurai Film." In *Reframing Japanese Cinema: Authorship, Genre, History,* ed. Arthur Nolletti, Jr., and David Desser, 145–64. Bloomington: Indiana University Press, 1992.
Diamond, Elin. "Brechtian Theory/Feminist Theory: Toward a Gestic Feminist Criticism." *Drama Review* 32, no. 1 (1988): 82–94.
Diderot, Denis, and William Archer. *The Paradox of Acting* and *Masks or Faces.* New York: Hill and Wang, 1957.
Dillon, Josephine (Gable). *Modern Acting: A Guide for Stage, Screen, and Radio.* New York: Prentice-Hall, 1940.
Donaldson, Peter S. "'In Fair Verona': Media, Spectacle, and Performance in *William Shakespeare's Romeo + Juliet.*" In *Shakespeare after Mass Media,* ed. Richard Burt, 59–82. New York: Palgrave, 2002.
Donalson, Melvin. *Black Directors in Hollywood.* Austin: University of Texas Press, 2003.
Drake, Philip. "Reconceptualizing Screen Performance." *Journal of Film and Video* 58, nos. 1–2 (2006): 84–94.
Dyer, Richard. *Stars.* New edition with supplementary chapter by Paul McDonald. London: British Film Institute, 2001.

Eisenstein, Sergei. *Film Form: Essays in Film Theory.* Ed. and trans. Jay Leyda. New York: Harcourt, Brace and World. 1949.

Ekman, Paul. *Explaining Emotions.* Berkeley and Los Angeles: University of California Press, 1980.

Elam, Keir. *The Semiotics of Theatre and Drama.* 2nd ed. New York: Routledge, 2002.

Elliott, Kamilla. *Rethinking the Novel/Film Debate.* New York: Cambridge University Press, 2003.

Emmert, Richard. "Expanding *No*'s Horizons: Considerations for a New *No* Perspective." In *No and Kyogen in the Contemporary World,* ed. James R. Brandon, 19–35. Honolulu: University of Hawaii Press, 1997.

Ergenbright, Eric, and Jack Smalley. "Star Factory." *Ladies Home Journal,* July 1937, 14–15, 54–55.

Esslin, Martin. *The Field of Drama: How the Signs of Drama Create Meaning on Stage and Screen.* New York: Methuen, 1987.

Falsetto, Mario. *Stanley Kubrick: A Narrative and Stylistic Analysis.* Westport, Conn.: Praeger, 1994.

Fell, John L. *Film and the Narrative Tradition.* Norman: University of Oklahoma Press, 1974.

Felperin, Leslie. "Smoke Opera." *Sight and Sound* 6, no. 4 (1996): 6–9.

Flinn, Denny Martin. *How Not to Write a Screenplay.* Hollywood: Lone Eagle Publishing, 1999.

Frank, Stanley. "Knockouts to Order." *Saturday Evening Post,* 3 January 1948, 12.

Frith, Christopher D., and Daniel M. Wolpert, eds. *The Neuroscience of Social Interaction: Decoding, Imitating, and Influencing the Actions of Others.* New York: Oxford University Press, 2004.

Gainor, J. Ellen. "Rethinking Feminism, Stanislavsky, and Performance." *Theatre Topics* 12, no. 2 (2002): 163–76.

Genette, Gérard. *Narrative Discourse: An Essay in Method.* Trans. Jane E. Lewin. Ithaca, N.Y.: Cornell University Press, 1980.

Genette, Gérard. *Narrative Discourse Revisited.* Trans. Jane E. Lewin. Ithaca, N.Y.: Cornell University Press, 1988.

Geraghty, Christine. "Re-examining Stardom: Questions of Texts, Bodies, and Performance." In *Reinventing Film Studies,* ed. Christine Gledhill and Linda Williams, 183–201. London: Arnold, 2000.

Gledhill, Christine, ed. *Stardom: Industry of Desire.* London: Routledge, 1993.

Goodwin, James, ed. *Perspectives on Akira Kurosawa.* New York: G. K. Hall, 1994.

Graham, Bob. "Denzel Gets Dangerous." *San Francisco Chronicle,* 5 October 2001, C1.

Granville-Barker, Harley. "Alas, Poor Will!" *The Listener,* 3 March 1936, 387–89.

Graver, David. "The Actor's Bodies." *Text and Performance Quarterly* 17, no. 3 (1997): 221–35.

Grotowski, Jerzy. *Towards a Poor Theatre.* Ed. Eugenio Barba. London: Methuen, 1975.

Hacker, Jonathan, and David Price. *Take Ten: Contemporary British Film Directors.* New York: Oxford University Press, 1991.

Hansen, Miriam. *Babel and Babylon: Spectatorship in American Silent Film.* Cambridge: Harvard University Press, 1991.

Hasse, Cathy. *Acting for Film.* New York: Allworth Press, 2003.

Heath, Stephen. *Questions of Cinema.* Bloomington: Indiana University Press, 1981.

Hecht, Patsy Ann Clark. "Kinetic Techniques for the Actor." Ph.D. diss., Wayne State University, 1971.

Herrington, Joan. "Directing with the Viewpoints." *Theatre Topics* 10, no. 2 (2000): 155–68.

Higson, Andrew. "Acting Taped—an Interview with Mark Nash and James Swinson." *Screen* 26, no. 5 (1985): 2–25.

Hirsh, Foster. *Laurence Olivier on Screen.* New York: Da Capo, 1984.

Hirsh, Foster. *A Method to Their Madness: The History of the Actors Studio.* New York: Da Capo, 1984.

Hodge, Alison, ed. *Twentieth Century Actor Training.* New York: Routledge, 2000.

Hodgson, John. *Mastering Movement: The Life and Work of Rudolf Laban.* New York: Routledge, 2001.

Holland, Peter. "Two-Dimensional Shakespeare: 'King Lear' on Film." In *Shakespeare and the Moving Image,* ed. Anthony Davies and Stanley Wells, 50–68. New York: Cambridge University Press, 1994.

Issacharoff, Michael. "Space and Reference in Drama." *Poetics Today* 2, no. 3 (1981): 211–24.

Issacharoff, Michael, and Robin F. Jones, eds. *Performing Texts.* Philadelphia: University of Pennsylvania Press, 1988.

Jones, David Richard. *Great Directors at Work: Stanislavski, Brecht, Kazan, Brook.* Berkeley and Los Angeles: University of California Press, 1986.

King, Barry. "Articulating Stardom." *Screen* 26, no. 5 (1985): 27–50.

Kingdon, Tom. *Total Directing: Integrating Camera and Performance in Film and Television.* Los Angeles: Silman-James Press, 2004.

Kirby, Michael. "On Acting and Not-Acting." *Drama Review* 16, no. 1 (1972): 3–15.

Kirby, Michael. "On Acting and Not-Acting." In *The Art of Performance: A Critical Anthology,* ed. Gregory Battcock and Robert Nickas, 97–117. New York: E. P. Dutton, 1985.

Kirby, Michael. "On Acting and Not-Acting." In *Acting (Re)Considered: Theories and Practices,* 2nd ed., ed. Phillip B. Zarilli, 40–52. New York: Routledge, 2002.

Klevan, Andrew. *Film Performance: From Achievement to Appreciation.* London: Wallflower Press, 2005.

Kliman, Bernice W., ed. *Hamlet: Film, Television, and Audio Performance.* London: Associated University Presses, 1988.

Kline, T. Jefferson. "Picking Dostoyevsky's Pocket: Bresson's Sl(e)ight of Screen." In *Robert Bresson,* ed. James Quandt, 235–73. Toronto: Toronto International Film Festival Group, 1998.

Klumph, Inez, and Helen Klumph. *Screen Acting: Its Requirements and Rewards.* New York: Falk, 1922.

Krasner, David. "I Hate Strasberg: Method Bashing in the Academy." In *Method Acting Reconsidered: Theory, Practice, Future,* ed. David Krasner, 3–39. New York: St. Martin's Press, 2000.

Krasner, David, ed. *Method Acting Reconsidered: Theory, Practice, Future.* New York: St. Martin's Press, 2000.

Krasner, David. "Strasberg, Adler, and Meisner: Method Acting." In *Twentieth Century Actor Training,* ed. Alison Hodge, 129–50. New York: Routledge, 2000.

Kuhn, Annette, and Mark Nash. "Editorial." *Screen* 19, no. 2 (1978): 5–7.

Kuleshov, Lev. *Kuleshov on Film: Writings by Lev Kuleshov.* Trans. and ed. Ron Levaco. Berkeley and Los Angeles: University of California Press, 1974.

Laban, Rudolf. *The Mastery of Movement.* 4th ed.. Revised by Lisa Ullmann. London: Macdonald and Evans, 1980.

Lamb, Warren, and Elizabeth Watson. *Body Code: The Meaning in Movement.* London: Routledge, 1987.

Langer, Suzanne K. *Feeling and Form.* New York: Charles Scribner's Sons, 1953.

Law, Alma, and Mel Gordon. *Meyerhold, Eisenstein and Biomechanics: Actor Training in Revolutionary Russia.* Jefferson, N.C.: McFarland, 1996.

Leach, Robert. "Meyerhold and Biomechanics." In *Twentieth Century Actor Training,* ed. Alison Hodge, 37–54. New York: Routledge, 2000.

Lewis, Robert. *Method or Madness?* New York: Samuel French, 1958.

Leyda, Jay. *Kino: A History of the Russian and Soviet Film.* 3rd ed. Princeton, N.J.: Princeton University Press, 1983.

Litvinoff, Valentina. "The Natural and the Stylized: In Conflict or Harmony?" In *Movement for the Actor,* ed. Lucille S. Rubin, 101–22. New York: Drama Book Specialists, 1980.

Lotman, Jurij. *Semiotics of Cinema.* Trans. Mark E. Suino. Ann Arbor: Department of Slavic Languages and Literature, University of Michigan, 1976.

Love, Lauren. "Rejecting the Organic: A Feminist Actor's Approach." In *Acting (Re)Considered: A Theoretical and Practical Guide,* 2nd ed., ed. Phillip B. Zarrilli, 277–90. New York: Routledge, 2002.

Lovell, Alan, and Peter Krämer, eds. *Screen Acting.* London: Routledge, 1999.

Maletic, Vera. *Body Space Expression: The Development of Rudolf Laban's Movement and Dance Concepts.* New York: Mouton de Gruyter, 1987.

Maltby, Richard. *Hollywood Cinema.* 2nd ed. Malden, Mass: Blackwell, 2003.

Manvell, Roger. *Shakespeare in Film.* New York: Praeger, 1971.

Margulies, Ivone. "John Cassavetes: Auteur Director." In *The New American Cinema,* ed. Jon Lewis, 275–306. Durham, N.C.: Duke University Press, 1998.

Matejka, Kadislav, and Irwin R. Titunik, eds. *Semiotics of Art: Prague School Contributions.* Cambridge: MIT Press, 1976.

Mayo, Virginia. Interview. 30 November 1973. Performing Arts Oral History Collection. Southern Methodist University.

McDonald, Keiko I. *Japanese Classical Theater in Films.* Cranbury, N.J.: Associated University Presses, 1994.

McDonald, Paul. "Film Acting." In *The Oxford Guide to Film Studies,* ed. John Hill and Pamela Church Gibson, 30–35. New York: Oxford University Press, 1998.

McDonald, Paul. "Stars in the Online Universe: Promotion, Nudity, Reverence." In *Contemporary Hollywood Stardom,* ed. Thomas Austin and Martin Barker, 29–44. London: Arnold, 2003.

McDonald, Paul. "Supplementary Chapter: Reconceptualising Stardom." In Richard Dyer, *Stars,* new ed. 175–200. London: British Film Institute, 1998.

McDonald, Paul. "Why Study Film Acting? Some Opening Reflections." In *More Than a Method: Trends and Traditions in Contemporary Film Performance,* ed. Cynthia Baron, Diane Carson, and Frank P. Tomasulo, 23–41. Detroit: Wayne State University Press, 2004.

McGilligan, Patrick. "James Cagney: The Actor as Auteur." *Velvet Light Trap* 7 (Winter 1972–73): 3–20.

McKenzie, Scott. "Wayne Wang." In *Fifty Contemporary Filmmakers,* ed. Yvonne Tasker, 370–78. New York: Routledge, 2002.

McQuire, Scott. "Digital Dialectics: The Paradox of Cinema in a Studio without Walls." *Historical Journal of Film, Radio, and Television* 19, no. 3 (1999): 379–97.

McTeague, James H. *Before Stanislavsky: American Professional Acting Schools and Acting Theory, 1875–1925.* Metuchen, N.J.: Scarecrow Press, 1993.

"Meet the Madame." *Modern Screen,* November 1940, 6, 89.

Menendez, Francisco. "Redefining Originality: Pearce and Luhrman's Conception of Romeo and Juliet." *Creative Screenwriting* 5, no. 2 (1998): 36–41.

Metz, Christian. *Film Language: A Semiotics of the Cinema.* Trans. Michael Taylor. New York: Oxford University Press, 1974.

Mitry, Jean. *Semiotics and the Analysis of Film.* Trans. Christopher King. Bloomington: Indiana University Press, 2000.

Moore, Carol-Lynne, and Kaoru Yamamoto. *Beyond Words: Movement Observation and Analysis.* New York: Gordon and Breach, 1988.

Morgan, Anna. *An Hour with Delsarte.* Boston: Lee and Shephard, 1891.

Moston, Doug. *Coming to Terms with Acting: An Instructive Glossary.* New York: Drama Book Publishers, 1993.

Mukařovský, Jan. *Aesthetic Function, Norm and Value as Social Facts.* Trans. Mark E. Suino. Ann Arbor: University of Michigan Press, 1970.

Mukařovský, Jan. *Structure, Sign, and Function: Selected Essays by Jan Mukařovský.* Trans. and ed. John Burbank and Peter Steiner. New Haven: Yale University Press, 1978.

Mukařovský, Jan. *The Word and Verbal Art: Selected Essays by Jan*

Mukařovský. Trans. and ed. John Burbank and Peter Steiner. New Haven: Yale University Press, 1977.

Mumford, Meg. "Brecht Studies Stanislavski: Just a Tactical Move?" *New Theatre Quarterly* 11 (August 1995): 241–58.

Musser, Charles. *Before the Nickelodeon: Edwin S. Porter and the Edison Manufacturing Company.* Berkeley and Los Angeles: University of California Press, 1991.

Naremore, James. *Acting in the Cinema.* Berkeley and Los Angeles: University of California Press, 1988.

Ndalianis, Angela. *Neo-Baroque Aesthetic and Contemporary Entertainment.* Cambridge: MIT Press, 2004.

Newlove, Jean. *Laban for Actors and Dancers.* New York: Routledge, 1993.

Newlove, Jean, and John Dalby. *Laban for All.* New York: Routledge, 2004.

Nichols, Bill. "Mise-en-scène Criticism." In *Movies and Methods,* ed. Bill Nichols, 311–13. Berkeley and Los Angeles: University of California Press, 1976.

"Nova Science NOW: PBS Airdate January 25, 2005." http://www.pbs.org/wgbh/nova/transcripts/3204_science.html, consulted 10 March 2005.

Ortolani, Benito. *The Japanese Theatre: From Shamanistic Ritual to Contemporary Pluralism.* Rev. ed. Princeton, N.J.: Princeton University Press, 1995.

Oudart, Jean-Louis. "Suture and Cinema." *Screen* 18, no. 4 (1977–78): 35–47.

Partsch-Bergsohn, Isa. *Modern Dance in Germany and the United States: Crosscurrents and Influences.* Chur, Switzerland: Harwood, 1994.

Pavis, Patrice. *Analyzing Performance: Theater, Dance, and Film.* Trans. David Williams. Ann Arbor: University of Michigan Press, 2003.

Pearson, Roberta E. *Eloquent Gestures: The Transformation of Performance Style in the Griffith Biograph Films.* Berkeley and Los Angeles: University of California Press, 1992.

Perkins, V. F. *Film as Film: Understanding and Judging Movies.* Harmondsworth: Penguin, 1972.

Phillips, William H. *Film: An Introduction.* 2nd ed. Boston: Bedford/St. Martin's Press, 2002.

Pilkington, Ace. "Zeffirelli's Shakespeare." In *Shakespeare and the Moving Image,* ed. Anthony Davies and Stanley Wells, 163–79. New York: Cambridge University Press, 1994.

Powell, Brian. *Japan's Modern Theatre: A Century of Change and Continuity.* London: Japan Library, 2002.

Preston-Dunlap, Valerie. *Rudolf Laban: An Extraordinary Life.* London: Dance Books, 1998.

Pudovkin, Vsevolod. *Film Technique and Film Acting: The Cinema Writings of V. I. Pudovkin.* New York: Bonanza, 1949.

Quandt, James. Introduction to *Robert Bresson,* ed. Quandt, 1–15. Toronto: Toronto International Film Festival Group, 1998.

Quinn, Michael L. *The Semiotic Stage: Prague School Theater Theory.* New York: Peter Lang, 1995.

Richie, Donald. *The Films of Akira Kurosawa.* Berkeley and Los Angeles: University of California Press, 1965.

Richie, Donald. *Japanese Cinema: An Introduction.* New York: Oxford University Press, 1990.

Rizzolatti, Giacomo, and Laila Craighero. "The Mirror Neuron System." *Annual Review of Neuroscience* 27 (2004): 169–92.

Roach, Joseph R. *The Player's Passion: Studies in the Science of Acting.* Newark: University of Delaware Press, 1985.

Rosenbaum, Jonathan. *Placing Movies: The Practice of Film Criticism.* Berkeley and Los Angeles: University of California Press, 1995.

Rosenstein, Sophie, Larrae A. Haydon, and Wilbur Sparrow. *Modern Acting: A Manual.* New York: Samuel French, 1936.

Ross, Lillian, and Helen Ross, eds. *The Player: A Profile of an Art.* New York: Limelight, 1984.

Rothman, William. "Against 'The System of Suture.'" In *Film Theory and Criticism,* 5th ed., ed. Leo Braudy and Marshall Cohen, 130–36. New York: Oxford University Press, 1999.

Rozik, Eli. *The Roots of Theatre: Rethinking Ritual and Other Theories of Origin.* Iowa City: University of Iowa Press, 2002.

Sabatine, Jean. *Movement Training for the Stage and Screen.* New York: Back Stage Books, 1995.

Saynor, James. "Accidental Auteur." *Sight and Sound* 3, no. 4 (1993): 3–8.

Scheuer, Philip K. "Franchot Tone More Than Just 'Man Joan Married.'" *Los Angeles Times,* 24 November 1935, n.p.

Schwartz, Hillel. "Torque: The New Kinaesthetic of the Twentieth Century." In *Incorporations,* ed. Jonathan Crary and Sanford Kwinter, 70–127. New York: Zone, 1992.

Schwartz, Vanessa R. "Cinematic Spectatorship before the Apparatus: The Public Taste for Reality in *Fin-de-Siècle* Paris." In *Cinema and the Invention of Modern Life,* ed. Leo Charney and Vanessa R. Schwartz, 297–319. Berkeley and Los Angeles: University of California Press, 1995.

Shaffer, Lawrence. "Some Notes on Film Acting." *Sight and Sound* 42, no. 2 (1973): 103–6.

Shawn, Ted. *Every Little Movement.* New York: Dance Horizons, 1963.

Sherman, Eric, ed. *Directing the Film: Film Directors on Their Art.* Los Angeles: Acrobat, 1976.

Shevey, Sandra. "Lillian Burns Sidney—She's Drama." *Los Angeles Times,* 18 December 1977, Calendar 88–90.

Shields, Ronald E. "Acting Prima Donna Politics in Tomás Gutiérrez Alea's *Strawberry and Chocolate.*" In *More Than a Method: Trends and Traditions in Contemporary Film Performance,* ed. Cynthia Baron, Diane Carson, and Frank P. Tomasulo, 219–46. Detroit: Wayne State University Press, 2004.

Silberman, Marc. "The Actor's Medium: On Stage and in Film." *Modern Drama* 39 (1996): 558–65.

Spolin, Viola. *Improvisation for the Theater.* Evanston, Ill.: Northwestern University Press, 1983.
Staiger, Janet. "The Eyes Are Really the Focus: Photoplay Acting and Film Form and Style." *Wide Angle* 6, no. 4 (1984): 14–23.
Stam, Robert, Robert Burgoyne, and Sandy Flitterman-Lewis. *New Vocabularies in Film Semiotics.* New York: Routledge, 1992.
Stam, Robert, and Toby Miller, eds. *Film and Theory: An Anthology.* Malden, Mass.: Blackwell, 2000.
States, Bert O. *Great Reckonings in Little Rooms: On the Phenomenology of Theater.* Berkeley and Los Angeles: University of California Press, 1985.
States, Bert O. *The Pleasure of the Play.* Ithaca, N.Y.: Cornell University Press, 1994.
Steiner, Peter. "Jan Mukařovský's Structural Aesthetics." In *Structure, Sign, and Function: Selected Essays by Jan Mukařovský,* ed. and trans. John Burbank and Peter Steiner, ix–xxxix. New Haven: Yale University Press, 1978.
Sterritt, David, ed. *Robert Altman: Interviews.* Jackson: University Press of Mississippi, 2000.
"The Strange Doings of Actress at Practice: Friends Help Natalie Wood Polish Dramatics." *Life,* 28 January 1957, 96–98, 100.
Strasberg, Lee. *A Dream of Passion: The Development of the Method.* Boston: Little, Brown, 1987.
Suzuki, Tadashi. *The Way of Acting.* Trans. J. Thomas Rimer. New York: Theatre Communications, 1986.
Sylwester, Robert. "Mirror Neurons." August 2002. http://www.brainconnection.com/content/181, consulted 10 March 2005.
Taylor, Neil. "The Films of Hamlet." In *Shakespeare and the Moving Image,* ed. Anthony Davies and Stanley Wells, 180–95. New York: Cambridge University Press, 1994.
"Terry Hunt's Job Is to Keep Movie Stars Thin and Healthy." *Life,* 15 July 1940, 55–57.
Thompson, Grahame F. "Approaches to 'Performance': An Analysis of Terms." *Screen* 26, no. 5 (1985): 78–90.
Thompson, John O. "Beyond Commutation—a Reconsideration of Screen Acting." *Screen* 26, no. 5 (1985): 64–76.
Thompson, John O. "Screen Acting and the Commutation Test." *Screen* 19, no. 2 (1978): 55–69.
Thompson, Kristin, and David Bordwell. *Film History: An Introduction.* New York: McGraw-Hill, 1994.
Tomasulo, Frank P. "'The Sounds of Silence': Modernist Acting in Michelangelo Antonioni's *Blow-Up.*" In *More Than a Method: Trends and Traditions in Contemporary Film Performance,* ed. Cynthia Baron, Diane Carson, and Frank P. Tomasulo, 94–125. Detroit: Wayne State University Press, 2004.
Tomlinson, Doug, ed. *Actors on Acting for the Screen.* New York: Garland, 1994.
Tomlinson, Doug. "Performance in the Films of Robert Bresson: The Aesthetics of Denial." In *More Than a Method: Trends and Traditions in Contem-*

porary Film Performance, ed. Cynthia Baron, Diane Carson, and Frank P. Tomasulo, 71–93. Detroit: Wayne State University Press, 2004.

Tomlinson, Doug. "Studies in the Use and Visualization of Film Performance: Alfred Hitchcock, Robert Bresson, Jean Renoir." Ph.D. diss., New York University, 1986.

Travis, Mark. *Directing Feature Films: The Creative Collaboration between Directors, Writers, and Actors.* Studio City, Calif.: Michael Wiese, 2002.

Tucker, Patrick. *Secrets of Screen Acting.* 2nd ed. New York: Routledge, 2003.

Universal International Collection. Talent School Files. Cinema-Television Library, University of Southern California.

Vardac, A. Nicholas. *Stage to Screen: Theatrical Origins of Early Film: David Garrick to D. W. Griffith.* Cambridge: Harvard University Press. New York: Da Capo, 1987.

Veltruský, Jirí. "The Prague School of Theory of Theater." *Poetics Today* 2, no. 3 (1981): 225–35.

Vineberg, Steve. *Method Actors: Three Generations of an American Acting Style.* New York: Schirmer, 1991.

Waller, Gregory A. *The Stage/Screen Debate: A Study in Popular Aesthetics.* New York: Garland, 1983.

Watson, Ian. "'Reading' the Actor: Performance, Presence, and the Synesthetic." *New Theatre Quarterly* 11 (1995): 135–46.

Weston, Judith. *Directing Actors: Creating Memorable Performances for Film and Television.* Studio City, Calif.: Michael Wiese, 1996.

Weston, Judith. *The Film Director's Intuition: Script Analysis and Rehearsal Techniques.* Studio City, Calif.: Michael Wiese, 2003.

Wexman, Virginia Wright. *Creating the Couple: Love, Marriage, and Hollywood Performance.* Princeton, N.J.: Princeton University Press, 1993.

Wexman, Virginia Wright. "The Rhetoric of Cinematic Improvisation." *Cinema Journal* 20, no. 1 (1980): 29–41.

Wikander, Matthew H. *Fangs of Malice: Hypocrisy, Sincerity, and Acting.* Iowa City: University of Iowa Press, 2002.

Williams, Raymond. *Drama in Performance.* New intro. and bib. Graham Holderness. Philadelphia: Open University Press, 1991.

Wojcik, Pamela Robertson, ed. *Movie Acting: The Film Reader.* New York: Routledge, 2004.

Wolford, Lisa. "Grotowski's Vision of the Actor: The Search for Contact." In *Twentieth Century Actor Training,* ed. Alison Hodge, 191–208. New York: Routledge, 2000.

Yacomar, Maurice. "Actors as Conventions in the Films of Robert Altman." *Cinema Journal* 20, no. 1 (1980): 14–28.

Yacomar, Maurice. "An Aesthetic Defense of the Star System in Films." *Quarterly Review of Film Studies* 4, no. 1 (1979): 39–52.

"Young Starlets Learn to Act." *Life,* 13 November 1937, 36–38.

Zarrilli, Phillip B., ed. *Acting (Re)Considered.* 2nd ed. New York: Routledge, 2002.

Zolotow, Maurice. "The Stars Rise Here." *Saturday Evening Post,* 18 May 1957, 44–45, 83–84, 86, 88.

Zorn, John W., ed. *The Essential Delsarte.* Metuchen, N.J.: Scarecrow Press, 1968.

Zucker, Carole. "The Concept of 'Excess' in Film Acting: Notes toward an Understanding of Non-naturalistic Performance." *Post Script* 12, no. 2 (1993): 54–62.

Zucker, Carole, ed. *Figures of Light: Actors and Directors Illuminate the Art of Film Acting.* New York: Plenum, 1995.

Zucker, Carole, ed. *Making Visible the Invisible: An Anthology of Original Essays on Film Acting.* Metuchen, N.J.: Scarecrow, 1990.

INDEX

Page numbers in italics refer to figures.